D1085179

Black Women and Politics
in New York City

Black Women and Politics in New York City

Julie A. Gallagher

University of Illinois Press
Urbana, Chicago, and Springfield

Library of Congress Cataloging-in-Publication Data
Gallagher, Julie A.
Black women and politics in New York City /
Julie A. Gallagher.
p. cm. — (Women in American history)
ISBN 978-0-252-03696-5 (hardback) —
ISBN 978-0-252-09410-1 (e-book)
1. African American women—Political activity—
New York (State)—New York. 2. African American
women—Civil rights—New York (State)—New York.
I. Title.
E185.93.N56G35   2012
323'.042082097471—dc23   2011045140

Contents

Acknowledgments / vii

Introduction / 1

1. Fighting for Rights in the 1910s and 1920s / 11

2. Strides Forward in Times of Crisis in the 1930s and 1940s / 46

3. Pushing Through the Doors of Resistance in the 1950s / 87

4. Feminism, Civil Rights, and Liberalism in the 1960s / 121

5. On the Shirley Chisholm Trail in the 1960s and 1970s / 157

Conclusion / 191

Appendix / 201

Notes / 205

Index / 241

Illustrations follow page 120

Acknowledgments

The conclusion of a project long in the making, as this book was, offers a much-anticipated moment of rest and more than that, a chance to reflect on the journey that brought it about. I have been fortunate on so many fronts, and it is a pleasure to acknowledge the people who have helped me get to this point. I want to start with Laurie Matheson at University of Illinois Press who believed in this project from the first time we met. Not only did she wait patiently for me to finish it, but she also offered sage advice at critical moments, which made this process relatively painless. I am indebted as well to the two readers of the manuscript for their valuable feedback and enthusiasm for the book.

I want to recognize the centrality of the Antioch College community to this book as an intellectual and political project. Colleagues and friends, especially Jean Gregorek, Marianne Whelchel, Suparna Bhaskaran, Chris Hill, Anne Bolin, and Iveta Jusová, demonstrated a commitment to learning and to justice that routinely inspired me to dig deeper, think harder, and see the world and ideas in broader and more complex ways. Two of my former Antioch students, Amy Campbell and Michaella Rey, were especially excited about my book, but that did not keep them from asking me challenging questions. I thank all of them, as well as many others on the faculty and staff, for their support and friendship throughout my years there.

Penn State Brandywine offered further opportunities, especially invaluable course release time and research support. The warm welcome I received made my transition easy, and I am particularly indebted to Phyllis Cole, Steve Cimbala, and Arnold Markley, a friend and accomplished colleague whose time on earth was cut tragically short by illness. Students in my upper-level history seminars made going to work a true delight. Their excitement, sincere interest, and at times distress about what we grappled with as we waded deep into the social and political history of the twentieth century reminded me why this work really does matter. Librarians Susan Ware, Sara Whilden, and Mary Fran McLaughlin always made sure I had every resource I needed to do my work, and they were extremely supportive along the way.

The origins of this book are rooted in my graduate studies at the University of Massachusetts. To the extent that I hit the high bar of scholarly rigor, it is because I learned from such dedicated intellectuals, including Kathy Peiss, Kevin Boyle, Manisha Sinha, Carl Nightingale, David Glassberg, Joyce Berkman, Bruce Laurie and Joye Bowman. I benefit still from the wisdom and generosity of my friends and colleagues from UMass, including Marian Mollin, Julia Sandy-Bailey, Jacqueline Castledine, and Richard Gassan.

I have presented aspects of this book at numerous conferences over the years. I learned very much from co-panelists and appreciated their questions, suggestions, and encouragement of my work. These include Prudence Cumberbatch, Stephanie Evans, Tiffany Gill, Stephanie Gilmore, Melanie Gustafson, Susan Hartmann, Erik McDuffie, Michele Mitchell, Premilla Nadasen, Mark Naison, Elisabeth Israels Perry, Barbara Ransby, and Barbara Savage. Along the way I met a handful of special people through the Coordinating Council for Women in History (CCWH) who became not just mentors but also friends, particularly Eileen Boris, Lisa DiCaprio, Katie Parkin, and Jen Scanlon. I have learned many life lessons from them but especially how much a supportive word can mean when you are deep in the tunnel of work and the light at the end is not yet in sight. Jen is not only a dear friend but at a critical juncture she carefully read the book manuscript and gave me much appreciated feedback. Barbara Winslow's support of my work on Shirley Chisholm has been tremendous. Not only that, she has taught me a great deal about feminist activism, social justice, and Brooklyn politics. One person deserves special mention: I am deeply indebted to Kathleen Laughlin, whom I was lucky to meet when she was a fellow at the Five College Women's Studies Research Center at Mount Holyoke and I was in the midst of writing my dissertation. She supported my growth as a person and a scholar in so many ways, and I cannot thank her enough.

In an age when the Internet and social media deliver information with the tap of a finger, we can too easily forget how vital archives, archivists, and librarians are to the production of new knowledge. I want to thank especially the archivists at the Schomburg Center for Research in Black Culture, the Schlesinger Library, Rutgers University Special Collections, the John F. Kennedy Presidential Library, the Moorland-Spingarn Research Center, and the Brooklyn Public Library. As I searched for photos to include in the book, I found Charles Wash, a gem of an archivist at the National Afro-American Museum and Cultural Center in Wilberforce, Ohio. I would also like to acknowledge the numerous individuals who generously shared their memories of New York City's political life with me, including Andy Cooper, Jocelyn Cooper, Joan Maynard, Constance Rose, and Jeanne Noble.

Maintaining balance in life, especially while writing a book, is not always easy. To the extent that I have, I owe much to cherished friends, including Virginia Oran-Sabia, Anthony Sabia, Christine Corriston, Kristin Long, and Lee Evans. Many of them are activists who have dedicated their lives to making the world a fairer, more just place. Our conversations often leave me thinking for days about new ideas or rethinking old ones. But they also know how to find humor in life and remind me of the healing power of a good laugh. Time spent in their company is always restorative.

I was privileged to grow up in a family where I was encouraged to seize every opportunity and take chances, not only to study and work hard, but also to seek a path that brings happiness and has meaning, and to live each day fully. My mother was always my biggest cheerleader, and to this day, all I have done has been profoundly influenced by her love. My father has spent more than half a century involved in civic life, and he has modeled, through his extraordinary dedication, how important it is to be engaged in the communities we live in. After all these years, the values that my parents instilled in us have remained the bedrock upon which my five siblings and I engage the world. I am continuously humbled and inspired by the ways my brother and sisters have passionately pursued their paths in life. I have not only learned from them, but I have been enriched by their love, dedication, and in various ways, support of this book.

My closing thoughts and greatest thanks are for my partner in all of life's journeys, great and small, Jane Berger. I love her for her deep intellect and commitments to justice and fairness, but also for so much more. She is patient and generous, thoughtful and loving, creative and fun. She shouldered the bulk of the parenting load at critical times, especially when I decamped to Ithaca to a room of my own, where I wrote to my heart's content and got this book all but done. Of all that we have done together, the most amazing experience by far has been raising our daughter Leighanne. Jane is a remarkable parent and Leighanne is a wonder beyond words. Together they have made my life fulfilled in more ways than I can count, and I am very, very lucky.

Introduction

"I stand before you today as a candidate for the Democratic nomination for the Presidency of the United States. I am not the candidate of Black America, although I am Black and proud. I am not the candidate of the Women's Movement of this country, although I am a woman, and I am equally proud of that. . . . I am the candidate of the people and my presence before you now symbolizes a new era in American political history," Shirley Chisholm declared to an enthusiastic crowd at Brooklyn's Concord Baptist Church on January 25, 1972.[1] The first black woman elected to Congress and the first to run for president on a national party ticket, Chisholm was justifiably recognized as a political trailblazer. At the same time, her designation as a "first" tended to obscure the efforts of generations of politically active black women who came before her. Victoria Earle Matthews and Irene Moorman Blackstone, who fought for women's suffrage in the early twentieth century, would likely have been thrilled to see Chisholm confidently standing at the podium announcing her candidacy. Layle Lane and Sara Pelham Speaks, who ran for Congress in 1934 and 1944, respectively, might have been disappointed that Chisholm's election to Congress came only in 1968, but these two political stalwarts would have been proud of her unprecedented run for president just four years later. On that momentous winter's day in 1972 the congresswoman from Brooklyn concluded an important and until now untold story about politically active black women in New York City who, over the course of six decades, waged struggles for justice, rights, and equality.

This book tells four interconnected stories that together make a number of innovative contributions to U.S. political history, the emerging scholarship on the Northern civil rights struggle, and women's history. Black women have historically worked through a variety of grassroots and women's organizations wherever they lived—North or South, in cities and in rural communities—for racial and gender equality, social, economic and political rights, and fundamental dignity.[2] However, starting with the fight for women's suffrage in New York City in the 1910s and through the waning years of Chisholm's political career in Washington, D.C., in the late 1970s, they also engaged in formal politics at an unprecedented level.[3] In their state-centered activism, which targeted lawmakers, the courts, and government bureaucracies, women like Anna Arnold Hedgeman, Dorothy Height, Eunice Hunton Carter, and Pauli Murray contended with the intersectional dynamics of racism and sexism. This intersectionality created not merely an additive level of discrimination, namely the combining of racism and sexism, but a wholly different and more complex experience of subordination for black women.[4] Undeterred and armed with the right to vote, they worked to get political parties to take them seriously as constituents and eventually as candidates. Their communities in Harlem and Brooklyn often needed far less convincing; on the contrary, they turned to women like Hedgeman, Ada B. Jackson, and Maude Richardson, and urged them to run for elected office. This new chapter of political history chronicles black women's emergence in party politics in New York City, in government agency work, and their candidacies for elected office. In the course of sixty years, they made impressive strides, breaking through longstanding barriers that were designed to keep them outside the arenas of political power. At the same time, they confronted serious challenges because of power dynamics embedded in the political culture, and because they lacked the kinds of institutional networks that could readily move their goals forward. This story reveals the political changes women helped bring about, and it underscores the limits of what they were able to achieve.

Between the legal and de facto Jim Crow dimensions of American society, South *and* North, African Americans had a deep appreciation for the gap between the promises of equality and the practices of discrimination. As part of their response to that reality, this book argues, black women in New York City developed a broad vision of politics that included a strategic engagement with various arms of the state, especially the legislative branch of government. They were primarily motivated to allocate economic, social, and political resources through the government to the black communities they lived in, and to undo the system of racial inequality everywhere and at all levels. They joined with national efforts to eradicate the scourge of lynching and disfranchisement; at the local level they demanded access to decent employment, affordable housing, neighborhood safety, reliable childcare, good schools, the full eradication of racial discrimination, and responsive political representation. The private sector fell far short of delivering many of these fundamental needs to predominantly black communities time and again, so women like Layle Lane, Ruth Whitehead Whaley, Ella Baker, Constance Baker Motley, and Shirley Chisholm purposefully turned to the state to act as mediator when possible, and provider when necessary. They understood that if they were not at the table raising concerns especially on behalf of black women, no one would. They tended to be more pragmatic than ideological, and they were not naïve. While they embraced the ballot, ventured into political clubhouses, initiated legal cases, petitioned legislators, and ran for office, most black women in New York did not expect the political process to transform the injustices of society immediately or completely.[5] At the same time, their ideas about the expansive role government could play in creating a more just society were more ambitious than those of liberalism's boldest leaders, even during the periods of greatest state activism in the New Deal of the 1930s and the Great Society of the 1960s.

Moreover, as this story demonstrates, through their political activism black women in New York City influenced the Democratic Party and policymaking processes including, by the 1960s, at the national level. Although African Americans had been loyal to the party of Lincoln since the end of the Civil War, after 1877 Republicans did little for them, either nationally or in Northern cities where black men could still exercise the right to vote. By the late 1910s, significant numbers of black voters in New York City migrated to the Democratic Party—long before the national realignment in the 1930s.[6] Newly enfranchised black women like Ruth Whitehead Whaley played an important role in this change and fought to expand the party's agenda to address the needs of women, especially women of color, and to more effectively respond to problems faced by African Americans, the working class, and the poor. Decades later when Cold War anticommunists targeted left-leaning activists and forced a narrowing of the political debate, scholars generally argue that struggles for economic rights were displaced by the more moderate goal of civil rights.[7] Yet as a number of politically active black women in New York City demonstrate, progressive ideas were hardly extinguished. Bessie Buchanan, Constance Baker

Motley, and Shirley Chisholm, for example, who came to represent the most liberal wing of the Democratic Party, fought for a progressive vision of social, political, and economic justice that scholars have not previously recognized.

Additionally, black women contributed to and influenced the Northern civil rights movement and the women's movements in ways that have yet to be fully appreciated. While their work in the post–World War II civil rights movement in the South has been well documented, black women's contributions to the struggles for racial equality in the North and to the national welfare rights movement have only recently begun to receive scholars' attention.[8] This book adds to these efforts, but it also demonstrates that women were even more actively involved in battles against racial injustice and at an earlier time than historians have generally recognized. In grassroots struggles and through their newly won seats in government, Buchanan, Chisholm, and Motley tried to shape legislative outcomes to eradicate racial inequalities that persisted into the 1970s, long after the period conventionally known as the civil rights era.

At the same time, Murray, Height, Hedgeman, Chisholm, and Jeanne Noble, whose formative intellectual and political years were spent in New York City, influenced the post–World War II women's movements in ways that are unappreciated in the literature and in the popular narrative.[9] These women raised concerns about the challenges women of color faced in the labor force, in politics, in the media, and in the culture more broadly. They did so in a variety of arenas, including liberal political establishments like the President's Commission on the Status of Women (PCSW) and the U.S. Congress; in pressure groups like the National Organization for Women (NOW), the National Association for the Repeal of Abortion Laws (NARAL), the National Women's Political Caucus (NWPC), and the National Black Feminist Organization (NBFO); and in their civic and church-based work for civil rights. Chisholm most fully embraced the mantle of feminism in the 1960s, but others also pushed U.S. presidents, members of Congress, and white feminists to consider the concerns of poor women and of women of color. Although African American women are not given extensive treatment in histories of women's activism, they deserve to be. There is also room to expand the framework of black feminist history to more fully include women like Murray, Chisholm, and Hedgeman who worked most often in organizations considered mainstream or liberal but who nevertheless substantively expanded the intellectual traditions and public conversations about black women's histories and their lives through their writings and activism.

While this is primarily a study of black women's political activism, it is also in part a collective biography. It briefly explores the backgrounds and political ideas of more than fifteen black women who came of age in Harlem's and Bedford-Stuyvesant's dynamic institutions and organizations. Most, but not all, of these women married. Fewer had children. Additionally, almost all of these women pursued higher education as well as advanced degrees—many at one of New York City's universities. As a result of their exceptional educational and professional opportunities, they were in a different class than the majority of poor and working-class African American women in the city. Particularly in the first two decades of the century, a number of these women were raised in or circulated in environments that embraced a politics of respectability, which centered on reserved public behavior, temperance, hard work, piety, and chastity.[10] Their approaches to racial uplift at times exacerbated that class division. However, even though these women were particularly well educated, their class status did not lead them to a single political ideology. Some, for example, were identified as progressive or radical, including Layle Lane, a Socialist; Ella Baker, a political nonconformist who in the 1930s spearheaded a consumer cooperative movement and in the 1960s urged young civil rights activists to establish their own organization rooted in principles of participatory democracy; and Ada B. Jackson, a Republican turned American Labor Party candidate and an officer in the left-leaning Congress of American Women (CAW) in the late 1940s. A minority of these women, including Sara Speaks and Maude Richardson, remained faithful to the Republican Party into the 1950s, unconvinced that the Southern Dixiecrats could be effectively sidelined. More of them settled into the Democratic Party. Chisholm's presidential candidacy on the Democratic Party ticket and her arrival at the Democratic National Convention in Miami with more than one hundred delegates was a marker of black women's firm commitment to that party.

Finally, New York City itself is important to this story for two specific reasons. First, it was a central hub of progressive politics in the United States. Although it was most often dominated by the Tammany Hall Democrats in the first half of the twentieth century, the city could at times be quite open to and supportive of diverse political ideas until the beginning of the Cold War. For example, Socialists represented city districts in the New York State Assembly in the late 1910s, two Communists served in City Hall in the 1940s, and after the American Labor Party's emergence in 1936, it fielded successful candidates for many offices, including one who went to Congress from Harlem in the 1940s. Black women were active in all of these political parties. Second, the demographic shifts the city experienced in the first two decades of the twentieth century created significant political and cultural opportunities for African

Americans. Although they would lament the chasm between the city's promise of economic opportunity and its reality, the black women in this book who migrated to New York from the American South and the Caribbean, as well as those born within its borders, stayed because of the energy, ideas, institutions, and opportunities they found there. Harlem was the locus of America's most important civil rights, Black Nationalist, and African American cultural institutions in the first half of the twentieth century. After its 1909 founding, the NAACP established its headquarters in New York City. The Harlem YMCA and YWCA, the 135th Street branch of the New York Public Library (which became the Schomburg Center for Research in Black Culture), Marcus Garvey's Universal Negro Improvement Association (UNIA), and nightclubs like Small's Paradise, the Savoy Ballroom, and the Apollo Theater nurtured some of the century's most influential writers, artists, activists, and musicians. For all of these reasons, New York City was fertile ground for stimulating one's mind and sharpening one's political skills. Starting in the 1910s and for the next sixty years, politically active black women did both; in the process, they not only built networks that sustained them and their communities, but they helped transform the city's and the nation's political parties, its laws, and its legislative bodies.

Chapter 1 covers the dynamic period of the 1910s and 1920s in New York City. Not only did tens of thousands of African Americans migrate north to the city, but the nation participated in a world war, women won the right to vote, and Harlem birthed a cultural renaissance and a major Black Nationalist movement. During these years black women from various backgrounds, native New Yorkers and new arrivals alike, including Anna Arnold Hedgeman, Irene Moorman Blackstone, and Ruth Whitehead Whaley, stepped into the public sphere to fight for economic, social, and political rights. The chapter explores how these and other African American women viewed and tried to use the various branches of government in their grassroots and their formal political efforts, and the implications of their work on their communities, on New York's political machinery, on black women's collective struggles for equality, and on themselves. Their grassroots measures yielded halting but at times meaningful progress, particularly when housing needs were alleviated or jobs were secured; but women's efforts to engage with men inside political party clubhouses, which were the fundamental locus of political activism in the city, were met with a porous wall of resistance which simultaneously welcomed a few of them but gave up almost nothing. Politically engaged women quickly came to appreciate that changing the culture would be a long-term struggle. Nevertheless, attaining

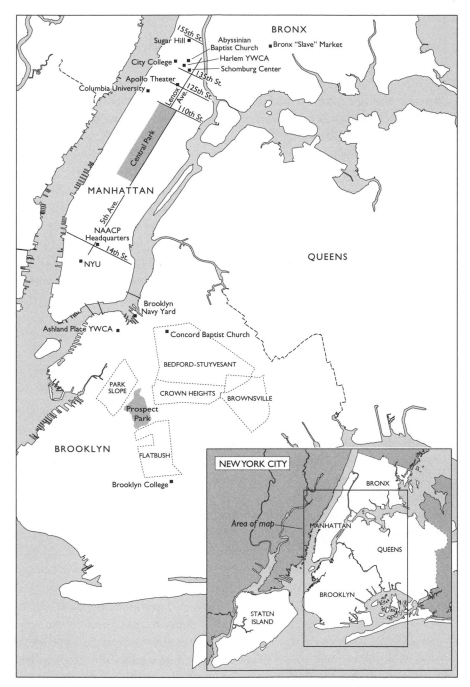

Map of New York City (post 1898). Some key institutions, especially in Harlem, and neighborhoods in Brooklyn noted.

the right to vote was an important step that their Southern sisters did not have, and they learned to use it effectively.

Chapter 2 explores the strides African American women made in government work and electoral politics during the Great Depression and World War II. While the economic crisis wreaked havoc on Harlem, it also created the space for college-educated women like Ella Baker, Dorothy Height, and Pauli Murray to find employment in the city's New Deal agencies. In addition to gaining useful experience, these women now had access to potentially influential arenas from which to pursue their ideas about economic fairness, human rights, and civil equality. Yet other women, including Eunice Hunton Carter, Layle Lane, and Sara Pelham Speaks, turned to electoral politics during the 1930s. Deciding that the time had come to forge forward in party politics, they ran for office on the Socialist, Republican, and Democratic Party ballots. The door they opened ajar in the 1930s was pushed further by Ada B. Jackson and Maude Richardson in the 1940s. The campaigns of these two Brooklyn women suggested that Bedford-Stuyvesant had become a politically important community by the war years. On their campaign trails every one of these women raised concerns about issues that plagued African Americans in New York City, including the lack of decent jobs and housing, racial discrimination, and minimal political party support for black leadership. Although they lost their elections, by the time the economy stabilized and World War II ended, black women in New York City had attained significant political experience.

Chapter 3 follows a number of African American women in the postwar period further into party politics and into city government, and it charts the efforts of local renegades to launch political insurgencies that sought to bring down entrenched Democratic bosses and improve African Americans' and women's access to political power. By the time Bessie Buchanan took her oath of office to become the first black woman in the New York State Assembly in 1954, Anna Arnold Hedgeman had already served her first year in Mayor Wagner's cabinet. Shirley Chisholm helped undo the stranglehold the old-guard Democratic Party bosses had on Brooklyn's political machine. Constance Baker Motley parlayed an impressive string of civil rights legal victories into a New York State Senate seat. Despite the challenges they faced, African American women who were committed to creating a more just society through formal politics were extremely busy in the 1950s and 1960s. They introduced new issues into the political discourse as elected officials and government administrators, they pressured political leaders through protests, and they effectively used the courts. Through their examples of leadership and methods of organizing, they also encouraged historically disempowered people, especially black women, to engage in politics and to demand change from various state actors, including politicians, judges, police chiefs, school administrators, and municipal and state bureaucrats.

Chapter 4 charts the impressive leap that African American women, including Dorothy Height, Pauli Murray, Jeanne Noble, Anna Arnold Hedgeman, and Constance Baker Motley, made into national arenas of political power starting in the early 1960s. Racial discrimination and social injustices in jobs, housing, education, and politics—problems that women had been fighting for the past four decades—were now raised before leaders of the liberal political establishment at the national level. Invited for the first time to participate in these national conversations, Height, president of the National Council of Negro Women (NCNW), Murray, a legal activist, and Noble, national president of the Delta Sigma Theta sorority, made important contributions to the PCSW meetings as well as the policy recommendations that resulted from them. Motley made history by attaining a federal judgeship. When time passed and many of the changes women hoped for were not forthcoming, women like Hedgeman did what they had done in the past: they utilized outside pressure groups and organized constituents to demand change and to hold leaders accountable. Additionally, these women, who had always understood their struggles for justice and equality through a prism of race, had to determine their individual and collective relationships to the burgeoning feminist movement they were helping usher in, especially in the wake of the PCSW. Contributors to national policy debates about racial and gender equality for the first time, these black women understood that their presence inside the federal-level branches of government created potential opportunities for influencing political change, but even more, given the traditions of the state to which they had not been party, they understood that it represented the beginning of the new level of activism.

Chapter 5 examines Shirley Chisholm's political career as part of this longer history of African American women in New York City politics. The first black woman elected to the U.S. Congress, Chisholm contributed to the breaking down of barriers that kept black women from powerful positions within the federal government. While she benefited from the changes that the civil rights and women's movements—and the eight years of Democratic Party dominance—had yielded, her success at the polls was the result of far more than a timely campaign. She won because of a combination of factors including her ideas about equality and justice, her political skills and strong personality, the consistent support she received from black women in her district, the tireless activism of two generations of politically inclined women who came before her, and the support of the Democratic Party. Chisholm was a vocal advocate for an activist government to redress economic, social, and political injustices, and she frequently used her national prominence to bring attention to racial, sexual, and class-based inequality. At the same time, she collided into well-established and powerful forces that made it hard to effect change, and she arrived in Congress at the moment when the New Deal coalition began to fall apart. Although her impact as a liberal Democrat would be blunted by the larger political forces surrounding her, Chisholm's influence on the predominantly white women's movement was substantial.

This is the story of three generations of black women in New York City who endeavored to work through the structures of government to undo entrenched racial and gender-based discrimination and to help create better opportunities for women, the poor, and for African Americans in their communities and across the nation. They were women of action, unwilling to sit on the sidelines of politics. Until now unacknowledged, their efforts contributed to the reconfiguration of political parties, the passage of laws that addressed economic, race-related, and gendered inequalities, and for the first time, they attained positions within the state and served as judges, high-level government administrators, and elected officials. By the time this story concluded, only the U.S. presidency eluded them, but not because they did not try for it. At the same time, while the acquisition of these positions was vitally important, it represented only a partial victory. They ran up against power brokers and deeply rooted structural forces that together worked to undermine the potential for change that these new arrivals in the state hoped to enact. It would take more than the hard won seats at the table for these women, marginalized by the interconnected forces of racism and sexism into the 1970s, to be able to fully enact their visions of politics that were fundamentally about racial and gender equality, social justice, and human rights. But, in sixty years' time, they had made an impressive amount of headway, and they were ready to press on.

CHAPTER ONE

Fighting for Rights
in the 1910s and 1920s

"I could see only one way to freedom—nationalism. Although the word 'nationalism' was not in my vocabulary, I knew that somehow the great talent and spirit of Negroes must be developed into a unified voice to demand not alms, but its birthright. This was my mood as I joined the professional staff of the Harlem YWCA," asserted Anna Arnold Hedgeman, a lifelong human rights and civil rights advocate, as she reflected on her migration to New York in the 1920s. "Cecelia Cabaniss Saunders, my new executive, talked to me of the movement of Negroes from many parts of the South in search of education, work and greater freedom . . . [She] put my thought into words when she said: 'There isn't the freedom here that they expect. But we are going to prepare them to go after the things which are their due.'"[1]

Many activists in New York City, including Hedgeman and Saunders, spent their lives pursuing for themselves, and even more for their communities, their "birthright" and their "due." These included being treated with fundamental human decency and respect; the elimination of racial, class, and gender discrimination in the workplace, schools, hospitals, and all public spaces; the right to live without fear of being beaten by police, maligned in the press, or exploited by landlords and shopkeepers. And their "birthright" and their "due" as Americans meant full access to the rights of citizenship, which included the ability to cast one's vote without risk of reprisals and to pursue elected office in an effort to bring one's political vision into reality.

Over the course of two decades, from the Great Migration in the 1910s through the Harlem Renaissance and New Negro movement of the 1920s, black women of diverse backgrounds and social positions in New York repeatedly stepped into the public sphere to fight for economic, civil, and political rights. A generation of women acquired important experience as they waged their struggles at the grassroots level, worked in community-based organizations, and learned to navigate formal political institutions. A number of these women, among them native New Yorkers, migrants from the South, and immigrants from the Caribbean, were middle class. Not only were they college educated, they were frequently schooled by their families, churches, and women's clubs in the politics of respectability that centered on reserved public behavior, temperance, hard work, piety, and chastity.[2] These well-mannered women were sensitive to the class chasm between themselves and the poor and working class people who were also settling into northern cities in unprecedented numbers. Yet while they hoped, in part, to wear down foundations of racial discrimination and segregation with their middle-class respectability and their programs designed to uplift the race, they also pursued new political opportunities that opened up as they settled in.

At the same time, poor and working-class migrants were determined to forge a better life in the North than was possible south of the Mason-Dixon Line, but in so doing they were not particularly deferential to this "talented tenth" and their approaches to racial equality.[3] Modest though their material means often were, many migrants brought the organizing skills that had enabled them and their communities to more than survive in a caste system designed to keep them fully oppressed. Yet others brought their artistic talents; and more, their faith traditions. The vast majority brought a deep desire for life with not just more economic and political opportunity, but also human dignity and freedom from violence.[4]

Class, ideology, and regional differences created tensions; but they also meant that the hydra of racism would be assaulted from an increasing number of directions and through a variety of new approaches. Native New Yorkers who had long been fighting for better community resources, safety, opportunity, and racial equality now had new allies, albeit it complicated allies, in African American migrants from the South and immigrants from the Caribbean who chose to settle in Harlem and to a lesser extent in Bedford-Stuyvesant, Brooklyn.[5] The significant majority of women in public leadership roles, regardless of whether they hailed from the working class or middle class, had to contend with the challenges of being black and female, a distinct social positioning that meant having to negotiate the discriminatory forces at the intersection of racism and gendered oppression. Those who believed that political organizations and the government were necessary allies in their struggles for justice faced considerable hurdles in getting these institutions to take them seriously as activists.

This chapter explores the issues over which African American women were compelled to take action in the public sphere, how they viewed and used the government in their formal political and their grassroots efforts, and the implications of their work on their communities, on New York's political machinery, on black women's collective struggles for equality, and on themselves. Their activism was multidimensional, and it stemmed from no single political ideology; yet challenging racial discrimination was integral to nearly all they did. Grassroots measures often yielded perceptible though frequently impermanent change. On the other hand, women's efforts to engage with men inside the political machinery once they secured the right to vote was met with a porous wall of resistance which simultaneously welcomed a few of them in but gave up almost nothing. Changing the political culture would be a long-term struggle, of which suffrage was but one important step. At the same time, even though black women's public demands were rarely explicitly feminist, women like Hedgeman and Saunders, by their very presence in the public sphere as poll watchers, plaintiffs, progressive reformers, or protesters, challenged deep-rooted and devastatingly negative stereotypes that had helped sustain the cultural and structural gender discrimination African American women routinely experienced.

Myriad challenges did not keep black women from trying to bring about a more just society; in fact, they spurred an increasing number of women to action. And so in the tumultuous context of the Progressive Era, World War I, the Great Migration, and the concluding years of the struggle for women's enfranchisement, black women in New York City escalated their political activism through the suffrage campaign and through a number of grassroots struggles in an effort to redefine the boundaries of politics and to garner a degree of social, political, and cultural capital for themselves and their communities. There was much to do because, despite Gotham's geopolitical identity as a *Northern* city, Jim Crow had taken up residence at slavery's end, though perhaps with less fanfare and fewer formal political trappings than it did in the South. And it was loath to leave without a fight.

African Americans and New York City:
The Social and Political Context

New York City, a longstanding center of struggle for racial equality and a hub of what has become known as the northern civil rights movement, was historically a racially and ethnically complex city. It promised opportunity and relative freedom to those who settled within its borders. At the same time, work options for black women and men did not correlate with the most limited possibilities open to the new European arrivals. Immigrants from Italy, Russia, Poland, or Germany could find numerous ways to eke out a living, especially in niche production like cigar making and textiles, and on New York City's bustling docks. Not so for African Americans. Even exploitive factories like the Triangle Shirtwaist that tragically went up in flames in 1911 excluded black women.[6] For them, the only welcome mat was at the back door of white people's private homes. Domestic workers were always in demand. In 1910, a staggering 85 percent of African American women worked in "domestic or personal" service while just over 1 percent worked in professional jobs such as teaching, and less than 0.25 percent worked in factories.[7] By 1920 there had been a little improvement in black women's employment options, but the vast majority remained in the under-paid, insecure, and professionally dead-end jobs.[8] Men found a few more possibilities, namely as porters, cooks, and laborers.[9] The gendered division of labor guaranteed them slightly better-paying and varied jobs; but racial discrimination denied black men steady access to them. As the twentieth century dawned, most African Americans found shop and factory doors closed wherever they turned.[10]

Racism could manifest itself in countless ways, but one of the most terrifying was the periodic, explosive riot. On a summer night in 1900, for example, African Americans on the west side of Manhattan found themselves targets of yet another violent uprising. (Those who had lived through the Civil War Draft Riot of 1863 still had vivid memories of the devastation it wrought on an economically and politically fragile black community.) Writing about the violence and destruction of 1900, historian James Weldon Johnson suggested it was "a brutish orgy, which if it was not incited by the police, was, to say the least, abetted by them."[11] In commenting on the role of the police, Johnson underscored one of the recurring and deeply troubling problems African Americans would have to contend with throughout the entire twentieth century in New York and other cities, including Philadelphia, Detroit, Chicago, and Los Angeles.[12] In the riot's aftermath, African Americans sought a new, safer neighborhood, one they hoped had more space and better housing. Under the stewardship of real estate entrepreneur Philip Payton, the exodus to northern Manhattan—to Harlem—began.

As the new century unfolded, African Americans poured the foundations of both local and national black institutional life. A growing number of churches, clubs, organizations, and talented individuals sustained their communities and advocated for equality and opportunity, just as previous generations had done before in the American South as well as in New York's small black neighborhoods like Weeksville in Brooklyn and Greenwich Village in Manhattan.[13] The NAACP, founded in 1909, located its national headquarters in New York City and appointed W. E. B. DuBois to serve as the organization's director of publicity and research, as well as the editor of its monthly magazine, *The Crisis.* Johnson noted that with the NAACP's founding in New York, the city "became again the centre of the organized forces of self-assertion of equal rights and of insistence upon the impartial application of the fundamental principles of the Republic, without regard to race, creed, or colour."[14] The Empire State Federation of Women's Clubs founded in 1908, an affiliate of the National Association of Colored Women's clubs (NACW), segregated branches of the YWCA and the YMCA, the National Urban League (NUL), established in 1910, and various settlement houses and local aid organizations provided those in need with a safe place to seek a meal, temporary housing, a social network, or a job referral.[15] Institutional and cultural life thrived as the number of Harlem residents swelled.

When the brutal fighting of World War I slowed the flow of European immigrants to a trickle, African Americans began the Great Migration. Over half a million men, women, and children from the South left their familiar surroundings to seek stability, prosperity, and safety in the nation's urban metropolises. Ultimately orienting north, they put down their bags as well as new roots in cities like Detroit, Chicago, Milwaukee, Buffalo, Pittsburgh, and Philadelphia.[16] They also headed to New York City in numbers so substantial that it became the "Mecca of the New Negro."[17] The shift was swift and dramatic. Prior to 1910 African Americans represented less than 3 percent of the city's population, but by 1920 New York City had more African Americans living within its borders than any other city in the nation. In some sections of Harlem, black people quickly made up nearly 90 percent of the population.[18]

Brooklyn, located across the East River from Manhattan, also experienced dramatic growth. As one of the nation's major manufacturing centers, the borough's population doubled from 1890 to 1940, due in large part to European immigration, but its African American inhabitants also increased tenfold in that time.[19] The Brooklyn Bridge, completed in 1883, and later the subway system, both of which linked the island of Manhattan with Brooklyn, enabled the growing black middle class to take advantage of the comparative breathing room they found across the river. Yet Brooklyn's racial climate was hardly welcoming. Kings County had had the highest number of enslaved people in the state of New York on the eve of the American Revolution. As the reform impulses of the early nineteenth century spread across the Northeast, the New York state legislature debated outlawing slavery. In 1827, it finally ended. Brooklyn, however, had maintained the largest slave population in the state through the end.[20] Widespread racial discrimination prevented black families from making substantial economic and political advancements. Yet, in spite of the limitations they faced, newly freed people created pockets of community in Brooklyn throughout the nineteenth century, as they did in Manhattan. While new Harlem residents struggled with mounting residential overcrowding, Brooklyn offered an alternative, and by the 1920s, the outlines of the future black community of Bedford-Stuyvesant could be seen.[21]

In spite of Brooklyn's relative space, the burgeoning community in upper Manhattan remained the most popular and well-known destination for African Americans seeking a better life. As the black population in Harlem soared, it began to find not only its cultural stride, but its political footing as well. With voting rights secure in the North, black men sought to gain traction in New York City's power bases, especially in politics. To do this effectively they had to consider crossing the political divide to embrace the Democratic Party, an idea anathema to anyone, especially from the South, who cared about racial justice. Simultaneously, black women expanded their political efforts. Many newcomers joined the vanguard of black women who had long been fighting for women's suffrage, sometimes with white women's organizations, but because of racial discrimination more often on their own.[22] At the same time, a passionate minority of black women actively probed the outer boundaries of formal political circles to find a gateway inside. They too weighed the costs and benefits of shifting their political loyalties from the party of Lincoln to the Tammany Hall Democrats.

The Political Geography of New York City in the Progressive Era

New York City sustained waves of immigration and migration, economic booms and busts, and cultural renaissance in the first half of the twentieth century; it also nurtured and eventually saw the fall of the infamous Democratic Party political machine, Tammany Hall. Tammany Society, founded in the late eighteenth century, became the dominant political force in New York City in the mid-nineteenth century and continued to dictate local politics well into the twentieth. Known as "Tammany Tiger" (or simply "the Tiger") by the late 1860s, it controlled city jobs, made sure saloons and prostitutes functioned without interruption, oversaw the brisk trade at the city's docks, and, most important, sent politicians to office.[23] Tammany operatives routinely greeted recent arrivals and smoothed their entry into the unfamiliar new life for the promise of a vote. Through its strategic efforts to court and hold voters, Tammany Hall maintained, with rare moments of exception, a tight grip on Gotham's politics for nearly eighty years.[24]

Tammany reigned over New York City, which until 1898 included only the island of Manhattan and a small piece of neighboring Westchester County.[25] In that year, the New York state legislature implemented a major consolidation. The city land mass increased more than tenfold when neighboring Kings, Queens, Bronx, and Richmond Counties, otherwise known as Brooklyn, Queens, the Bronx, and Staten Island, were annexed to create Greater New York. But the consolidation was not universally welcomed. In particular, Brooklynites were proud of their city and wanted to maintain independence. Not only that, the population was exploding and the political leadership sought to expand its power.[26] The creation of the new municipality—New York City—jeopardized that goal, so in the late 1890s they tried to scuttle merger. They had reason to fear the Tiger's voracious appetite, but in reality Tammany risked losing power too because now it had to at least acknowledge other boroughs' Democratic leaders.[27]

Brooklynites' apprehension over Tammany's influence escalated in the early years of the new century. The Tiger was perceived to be strong-arming Democratic clubhouses across the city, and it adamantly resisted the mounting calls for social and political reform. Tammany politicians, especially "boss" Richard Crocker and Greater New York City's first mayor, Robert Van Wyck, were politically destroyed in scandals. In the 1902 mayoral election and again in the early 1910s the Democrats in every borough lost ground to reform candidates. Brooklyn leaders blamed Tammany Hall.[28] Charles Murphy, who assumed Tammany's leadership in 1902, conceded some authority to Brooklyn Democrats in order to keep peace, but they remained guarded about Tammany's will and potential to overwhelm them. Ultimately, Brooklyn Democrats remained fairly independent, but the "boss" in Manhattan dictated what the party would do. And Murphy was a masterful party leader. He read the winds of change during the era of reform in the 1910s and decided to redirect Tammany's path accordingly. As two major changes unfolded—the Great Migration of African Americans and women's attainment of the vote—the Tiger was well on its way to recovering its strength.

African Americans in the South and the North had been loyal to the party of Lincoln since the end of the Civil War.[29] In 1898, however, Edward E. Lee, along with a handful of other African American men who had grown frustrated with the total lack of political, economic, or social recognition from the New York City Republican Party, founded the club United Colored Democracy (UCD) in coordination with Tammany Hall to garner any benefits that Democratic Party patronage could yield. The UCD made its appeal to black male voters in overtly partisan and explicitly racial terms, arguing that while Republicans had abandoned black voters in New York, Democrats like Mayor Gaynor had served them well. They noted that Gaynor had called for an investigation of racial discrimination in hospitals and theaters, and he had addressed police brutality directed toward African Americans.[30] Although Tammany's claim was self-motivated and overstated, historian Richard Valelly suggests it was generally valid. Republicans dominated national politics at the very moment Southern Democrats inflicted their most lethal wounds on Southern black voters. At the national level, despite their relationship with Booker T. Washington, presidents McKinley, Roosevelt, and Taft, along with their Republican-dominated Congresses, did nothing to stop the near-total disenfranchisement of this loyal constituency.[31] In New York, Republicans did little for African Americans either, which had been the motivation for Lee and the others to found the UCD initially.

Though Democrats remained a minority within the African American community in New York City, they portended the possibility of political realignment. Moreover, the UCD was not the only example of African Americans' foray into the Democratic Party early in the twentieth century. In the 1912 presidential election, a number of national black leaders, including W. E. B. DuBois and William Monroe Trotter, decided to support Woodrow Wilson, appalled by both Roosevelt's and Taft's racism during their presidencies as well as Roosevelt's sanctioning of lily-white political clubs during his candidacy for president on the Progressive Party ticket.[32] But the move yielded nothing but disappointment. After his election, Wilson demonstrated his racist stripes by, among other things, segregating the nation's capital.

Given these national party dynamics, the UCD and Tammany Hall had to move strategically to win black voters' support. They distanced themselves from the president and the national Democratic Party with hard-hitting campaign fliers that called Wilson's actions toward African Americans "traitorous, un-American, unjust, undemocratic and hypocritical." Tammany argued that "the Wilson brand of democracy . . . ought to damn him eternally in the eyes of the Colored voter." The Tiger fashioned itself as something very different from the national Democratic Party. Simultaneously, it had to steer black men away from its local political competitors, especially the Fusion-Reform party.[33] Well ahead of the national reconfiguration of the Democratic Party in the 1930s and straddling a tricky political line, Tammany aggressively pursued black men's votes at the local level. Despite, or perhaps because of its provocative rhetoric, the Tiger's early efforts to woo African Americans helped chip away at the GOP's solid hold on this constituency.

Tammany's stance on race relations was strategic, not ideological, however. The Hall understood its political largesse as "kindness" that was to be repaid with votes. A UCD campaign flier concluded an appeal to black voters with a threat: "Will the Colored voters of this city have the intelligence enough to show their gratitude to Tammany Hall? If they do not, then for their base ingratitude and ignorance, Tammany Hall ought to withdraw its support from them."[34] Tammany's strong-arm tactics defined the terms by which it operated. For the African American voters who recently moved north, the choice was between a party that had helped liberate them from slavery but had since forsaken them or a party whose various coalition members represented both Jim Crow obstinacy and practical but conditional support.

Although overwhelmed by progressive reformers in the 1914 mayoral election, Tammany pressed forward. In return for Democratic Party loyalty, a handful of black leaders garnered a small but notable amount of patronage. For example, Ferdinand Q. Morton, leader of the UCD from 1915 through the 1920s won favor with Murphy. He was appointed head of the Indictment Bureau of the New York County district attorney's office and was the first black member of the Municipal Civil Service Commission.[35] Even the token gestures that the Democratic Party in New York City made were an improvement from the past, and African Americans began to migrate in increasing numbers from the Republican to the Democratic Party throughout the 1920s, particularly in local and state elections. When Tammany Mayor Hylan ran for re-election in 1921, for example, he won more than 70 percent of the black vote. Charles Murphy's protégé, Al Smith, won more than 60 percent in New York City when he ran for governor in 1922.[36] During that election year, an article in *The Crisis* reminded readers: "Ten years ago there was not a single Negro policeman in the metropolis of America. Today there are twenty or more. The Democrats gave them to us."[37]

In addition, Caribbean immigrants, who made up more than 15 percent of New York's black population, did not have the same ugly history with the Democratic Party as African Americans did. Marcus Garvey, the Jamaican born leader of the "Back to Africa" movement and founder of the Universal Negro Improvement Association (UNIA), supported Tammany Hall in the early 1920s. So did a number of other influential Caribbean immigrants who became Harlem leaders. These included Herbert Bruce, the first black Tammany district leader, and J. Raymond Jones, the first black Democratic county leader.[38]

In Brooklyn, the Democrats made inroads with black voters as well. The party secured the backing of the influential Rev. Thomas Harten, who led protests against racial discrimination in Brooklyn for more than two decades.[39] Harten determined that, at least at the local level, the Democrats had earned black people's support because they provided men with a variety of patronage jobs, including messengers, clerks, and street sweepers; just as important, Democrats provided women with teaching positions.[40] These appointments served as an early sign that when the Democratic Party reconsidered its position on race relations, there could be tangible benefits on both sides of the political equation.

While the party was busy courting black men in Harlem and Brooklyn, a second sizable constituency secured the right to vote. Tammany, the archetypal male political machine, had to decide how to handle women as voters and as potential political partners. And women, especially black women who had witnessed the disenfranchisement of their men, had to decide how to engage in politics.

Black Women and the Struggle for Suffrage

In a chapel just beyond the banks of the Seneca River in the "burned-over" district of New York State, Elizabeth Cady Stanton and Lucretia Mott brought together the nation's first formal gathering dedicated to women's rights in 1848. For the next seven decades, African American women and men, including the towering abolitionist, Frederick Douglass, and white women like Susan B. Anthony and Lucy Stone, fought for women's rights, above all the right to vote. At the end of the Civil War, African American leaders such as Mary Ann Shadd Cary, Charlotte Forten, Josephine St. Pierre Ruffin, and Sojourner Truth worked for suffrage in various Northern and border cities. As part of their efforts, they joined the two principal suffrage organizations, the National Woman Suffrage Association (NWSA) and the American Woman Suffrage Association (AWSA) to push the issue forward.[41] In the early 1870s, determined to exercise what they believed was their fundamental right of citizenship, Cary, Truth, Anthony, and other women attempted to vote. In Battle Creek, Michigan, Truth was denied a ballot; in Washington, D.C., Cary was denied as well; in Rochester, New York, Anthony and more than a dozen other women were arrested.[42]

Throughout the rest of the nineteenth century, efforts to secure women's enfranchisement continued, but they were hardly unified. Fault lines surfaced repeatedly over critical issues like the embrace or rejection of racial equality and over strategies like the targeting of the U.S. Congress or the states. Suffragists' debates regarding support of the Fifteenth Amendment, which enfranchised black men, fractured the movement in the immediate aftermath of the Civil War.[43] It took twenty years for the NWSA and AWSA to merge their efforts in the wake of that conflict and form the National American Woman Suffrage Association (NAWSA). Even when officially welcomed into suffrage organizations led by white women, black women rarely experienced equal treatment; at times they were excluded from or segregated during strategy sessions and public events.[44] The most striking examples of racism went beyond the exclusion of black women from meetings, however. In Southern states the goal was to exclude them from the right to vote itself.[45] Despite the myriad obstacles they faced, black women persevered.

In the Reconstruction South, black women had participated in a kind of family politics whereby they attended civic celebrations, discussed issues, and evaluated candidates with their husbands even though they could not vote. When they moved north to New York, Chicago, and Detroit, they retained their concerns about political and civic life and, despite some class tensions, joined their efforts with those of women, especially clubwomen in these cities who had taken up the suffrage cause.[46] In New York City, for example, Victoria Earle Matthews, a journalist for T. Thomas Fortune's newspaper the *New York Age*, was an ardent champion of women's suffrage. Born into slavery in Georgia and brought north through her mother's efforts, Matthews was a passionate and effective organizer. She co-founded the Women's Loyal Union in the wake of Ida B. Wells's 1892 anti-lynching speaking tour in New York, and she helped secure more than ten thousand signatures in support of a woman's suffrage resolution.

Sarah J. S. Garnet, a native New Yorker, was born twenty years before the Civil War. A teacher by profession and the first African American female principal in the New York City public school system, Garnet was a lifelong activist. In the 1880s, she fought to keep African American schools open and traveled to the state capital to protest against discrimination that black teachers faced. Although the widow of Henry Highland Garnet, the renowned abolitionist, minister, and diplomat, Sarah Garnet was respected in her own right for her breadth of activism. She started the Equal Suffrage League in the late 1880s, which was the only black women's organization in Brooklyn dedicated to the cause, and after the NACW's founding, she headed its Suffrage Department. She died in 1911, just as New York suffragists launched their final rounds of struggle, but her influence on black women was felt across the city and the nation. In keeping with Garnet's vision, Frances R. Keyser, first president of the NACW affiliate Empire State Federation of Colored Women's Clubs, was a dedicated suffragist as well. She guided her organization's racial uplift strategy. Not only did it include the embrace of respectability, but Keyser also ensured that it incorporated the acquisition of full citizenship rights for women, politically as well as socially.[47]

By 1910, Irene Moorman also joined the ranks of suffragists, although, like many women, she maintained a broad political agenda. Not only did she serve as president of the Negro Women's Business League, but she was also an early and enthusiastic Garvey supporter. Moorman became president of the New York UNIA Ladies' Division in 1917. At first Moorman doubted that white America would grant black women full political rights, especially given the devastating effects Jim Crow laws and vigilante violence had had on black men's right to vote in the South. But she was persuaded enough by a conversation she had with Alva Belmont, prominent white socialite and founder of the Political Equality League, that she organized a suffrage meeting at the Mount Olivet Baptist Church on West Fifty-Third Street in February 1910. Under Moorman's leadership, the meeting proved a success. That day more than one hundred women in the audience joined the Political Equality League and harnessed their energy to the suffrage fight.[48]

Historically, black women, like white women, had been denied the full rights of citizenship. But black women had a considerable set of challenges to contend with that white women did not. African Americans' physical safety was jeopardized when white people's racism boiled over into violent, riotous rage, as it did in Manhattan in 1863 and again in 1900. Their access to jobs, education, and decent housing was circumscribed by ideological color lines and restrictive covenants. Time and again, Moorman's and many other black women's skepticism about their attainment of real political power in New York and in cities across the North proved justified. A year after the Mount Olivet Baptist Church meeting, the *New York Times* reminded New Yorkers just how alive and well Jim Crow was in their city. When Harriet Alice Dewey, a white woman and wife of philosopher John Dewey, wanted to host an interracial suffrage meeting in her uptown apartment, the building owners demanded she cancel it, emphasizing that the problem was black women's attendance.[49]

Most often, however, black women met resistance from white women themselves rather than from outside obstacles. As historian Roselyn Terborg-Penn notes, even Belmont, who helped fund suffrage offices in black neighborhoods in New York, evinced racism. A Southerner by birth, she also gave money to the Southern Woman Suffrage Conference, which fought a federal suffrage amendment because it would enfranchise Southern black women.[50] Racism proved there was no such thing as sisterhood, but black women remained committed to women's enfranchisement and were cautiously willing to work with white women nonetheless.

New Yorkers first voted for a women's suffrage amendment in 1915. In anticipation of the election, black women, like white women, escalated their efforts. Lyda Newman opened the Negro Suffrage Headquarters in Manhattan as part of the coordinated effort with the New York Woman Suffrage Party. Not only did she encourage neighborhood mothers to get involved by providing childcare, but she also canvassed the district and organized street meetings to educate the community about women's suffrage. New Yorkers voted down the amendment in 1915, but suffragists made sure it was on the ballot again in 1917.[51]

Annie K. Lewis, president of the Colored Women's Suffrage Club of New York City, led the final push in Harlem. Yet even as the state's historic vote loomed, black women questioned their status in the suffrage movement in relation to white women. Tensions boiled over weeks before the 1917 election when Mary Sharperson Young, a Colored Women's Suffrage Club member and later leader in the UNIA, charged that she had been discriminated against during the statewide suffrage convention in Saratoga. Lewis called a meeting of the Colored Women's Club to discuss the matter and invited white suffrage leaders Anne Watkins and Annie Matthews to attend.[52] The meeting lasted well past midnight and generated a great deal of debate. Annie Lewis and Helen Christian, both of whom had also been at the Saratoga convention, disputed Young's interpretation of the event, arguing that black women had received equal treatment to white women. Others at the Harlem meeting, including a woman referred to in the meeting minutes only as "Mrs. Goode," shared Young's perspective of black women's lack of equal status. Goode sparked "quite a verbal battle" when she argued that black women should form an independent suffrage organization rather than work through the New York City Woman Suffrage Party. Lewis tried to silence Goode, arguing that she was not a member of the Colored Women's Suffrage Club and therefore not entitled to speak at the meeting. She and Christian wanted to maintain a positive relationship with the white leadership of the New York State Woman Suffrage Party. Interracialism versus black separatism was one of many ideological fault lines that divided black women and men at the same time that the commitment to racial equality united them. As a UNIA member with a strong sense of race pride, Young may have been more willing to forsake niceties to expose racist undercurrents.[53] Young's and Goode's advocacy of separatism did not prevail in this debate, however. By the meeting's end, the majority of participants concluded that black women's status was equal to white women's status in the New York suffrage organization, and they left with a rousing suffrage speech by Harlem's Helen Holman, a Colored Women's Club member and a Socialist, ringing in their ears.[54]

For black women who pursued leadership roles, especially those whose leadership took them face to face with white-led organizations, certain lessons were clear by the 1910s. The first lesson that all American women had to contend with was that at its root, public citizenship was a masculine domain. The Tiger had been against the enfranchisement of women for years. For example, when a group of white women initially asked Tammany favorite son Assemblyman Al Smith to support women's suffrage, he "shot a stream of tobacco juice at a spittoon and told them that as far as he was concerned a woman's place was at home."[55] In pursuing the franchise, women were hammering away at one of the foundations of male privilege and power, and men were determined to give as little ground as possible. Though hardly new, the second lesson was similarly challenging. White women could not be counted on to stand with black women in the struggle against racism or racialized gender discrimination that black women alone faced.[56] If black women wanted to engage in politics, they would have to wear an emotional coat of armor to fend off outward attacks and more subtle but equally pernicious slights from hostile men, black and white, and from white women.

The third lesson posed a distinct dilemma. Discord among African American women, it was increasingly clear, was draining but often unavoidable. Black women held diverse ideological positions, competed over strategies, and suffered from class tensions. Annie Lewis, for instance, faced criticism from black women outside the Colored Women's Suffrage Club. Her opponents argued, according to the *New York Age*, that Lewis was "not generally known as an educated woman," implying that she was unfit to lead the crusade in Harlem.[57] Moreover, Goode and Young had questioned her suffrage strategies and willingness to work with white women whose commitment to racial equality was thin or nonexistent. Gender, race, class, and ideological issues individually, and as interconnected dynamics, created daunting challenges to black women. The situation was familiar though disheartening. Their growing numbers and impending enfranchisement may have positioned them one big step closer to the levers of political power, but they understood there was much more terrain to cover before they garnered any real capacity to make lasting, structural changes.

At times working across the color line, but more often in separate organizations, suffragists ultimately attained their goal. The Republican-controlled legislature in Albany sent the suffrage amendment to the voters again. In addition to the women's steady efforts, a combination of forces gave the amendment a strong boost between the failed vote in 1915 and the successful vote in 1917. Although the national Democratic and Republican parties were unsupportive of the vote for women, the progressive reform spirit ran high in New York City. Activists had worked assiduously to wear down the resistance of the New York State legislature and that of male voters, especially during the 1910s.[58] In addition, in 1917 the Socialist Party fielded a number of successful candidates for the state assembly and a competitive candidate for mayor. It also actively supported women's suffrage.[59] Finally, although Tammany Hall was nothing if not a man's world, some of its leaders appreciated not only the momentum behind the suffrage amendment but also the possibility of capitalizing on new voters. In a demonstration of Murphy's strategic leadership, it was the vote in New York City—Tammany's stronghold—that gave the suffrage amendment its significant margin of victory.[60] With the amendment's passage, more than a million women in New York were enfranchised.

Citizenship Education for Women

Immediately after women's suffrage became law, voter education campaigns proliferated. The *New York Times* ran a series titled "The Woman Voter," which detailed numerous aspects of New York City politics, including the function of primary elections and party leaders. The series also explained how political power was determined.[61] The *New York Age* noted that "Colored women ... have begun to form clubs and are talking politics with zest and enthusiasm." On the eve of the first presidential election after the Nineteenth Amendment's ratification, the editors of the *Age* urged women to "learn all the preliminary steps to voting and to get the practice of marking a ballot." At the same time, they displayed their skepticism that women were fully ready to take on the franchise and argued that "there is no reason why they should not permit men to assist them in it."[62] Women continued to face paternalism and resistance long after they won the vote. Getting the majority of the press to take them seriously as political actors would prove to be a significant and intractable challenge. But that did not keep Harlem's women from moving forward. The YWCA hosted forums on "preparation for citizenship" and the NAACP urged women to learn all about the government and election laws in order to advance the race. *The Crisis*, its monthly publication, contended, "They may beat and bribe our men, but the political hope of the Negro rests on its intelligent and incorruptible womanhood." Though a heavy and intensely gendered burden, black women stood ready to respond.[63]

The significant shifts in the electoral demography that resulted from the Great Migration and women's suffrage posed unprecedented challenges and opportunities to party operatives across New York City. The political culture was both racialized as white and deeply masculine. Tammany Hall had its work cut out if it wanted to attract these untested constituents rather than concede them to the more reform-minded and ostensibly more supportive Republican Party.[64] At the same time, these new voters had to learn the political ropes. They had to determine how and when to participate in formal politics; they also had to cultivate strategies that would not only land them inside party clubhouses but also give them a say in evolving political agendas. The challenges were numerous, and access to political parties and the halls of government, women learned quickly, did not equal power.

Political Parties Respond

The varying degrees to which the Democrats, Republicans, and Socialists were willing to reconfigure their political structures in response to African Americans' and women's participation in electoral politics emerged over the next few years.[65] In 1918, the first election after women in New York won the right to vote, Tammany Hall courted African Americans and women. The groundwork it had laid with the UCD seemed to be paying off. After a successful stint in the state assembly, Al Smith sought the governorship. The NAACP gave Smith a glowing endorsement, noting that in Albany, Smith had "achieved a record for constructive and progressive legislation unsurpassed by any man."[66] Moreover, after 1917, when Edward A. Johnson, a Republican black man from Harlem, was elected to the New York State Assembly, Tammany began to run black men for the office.[67]

At the same time, in early 1918 a group of men and women formed the Independent Citizens' Committee for Alfred E. Smith. Among them were prominent white progressive reformers Belle Moskowitz and Frances Perkins, who had worked with Smith on safety legislation in the aftermath of the Triangle Shirtwaist fire, and suffragist Harriet Stanton Blatch.[68] Most politicians expected that women would vote as a bloc; Smith was no different. To win women's votes, Smith asked Moskowitz to set up a special Women's Division and advise him about how to speak to women's groups.[69] As a result of Tammany's foundational work courting black men's votes and Smith's cultivation of women's votes (there is no evidence he made overtures to black women specifically), he was elected governor of New York in November 1918.[70] Tammany was back on top in the city and in the state capital in Albany.

Tammany's outreach efforts through the UCD and the Women's Division were typical vote-getting approaches. It simultaneously pursued a second, novel strategy. The Tiger wanted to determine if it could win more women's votes if it ran female candidates, so it fielded a white female candidate in the 1918 election. It was only curious to a point, however. The Democrats ran Mary Lilly in a solidly Republican assembly district in Manhattan against Allen Ellenbogen, the Republican incumbent. Their political curiosity was not so strong as to risk a safe Democratic seat. A progressive reformer, Lilly showed her mettle, beating both Ellenbogen and the Socialist candidate, Robert Vogel, by a few hundred votes. One of the first two women elected to office in New York, Lilly headed to the state capital in Albany to represent the Seventh Assembly District.[71]

The Republicans also competed for African Americans' and women's votes. In 1917 they began to run black men for elected office in predominantly African American districts, and black men won. At the same time nearly seventy-five thousand black women were enfranchised in 1917, a sizable constituency that the party fought to hold. The GOP chose four African American women to serve as delegates and alternates for the New York State Republican convention. This was hardly a radical step, but it created the opportunity for black women officially to weigh in on the party's platform for the first time. Moreover, in the 1920 presidential campaign, the first after the Nineteenth Amendment's passage, Warren Harding made more of an effort to secure black voters in the North than most Republican candidates had in recent elections, and this effort included targeting black women. The party also wanted to secure white women's votes. As part of its strategy, it set up women's divisions at all levels to court the anticipated women's voting bloc, and party bosses selected New York City suffrage leader Mary Garrett Hay, a white woman, to chair the platform committee.[72]

The Republicans wanted also to see how African American and female candidates fared as candidates. The Nineteenth Assembly District was in the heart of Harlem. In 1917, the GOP fought to retain black men in the party by running an African American for office. They fielded Edward A. Johnson, former dean of Shaw University's law school, for the seat. Upon his victory, Johnson became the first black man elected to office in the state of New York. Johnson won with substantial African American support, but he also won at least some white support. A year later, Democratic challenger and Tammany operative Martin J. Healy, a white man, defeated both Johnson in his reelection bid and Socialist Party candidate and labor leader A. Philip Randolph. That the two black men held competing political views helped divide the black vote. But so did the controversial issue of prohibition. Johnson supported it. That may have helped him win over black women who worried about temperance, a central element of their racial uplift strategy. The majority of voters, however, preferred the anti-prohibition candidate, Healy. The extent to which voters, now including thousands of black women, made their decisions based on race or prohibition is impossible to measure, but Healy's victory was narrower than the racial divide, indicating that he won some African Americans' votes.[73] Prohibition may well have been the deciding factor.

Republicans in Manhattan wanted to test the new voters' electoral proclivities further. The Long Island GOP ran a successful female candidate for the State Assembly in the 1918 election. Ida Sammis, a white woman from Suffolk County, served in Albany with Mary Lilly. A year later Harlem Republicans put Marguerite Smith, a white woman, up for office for the Nineteenth Assembly District against the incumbent, Martin Healy. Prior to the primary, the Nineteenth Assembly Republican club negotiated a deal with the local leadership to run a black man for the board of aldermen and a white woman, Smith, for state assembly in an effort to capitalize on both black and female voters. Harlem residents unhappy with the party's strategy, however, wanted African American candidates to run for both, so Rev. R. M. Bolden, a black man from the district, was tapped to run against Smith in the primary election in a direct challenge to the party's wishes.[74] But with strong party backing and the *New York Age*'s endorsement, Smith defeated Bolden in a heated race and headed to the general election, where she also beat Healy. Tammany took a drubbing during the 1919 elections, and Smith was one of many Republicans that year who benefited from its temporary decline. Because Tammany's losses included its only female assemblywoman, Mary Lilly, Smith's cohort of women in the legislature remained tiny.

In sum, the Democrats and Republicans tried to capitalize on the new constituents flooding the voter rolls in the late 1910s. To win women's support they made small changes to the party structures and ran a handful of white women for the assembly. Fighting to secure black women's votes, the Republicans also selected African American women to represent their districts at the state and national party conventions. The success of even these modest gestures had important lessons to convey to the political parties—namely, that women were not only eager to participate in party politics, but they could win. Nevertheless, these lessons were willfully lost on both the Democrats and the Republicans. Lilly's and Smith's victories and the other work women did for the parties failed to change Democratic or Republican leaders' behavior toward women in any lasting or substantial way. The parties were more attentive to the lessons they learned about running black men for office. At least in predominantly African American districts, after 1917 the Democrats and Republicans fielded black male candidates for office on a fairly consistent basis. The racialized white nature of party politics changed more than its gendered masculine dimensions. For the black women who had shown their commitment to electoral politics and may have wanted to run for office, the interconnected dynamics of racism and gender discrimination kept them off the political parties' radar screens almost completely. No black women got the chance to show either Democrats or Republicans how they would fare at the polls because throughout the 1920s, neither party ran them for office. Resilient in the face of adversity and discrimination, black women pushed forward nonetheless, determined to make a space for themselves in the political arena and to have a say in the social, political, and economic landscapes of Harlem and Brooklyn.

African American men and women as well as white women looking for a more inclusive political home found it in the Socialist Party.[75] Not only had the party actively backed women's suffrage, but between 1917 and 1921, when Socialists in New York had representative presence in both city and state legislatures, they ran a significant number of African American and female candidates, including Grace Campbell, a black woman and head of the Harlem Negro Settlement House. Campbell ran for office at least twice. She ran unsuccessfully for the Twenty-First State Assembly District seat in 1919. The following year, Campbell challenged incumbent Marguerite Smith for the Nineteenth Assembly District seat.[76] Again she lost. Neither Campbell nor any of the other Socialist Party candidates, including the labor leader A. Philip Randolph, received positive coverage in black newspapers like the *New York Age*, which had a staunchly Republican editorial board. Campbell may have been the first African American woman to run for elected office in New York City, but because of her leftist political affiliation and the indifference the press had about women in politics, this historic marker passed without comment from the city's largest black newspaper.[77]

In the years following World War I and the Russian Revolution of 1917, an oppressive climate of intolerance settled upon the nation. Anti-immigrant advocates began a vigorous campaign to close the nation's gateways. In 1921 and even more robustly in 1924 Congress answered their call with a pair of laws that dramatically reduced the number of Europeans allowed into the country. In the wake of an unprecedented strike wave in 1919, labor unions and striking workers, including the Industrial Workers of the World (IWW) and the Boston police, were violently repressed. United States Attorney General A. Mitchell Palmer ordered the raids of radical organizations and labor unions. Over five thousand people were caught up in the dragnet. Anarchist activist Emma Goldman was deported; Socialist labor leader and five-time presidential candidate Eugene Debs was jailed. A near toxic Red Scare spread across the country.

The New York State Assembly was not spared from the witch hunt. In 1920, five state assembly members who had won their elections on the Socialist Party ticket were barred from taking their seats in the state house.[78] Suspicion ran so high that the state assembly passed a bill by a wide margin excluding the Socialist Party from participation in future elections. It was only Governor Smith's veto that kept the bill from becoming law.[79] The repressive environment did not keep Socialist candidates from trying to win elections, however. In addition to Campbell, a number of African Americans and women ran for city, state, and national office, including A. Philip Randolph and Harriet Stanton Blatch. But in the hostile climate, Socialists fared poorly at the polls. More so than the two major parties, third parties remained more supportive of those who had been historically marginalized, especially African American and female candidates; however, they did not lead women to electoral victories.[80] If women were going to win, it would be with the less welcoming Democratic and Republican parties.

In assessing the elections in the late 1910s, it is impossible to definitively identify why voters made the decisions they did. Their affinities with or concerns about candidates' racial or gendered identities likely played a contributing role in how people voted. African American candidates did well in predominantly black districts. Yet if black voters had cared only about racial solidarity, then Johnson would have held their loyalties in his reelection bid against Healy, and Bolden could have defeated Marguerite Smith in the primary campaign. Similarly, Grace Campbell could have beaten or at least seriously challenged Marguerite Smith and the white Democratic candidate. But political ideology was also an important factor in people's voting behavior. New Yorkers generally, and Harlemites particularly, did not support Socialist candidates, especially after 1919. Even Campbell's longstanding and respected community activism did not help her win over large numbers of black voters. At the same time, the gendered culture of clubhouse politics and the "gendered imagination" of the society in which they lived undermined women in electoral politics.[81] Even though organizations like Tammany made room for a handful of powerful white women, men continued to dominate national and state party conventions, clubhouse politics, and campaign slates. Mary Lilly and Marguerite Smith were the only women from New York City elected to the state assembly between 1918 and 1933.[82] During the same period, in contrast, black men not only ran for the state assembly and board of aldermen regularly, but more than a handful won.

While the vote was a significant step for the advancement of women's citizenship rights, it was clear that the Democrats and Republicans had no intentions of running black women for office. After Campbell's failed campaigns black women did not appear on party ballots for more than a decade. Instead, they worked in the limited ways they could to compel the parties, over time, to take them seriously as political actors and to pay attention to the issues they raised. These were very much uphill struggles. As the new decade dawned and the Progressive Era drew to a close with Warren Harding's presidential election, black women employed a variety of political strategies to make advances for their communities and themselves.

The 1920s—New Opportunities and New Complications for Black Women

By 1920 the war was over, but the nation did not know peace. Instead, horrific demonstrations of racist brutality and labor repression unfolded in cities across the country. Harlem Renaissance luminary and NAACP field secretary James Weldon Johnson, who had chronicled the viciousness of the 1900 New York City riot, now coined the phrase "Red Summer" to capture the scope of the violence and devastation that resulted from the 1919 riots. In that notorious year, from the birthplace of the old Confederacy in Charleston, South Carolina, to the sizzling summer streets of Washington, D.C., and Chicago, to the mining centers of the Southwest like Bisbee, Arizona, African Americans died at the hands of white aggressors, in some cases while they were still wearing their military uniforms.[83] In 1921, the most horrific exposition of racist violence unfolded in Tulsa, Oklahoma, when a white mob murdered more than two hundred African Americans and burned the black neighborhood of Greenwood to the ground.

The promises of citizenship that black men's participation in World War I and black women's patriotic war work were intended to yield never materialized. Instead, in response to the Great Migration, cities in the North and Midwest witnessed the reincarnation of Jim Crow and racial hatred.

Wiser for their war experiences on the battlefields and the home front, and politically stronger because of their concentrated numbers in northern cities, African Americans issued a powerful response of resistance. It was most clearly manifest in Harlem, the "Negro Mecca." As migrants settled in from the South and the Caribbean, they shared not only their labor but also their ideas about racial justice and their creative talents. Writers, musicians, and artists birthed a cultural renaissance that notably marked not just the city but also the nation. When Anna Arnold Hedgeman moved to Harlem to become the YWCA's membership secretary, she entered a world in which she had regular contact with the most dynamic minds of the era. At forums sponsored by the Harlem YWCA, Langston Hughes, looking like "a slim brown angel," read his poems, and W. E. B. DuBois talked about Africa and pan-Africanism. "James Weldon Johnson was our authority on the history of the Negro," Hedgeman recalled. And William Pickens, who was affectionately known as "The Dean," lectured about the ongoing challenges that the NAACP faced in the Jim Crow South.[84] Through these frequent encounters as well as the regular stories published in *The Crisis* and the *New York Age*, Hedgeman and numerous other women who were fighting for racial equality and community betterment locally could see their activism as part of the larger national effort to bring about equality and justice.[85]

At the same time, African American women found themselves in an increasingly complex sociopolitical landscape in the 1920s. The emerging New Negro movement and Black Nationalism had distinct gendered dynamics that politically minded black women had to carefully negotiate. The NAACP's W. E. B. DuBois and Jamaican-born poet Claude McKay encapsulated the masculinist spirit of the era in a pair of writings published in 1919. Speaking on behalf of black *men* in his article "Returning Soldiers," DuBois decreed, "We are returning from war! . . . This country of ours, despite all its better souls have done and dreamed, is yet a shameful land. . . . We are cowards . . . if . . . we do not marshal every ounce of our brain and brawn to fight a sterner, longer, more unbending battle against the forces of hell in our own land. . . . We return fighting."[86] McKay's poem "If We Must Die" was equally unambiguous in its assertion of masculinity:

If we must die, let it not be like hogs
Hunted and penned in an inglorious spot,
While round us bark the mad and hungry dogs. . . .
If we must die, O let us nobly die, . . .
Like men we'll face the murderous, cowardly pack,
Pressed to the wall, dying, but fighting back![87]

And finally, the changes were characterized by the ascendance of Jamaican-born leader Marcus Garvey and his proudly patriarchal organization, the UNIA. In this shifting environment and in response to Red Summer, black men in Northern cities gained political agency and cultural capital. At the same time, black clubwomen, who had long worked for racial uplift through the politics of respectability and the elevation of women's status, were displaced as race leaders.[88]

Many politically minded women adapted. Some refocused their priorities, others created new ways to practice their activism.[89] Former suffragists Mary Sharperson Young and Irene Moorman Blackstone, for example, embraced Garveyism and assumed some of the leadership positions open to women within the UNIA. Young helped build ways for women to participate in the organization's pageantry by founding the UNIA Women's Elite Royal Court of Ethiopia in New York City. The organization's newspaper, the *Negro World*, featured a photograph of Young sitting regally adorned. The image reinforced the UNIA's belief that black women and womanhood were to be protected and celebrated.

Its subtler message, however, was that they were no longer the public leaders of the race.[90] Blackstone's role in the movement suggested that gender roles were at least a little fluid despite the UNIA's rigid structure. When Garvey first settled into New York City, Blackstone was one of his earliest followers. In 1917, she served as the president of the New York UNIA Ladies' Division. After that she remained, according to the *Negro World*, "an unusually bold and race-loving character, who is not happy unless doing something to promote the interests of her race." To that end, she gave an inspiring speech to the New York chapter of the UNIA in 1923. Attentive to the economic and political power of consumer-based activism, she advocated black-owned businesses and the boycotting of white-owned stores. "Why," she pointedly asked the audience, "should all the white men come up here on your main streets—Fifth Avenue, Lenox Avenue, Seventh and Eighth Avenues [in Harlem]—and have all of the business places? . . . White men paying rent to have stores to keep you waiting to be waited on. . . . If you would boycott the white business man in Harlem, you would find black businesses on the avenue." Additionally, she urged black women to leave white women's kitchens and realize their own strength and ingenuity. Blackstone embodied the very essence of the New Negro movement. "I am American. I am black, and I am proud that I am black," she proclaimed.[91] Her embrace of her "twoness" was absent the tension DuBois documented in his powerfully written *Souls of Black Folk* twenty years earlier.[92] Yet, in line with the times, Blackstone did not situate black womanhood as an explicit element in her framework of race politics.

Other black women, who may have appreciated the critiques that Black Nationalism had to make of white America, were nonetheless more inclined to pursue politics through other avenues—in interracial political clubhouses, in civic organizations, and in grassroots groups. Hedgeman was such an example. She expressed separatist sentiments but worked for the YWCA, an organization ostensibly committed to racial equality and integration. Shortly after her arrival in New York she, like other civic activists, began to appreciate the "value of political power" that the increased African American population yielded in Harlem. Hedgeman mounted countless stairs, conducted informal civics lessons, collected signatures on petitions, and hosted meetings for the community to meet with candidates.[93] Through efforts like hers, both the Republicans and Democrats experienced an increase in support from African American women. Along with their support, however, these women brought more public scrutiny. The parties, at least at the local level, were held to greater account, particularly—but not exclusively—on issues of race.

Throughout the 1920s, Republican women formed local clubs to raise concerns about economic inequality and civil rights issues. That was what the Roosevelt Women's Republican League did, for example. Harlem local Julia Coleman and Brooklynite Maria C. Lawton, a longstanding leader in the clubwomen's movement, collaborated to form the Professional Women's Republican Club to give middle class women an opportunity to discuss and weigh in on political issues. A third Republican organization, the Colored Women's Hoover-Curtis Committee of Manhattan, emphasized the need for women to learn the fundamentals of civic life. Its members worked aggressively to register women to vote, particularly first-time voters.[94] Women's voter education and registration work was so effective that during the 1928 election, the *New York Age* acknowledged, "Never before in the history of political campaigns have the women of the country taken such an active part."[95]

At the same time, women often challenged racism within the GOP and weighed their votes in light of it. Editors of the *New York Age* and the *New York Amsterdam News* urged women in Harlem to vote Republican. But several female leaders refused to give their loyalty automatically to the GOP, as was evidenced by the substantial black vote for New York Democrats John Hylan for mayor and Al Smith for governor in the late 1910s and early 1920s. It was also clear in the halls of the YWCA, one of the most important social spaces for women in Harlem. Cecelia Cabaniss Saunders, the Harlem YWCA director with whom Hedgeman worked, spoke about the importance of the vote and declared that although she was an "enrolled Negro Republican," she emphasized "'Negro' and stated that she has more ties to bind her to the Negro race than to the Republican or any other party or organization."[96] The same caution was evident at the national level. During the NACW's 1920 convention, for example, the association's members defeated a resolution to endorse the Republican Party platform because it did not take a strong stand against lynching.[97] Those who expressed wariness about the Republican Party found they were vindicated. By the 1920s the party of Lincoln had abandoned even a pretense of concern for African Americans' social, political, or economic rights. One such example transpired after the 1928 presidential election. Although the Republican leadership deployed African American women as foot soldiers to campaign for Hoover, they asked the women to give back invitations to one of the presidential inaugural balls that had been sent to them "accidentally."[98]

Many African Americans in New York City left the party. Others tried to reform it. After a protracted struggle over the Republican Party leadership in Harlem, black women and men under politico Fred Moore's direction finally displaced the white-dominated political machine.[99] At least in one arena of city politics, African Americans made headway. New York City was still dominated by Democrats, however, and for a growing number of black New Yorkers, the Republican Party was the wrong vehicle for change.

Inasmuch as many black women joined the GOP after they won the right to vote, a number of politically oriented women joined Democratic Party clubhouses and created new organizations throughout New York City. One such woman was North Carolina native Ruth Whitehead Whaley, a trailblazer in the legal profession and later mentor to feminist legal activist Pauli Murray. Whaley was the first black woman to graduate from Fordham Law School. She learned quickly that despite her migration north and her superlative academic success, she was not protected from the vagaries and humiliations of racism. As a top student in her graduating law class, Whaley was supposed to receive a free set of law books, but the school and the publisher delayed the award, demanding that she submit to an unprecedented extra round of competition. Whaley charged them with racism. Her graduation day, which should have been a moment of celebration and historic significance, was instead shadowed by discrimination.[100]

The Fordham conflict was frustrating, but it certainly did not dissuade Whaley, who forged forward into public life. When she moved to Harlem, Whaley made her political home in the Democratic Party, earlier than most nationally prominent African American women. She worked for the party during Al Smith's 1928 presidential campaign, serving as the vice chairman of the Smith for President Colored League.[101] Yet Whaley, like scores of black women, was neither blind to her party's racism nor silent about it. When she found it necessary, she distanced herself from the Democrats and argued that the only way to get the political parties to support African American candidates for judgeships was to organize an independent movement. Without a threat to their power, "old line politicians," Whaley contended, would not nominate or appoint black judges. So convinced was she of the need to strike out on a separate path, she offered her time and energy to any black candidate willing to take a stand.[102] Interestingly, Whaley did not run herself. Either she determined that the time was not right for a black female candidate, or she was not ready to jump into the fray at that level. She would be ready later, but not in the 1920s.

In New York City, just as in the rest of the country, the Democratic Party was known for its racist practices. The Tammany Hall club in Harlem's Nineteenth Assembly District remained under the control of two white operatives, William Allen and Annie Matthews, the former suffrage leader who attended the 1917 Colored Women's Suffrage Club meeting the night the organization deliberated its status vis-à-vis white women. In 1924, Allen and Matthews demonstrated remarkable enmity toward African Americans when they hosted a dinner for six thousand city Democrats, and not a single one of the attendees was black.[103] Moreover, although Charles Murphy, Al Smith, and a number of other white leaders garnered support among black voters, many Tammany candidates refused to cross the color line even for the good of the party. Knowing that victorious black candidates like Johnson and Anderson had won their elections with at least a little support from white voters, some white candidates deployed racist campaign tactics to scare them. For example, a 1922 campaign flier with photos of the black candidate and the white candidate read, "So That You Might Know Before Voting—CONSIDER and Make Your Choice" (emphasis in original). Despite the NAACP's support of Governor Smith in the early 1920s, DuBois noted in a *Crisis* editorial that the Democrats, including Smith, failed African Americans as often as Republicans did. He made neither political appointments nor legislative proposals to benefit African Americans.[104] Smith's recognition of African Americans was so minimal that when he ran for president in 1928, with the exception of Massachusetts and Rhode Island, he carried only Southern states. Belle Moskowitz, his closest advisor, told Walter White that "Smith thought he should have made a stronger bid for the black vote."[105] This was at best an understatement. Black leaders like Whaley locally and DuBois nationally publicly exposed machinations of discrimination and voiced skepticism about remaining loyal to either party, even as they endeavored to make them fairer.[106]

Black politicos were left uncertain about where to cast their political fortunes as the 1920s wore on. The GOP failed to pass an anti-lynching bill, it tolerated Jim Crowism in the Southern branches of the party, and it did next to nothing to create economic or political opportunities for African Americans in the North.[107] Yet, despite their experiments outside the GOP at city and state levels in the North, black voters still found it nearly impossible to pull the lever for the Democratic Party in national elections when Southern racists remained so dominant and so vocal. One particularly stark reminder about the party's limits transpired during the 1928 Democratic National Convention. Black Democrats were corralled into a segregated area of the convention floor that had been cordoned off with chicken wire. African American men and women were ready to migrate from the Republicans, but there was no new viable political home on the horizon.[108]

As black activists contended with the realities of racism within political parties, the women among them had a number of distinct challenges to grapple with at the same time. There was a highly gendered culture in clubhouse politics that successfully absorbed women's participation without conceding much real decision-making power.[109] Only two women over a sixteen-year period, both of whom were white, were elected to the state assembly. Not only that, by 1928 the percentage of female delegates chosen for the Democratic and Republican Party national conventions had settled in between 10 and 15 percent.[110] Men continued to dominate national and state party conventions, clubhouse politics, and campaign slates. Taken together, these experiences, along with the racism embedded in political parties, explain why black women made, at best, very modest advances in formal political circles through the 1920s. They got a big toe inside the doors of both the Democratic and Republican Party machines working as poll watchers, campaign workers, and, when possible, as critics of racist practices. But while these activities provided important experience, they represented the limits of women's forward movement.[111] At least in the public record, African American women remained silent about these limitations. There is little evidence beyond the suffrage campaign that breaking down gendered walls of discrimination in politics was one of their main concerns. Only the very efforts to participate in New York's political life by women like Cecelia Cabaniss Saunders, Julia Coleman, Irene Moorman Blackstone, and Ruth Whaley demonstrate their belief that women had a right to have a say in politics. For black women especially, the attainment of their "birthright" and their "due" was still a long way off.

People's Politics—Reform and Resistance at the Grassroots Level

Although a few worked through formal political channels, most black women tried to exert influence through a different, familiar form of politics—grassroots organizing. Some activists hailed from the middle class and embraced the politics of racial uplift. Creating new organizations and facilities, these women endeavored to improve their communities' physical and moral well-being. Others were grounded in a more assertive politics of race pride. Taking advantage of the comparatively safer space in the North, they marched, they lobbied, and they organized. Whether the need was for housing, jobs, or community betterment, in the 1910s and 1920s women were regularly in the vanguard of the fight. Many operated in ways that were very much in keeping with larger Progressive Era reform efforts of the day. At the same time, even when the nation sought "normalcy" and the curtailment of government intervention after World War I, these grassroots activists persisted apace.

As soon as they migrated to Harlem, women organized and led lobbying efforts for housing. They needed to because they faced housing shortages, exorbitant rents, and at times appalling physical conditions. Some brought with them years of community or church-based experience but had had little or no opportunity for political activism in the South. Winnie Jones, for example, not only organized the tenants in her building on 143rd Street, she helped form a neighborhood association that collected signatures to protest unjust and dramatic rent increases. In conjunction with the National Urban League and the Negro Civic Improvement League, the association sponsored a mass meeting that drew more than fifteen hundred people who were anxious about losing the roofs over their heads. Similarly, even before she had won the right to vote, Helen Hanning, along with other leaders of the North Harlem Community Council, sponsored a resolution requesting that Mayor Hylan appoint a committee to investigate abusive rent practices and poor housing conditions.[112] Housing availability and affordability were matters of urgency to economically vulnerable migrants who were hoping to make a better life for themselves and their families in an unfamiliar city. But the safety of their homes was also a paramount concern: whether it was a lack of heat in winter or rats that menaced sleeping children, women committed to improving their communities organized protests and petitioned their legislators.[113] These women were quintessential progressive reformers who urged the government to take action and fought to literally clean up the streets of Harlem.

As the evidence began to stack up against exploitive and racist building owners, including one landlord who said she "would rather burn [her] house than have Negro tenants," renters made some headway. By the late winter of 1924, new construction was underway to alleviate some of the pervasive over-crowding. Moreover, from time to time landlords were forced to lower rents, one was sent to jail for failing to supply hot water, and legislators yielded to constituent demands and created laws designed to protect renters.[114] Tenants also took matters into their own hands, throwing "rent parties," taking in borders, forming a Consumers' Co-operative Housing Association, and sending every family member that could to work to cover the essential living expenses. Nonetheless, although protests yielded a little relief when landlords faced both civic and legal challenges, the gains were temporary because building owners knew they could always raise rents on their African American tenants who were hemmed in by racist practices. With no laws against residential segregation, black New Yorkers found they had to wage the struggle for affordable, livable housing over and over again.[115]

For those job seekers who made the long trip out of the Jim Crow South, hopes of leaving the color line behind were quickly dashed. Employment discrimination proved to be as great a hurdle as exploitation was in the housing market. But the community responded with equal fervor and found that, with the right combination of strategies, they could score some gains. Protest campaigns that tied job opportunities for African Americans in particular stores to their willingness to patronize those same shops, known in the 1930s as "Don't Buy Where You Can't Work" campaigns, were still a few years off when the citizens of Harlem demanded that local movie theaters hire black projectionists. And in 1919, when Coral Smith was hired as a nurse at Bellevue Hospital in Manhattan and then fired two days later because "colored nurses were not employed at that institution," she brought a legal suit against the hospital, charging that her dismissal was a violation of New York State's 1895 Civil Rights Act. The law was initially passed because of the efforts of African American Republicans, especially Charles Anderson, who had been the secretary to State Treasurer Colvin. Now it was being used to open the door to employment for African

American women. Although Smith's struggle to break down the Jim Crow door took more than a year, by May 1921 the hospital had been obliged to rethink its practices through further prodding by Harlem Alderman Charles Roberts, one of two African American legislators at the time. The hospital promised to hire African American nurses from that point forward.[116] Such was not the case for Natalie Stewart, however, who, despite passing civil service exams with top grades, was repeatedly passed over for jobs she was eminently qualified for. The Civil Service Commission refused to address the problem, arguing that it was "powerless to prevent discrimination" by city and state institutions.[117]

Anna Arnold Hedgeman led a broader effort to organize workers just prior to her move to Harlem. Her education on the injustices of racism and gendered labor discrimination came in a different form than Coral Smith's or Natalie Smith's, but its lessons shaped her life nonetheless. Raised in a Republican household by strict Christian parents in the nearly all-white town of Anoka, Minnesota, for the first twenty-five years of her life Hedgeman believed in the principles of American individualism and that success came only through one's own efforts. The first African American to graduate from Hamline University in Minnesota, she headed south to Holly Springs, Mississippi, in 1922 to teach at Rust College. She was eager to serve others and also to learn about the world of the South that her father had come from. Quickly exhausted by the endless needs of a school and a community worn thin by desperate poverty, and in despair over Mississippi's suffocating racial oppression, Hedgeman returned north after just two years of teaching. Yet, with newly opened eyes, she realized that Jim Crow wore many faces and that racism was everywhere. Her first job back in the North was at the "Negro" YWCA in Springfield, Ohio. There she learned that "'separate' meant inferior, despised and unequal." Even as a YWCA administrator she was unable to use the Central (white) YWCA's facilities. Hedgeman's frustration mounted when she gave lectures on race relations. She asked rhetorically, "How does one cope with white people who dare ask Negro Americans what they seek in this their own country? . . . Were there no white people who could understand that Negroes wanted no gifts, no charity, but merely their rights?"[118]

Professional ambition and anger against white America led Hedgeman to the East Coast. In 1926 she took a job as the director of the "Negro" branch of the YWCA in Jersey City, New Jersey. The last pillars of her old understanding of the world came crashing down when she accepted the challenge put to her by the Y's club president, May Ryan, to spend a week of her vacation as a laundry worker. Following the painful exercise, Hedgeman acknowledged, "My dearly cherished Midwestern ideas about the ability of the individual to accomplish on his own changed drastically." She embraced collective organizing as a solution to the domestic workers' and laundry women's abysmal plight and urged the YWCA's board of directors to support a union. Neither the board nor established unions were interested, however. Not only were these jobs low paying and hard to organize, but they were most often held by black women. The combined forces of class, gender, and racial discrimination left black women outside the doors of organized labor. The experience not only sensitized Hedgeman to the limited employment options the majority of poor women faced, it enraged her. As she prepared to move to New York she decided, "I had no choice but to reject all white people." She settled into the Harlem YWCA and pursued ways to put her recently learned lessons to work.[119]

These struggles against discrimination were important, but they were waged piecemeal, organized to achieve a specific victory or to redress a particular wrong rather than to deal with the systemic reality of race-based employment discrimination. As a result, precious human resources and capital were spent fighting iterations of the same battles repeatedly in both the public-sector and private-sector job markets.[120] As Hedgeman had come to realize, only collective efforts and comprehensive redress that ensured compliance and that included punitive measures for violations would stanch the persistence of discriminatory hiring.

As a growing number of scholars have documented, struggles against housing and employment discrimination were part and parcel of black life in Northern cities.[121] These were, after all, necessities of modern life. But it was the quality of that life and the dignity that one felt living it that preoccupied women like Grace Campbell, who founded the Empire Friendly Shelter for Girls (and who had run for State Assembly on the Socialist Party ticket); Mrs. Oliver who organized the 131st Street Block Association; Wilhelmina Adams, a leader in the Utopia Neighborhood Club; and the members of the Colored Women's Civic League. Unsightly garbage piles sat uncollected on busy residential streets, creating health hazards for the children who spent their afterschool hours playing on the sidewalks. Those same children often lacked adult supervision because households living on the knife's edge of poverty sent every able body into the waged labor force. During the "dry" decade of the 1920s, "hootch sellers" proliferated on the streets of Harlem. As progressive reformers, these women fundraised, organized, and lobbied city officials so that they could provide the space and programming to keep children well fed and safe when anxious mothers went off to work, to get the streets cleaned up, and to improve community safety—often by securing one traffic light or patrolman at a time.[122] Well into the Jazz Age, they enabled families, and most often other women, to go to work with a little peace of mind, they helped reduce the public health hazards that could cripple whole communities, and they gave many children the chance for a better future. The practitioners of a politics of racial uplift, infused with their clear middle-class sensibilities, left their mark on Harlem. But so did the advocates of Black Nationalism, who were becoming increasingly visible and strategic in the 1920s.

The discrimination that made good housing, stable jobs, and safe streets harder to come by for African Americans was often more subtle than the overt bigotry and violence that periodically disrupted daily life and left physical and psychological scars, but it also increased people's determination to eradicate racism. Not only were they victims of such hostilities, women of color were also principal actors in fighting against them. The work to protect the race took many forms. Brooklyn women, for instance, boycotted a Big Brother and Big Sister conference in Washington, D.C., when the management of the Roosevelt Hotel, which hosted the conference, declared that it would not allow African American delegates to walk through the hotel lobby. In their letter of protest, the Brooklyn Big Sisters affirmed that they could not "with justice or dignity, send any of its members to the meeting."[123] In another instance, Maybelle McAdoo, a *New York Age* editor, urged her female readers to fight neighborhood grocers who discriminated against them. Foremost she demanded that women be treated with respect. Moreover, she argued for fairness, asserting, "We intend to have just weights, fair prices and fresh goods." She concluded with a reminder that was hardly necessary for her audience, "If we don't protect our own interests, we can't expect others to do it."[124] The grocery stores, like the landlords, had to be continuously pressured to stop charging black patrons inflated prices, stop offering them inferior goods, and to stop treating them with a lack of respect.

Some people were inclined to take to the streets or to lobby legislators. Others made effective use of the state's civil rights law to bring suit against proprietors who discriminated on the basis of race. Anna Dawson, for example, who had been denied access to a tour bus, filed a suit against Greeley Sight-Seeing Bus Line for racial discrimination. The court found in her favor and ordered Greeley to pay Dawson $100 in damages. Similarly, Fannie White and several of her fellow parishioners from the National Baptist Church on 125th Street found it necessary to turn to the courts. While in downtown Manhattan on church business, the group of eight sat down to eat at Stanley's Lunch Room on Broadway. They were ignored for more than twenty minutes and then grossly mistreated. According to the waitstaff, the management had established as policy that black customers were to receive poor service and have "foreign substances" put in their food to discourage their patronage. White and the others found their food had indeed been subjected to such tampering. The restaurant decided to settle out of court rather than face a jury, and the plaintiffs received $1,000 for the discrimination they suffered.[125] These kinds of legal challenges persisted throughout the decade as plaintiffs and causes for action were both plentiful. But the issue that garnered the widest and most sustained activism was a blight that had left in its wake an even more treacherous reality.

During the 1890s, Mississippi native Ida B. Wells penned a series of newspaper editorials and three searing exposés, *Southern Horrors, A Red Record,* and *Mob Rule in New Orleans,* which revealed the illegality and inhumanity of lynching. Forced to flee her home in Memphis, Tennessee, shortly after the first was published, Wells sought refuge in the North. From that momentous night in October 1892 when she was honored by an appreciative and inspired audience of 250 African American women at a dinner in midtown Manhattan, women remained at the forefront of the fight to secure a federal law against the abominable crime. As one decade and then another passed without a federal response, African Americans increased their activism. In one dramatic show of racial solidarity, women in Harlem marched in the blazing sun and the pouring rain to protest massacres that left black communities in East St. Louis and Tulsa in ashes. Mary Talbert, former NACW president and director of the NAACP's anti-lynching campaign, organized a movement called A Million Women United to Stop Lynching. Another group called for a national sunrise prayer service to "wipe out the evil of lynching" and to get the Dyer Anti-Lynching Bill passed in Congress in 1922. Dyer, a Republican from Missouri, had introduced the legislation to make lynching a federal crime. With pressure mounting, the U.S. House of Representatives passed the bill, but the Senate let it die.[126]

Legislative stonewalling spurred further organizing efforts across the nation. Education pioneer and NACW division leader Mary McLeod Bethune, literary and political activist Alice Dunbar Nelson, and NAACP Executive Secretary James Weldon Johnson traveled to Brooklyn to address a meeting of the Brooklyn Women's Anti-Lynching Crusaders. The speakers called for racial solidarity. They also argued that African Americans should exercise political independence as a means to gain ground. Neither political party could be counted on to outlaw this scourge on the race and the nation; therefore, neither deserved African Americans' loyalty. Bethune appealed particularly to the women *as* women tapping into their sense of shared experiences and solidarity: "We black women feel the injustices meted out to us every day. We do not want to be treated as white women or as black women, we want to be treated as women," with all of the respect that the term implied.[127] When still no federal action came, Harlem activist Eleanor Johnson and a group of women formed yet another organization, the Colored Women's Stop Lynching League of New York City. Johnson issued a strong appeal to the women's sense of race pride, avowing, "We can do it. Do you think for one moment that white women would sit idly by and see their fathers and sons tarred, feathered, and burnt at the stake? A thousand times No."[128] Their commitment was deep and their efforts unrelenting, but the power and racist ideals of the Senate's Southern Democrats and the nation's Republican presidents were unmoved in the 1920s. The Dyer bill died in Congress. African Americans' demand for racial equality in housing, jobs, in their stores, and on their streets persisted despite repeated setbacks. Though the defeat of the anti-lynching legislation was a huge setback, other, more piecemeal victories indicated that change was possible nonetheless.

Conclusion

By the time the 1920s drew to a close, black women could look around the crowded streets of New York City and appreciate the scope of the changes they had helped bring about, as well as the barriers that remained between themselves and "the things which [were] their due." Only twenty years earlier most black families in Harlem had lived in places other than New York, and not a single woman in the state of New York could vote. While far too often unrecognized for their roles in bringing about these significant changes, black women were integral to both. As a result of these collective shifts, African Americans in New York City, especially black men, made subtle though important advances in the struggle for political power. At the same time, women steeped in middle-class values, as well as working-class and poor women, pragmatically used various branches of the government, including the courts and petitions to legislators, to try to secure better housing, more jobs, and safer streets. Enough of these piecemeal struggles yielded positive outcomes that many women continued in this vein. Most often associated with the era of progressive reform, black women's turn to the state to improve the lives of people in their communities persisted throughout the 1920s. Others took to the streets to protest injustices and racist violence. Even more passed along advice in the halls of the YWCA, the aisles of grocery stores, at church and association meetings, and on neighborhood blocks. African American women, native New Yorkers and newcomers alike, fought not just for community development but also for individual and collective dignity. All of these issues together made up their "birthright" and "their due," and despite their ideological and strategic diversity, they all demanded and collectively helped move toward those goals.

At the same time, even as they embraced the ballot, ventured into political clubhouses, or petitioned legislators, most black New Yorkers, men and women alike, did not expect the political process to transform the injustices of society substantially or immediately. With myriad manifestations of legal and cultural Jim Crow to point to in the North as well as the South, African Americans maintained a deep appreciation for the gap between the promises of equality and the practices of discrimination. Bold women like Anna Arnold Hedgeman and Irene Moorman Blackstone exposed the prevalence of racism in theoretically interracial organizations. In their own ways, both women embraced aspects of black separatism and nationalism. Not only racism but its intersection with gender discrimination circumscribed the ways African American women fought for change and the outcomes they could attain in formal politics and in grassroots activism. The repeated need to fight for housing, work, and community safety exposed the weakness of general political disempowerment and piecemeal struggle. The most dramatic reminder of racism's evil unfolded hundreds of miles from the heart of Harlem, to unknown men and women, in little-known towns of the American South. Lynchings horrified anyone committed to human rights. Women were often in the vanguard of that fight, especially on the streets of New York where they could level protest without fear of death. But throughout the 1920s their marching, organizing, protesting, and lobbying efforts failed to move Congress and three U.S. presidents to pass a federal anti-lynching law. Only structural changes in the law, the economy, and society at large would yield a degree of real security and indicate a permanent movement toward full citizenship rights, particularly for African American women, the most politically disempowered members of society because of the ways racism and gender discrimination together worked as a distinct and oppressive whole. The vote was one of those important structural changes, but on its own it was hardly enough. Women would need to attain more political and economic influence, let alone power, before they could help secure lasting gains for African Americans generally or for themselves in New York City and beyond its borders. There was an economic disaster percolating on the horizon. It would yield further, devastating challenges and unprecedented opportunities. Those black women who had spent years toiling in formal and informal political circles found new breaches in the walls of political resistance during this time of upheaval, and they were ready to push forward.

CHAPTER TWO

Strides Forward in Times of Crisis in the 1930s and 1940s

"The attitude of the public toward the woman in the professions," Ruth White-head Whaley explained in a 1931 interview with the *Afro-American*, "is still inimical. It puts her on the defensive. Men get the notion that because she has more freedom than the woman who makes her home her career, she is just as free in her morals. There are many things that the professional woman has to endure." She went on: "If she is serious, people say she is masculine; if she is natural, they accuse her of trading on her sex, and so it goes, she is put between the devil and the deep blue sea." Whaley, a Democratic Party activist and a lawyer by profession, also noted that she was often mistaken for her clients "because I was a woman." In the male and predominantly white worlds of politics and law, Whaley had to prove herself constantly, finding that to be taken seriously she and other female lawyers, both African American and white, had to be "better than the average man in the field and neither the community nor the profession will permit her to make many mistakes." Her frustrations, peppered as they were in the interview with bits of humor to take the edge off her social critiques, were shared by a small but growing number of well-educated African American women with professional goals and increasingly political aspirations. Yet despite pervasive double standards, Whaley believed that the future for women in the legal profession was bright. Not only that, she tried to find a silver lining amidst the gender discrimination, noting that when men "find out that they cannot take advantage of you, they have a wholesome respect for you and advertise it."[1]

Entrenched gender discrimination, which Whaley underscored, posed only one of the significant challenges the majority of black women faced as the age of the New Negro ended and the nation confronted first a devastating economic crisis and then a world war. In the face of oppression and adversity, however, talented, pragmatic women like Whaley also found or created opportunities. Just as in the era of the Great Migration, black women were integral participants and often leaders in community-based as well as state and national struggles for social, political, and economic justice. They maintained diverse political ideologies that spanned from Republicans to Communists and from integrationists to black nationalists.

In addition, government responses to the Great Depression enabled numerous college-educated black women in New York City to find new, politically valuable employment. After 1932, in addition to Mary McCloud Bethune, who has been recognized for her leadership in President Roosevelt's "Black Cabinet," future leaders Anna Arnold Hedgeman, Ella Baker, Dorothy Height, and Pauli Murray secured jobs in New Deal agencies in the city. Not only did this work provide them with important professional experience and networks, but it also gave them a forum from which to pursue their ideas about economic fairness, human rights, and civic equality. Finally, the decade was a turning point for African American women and electoral politics. An exceptional number of black women engaged in politics, not as campaign workers or poll watchers, but in a change from the past, as candidates.

Some women—Layle Lane, Eunice Carter, and Jane Bolin, for example—ran with their respective party's backing. Sara Pelham Speaks and Ruth Whitehead Whaley, in contrast, forged ahead in their first campaign efforts with little or no support from their parties. Others still, including Ada B. Jackson and Maude Richardson, were beckoned to politics by community members who were eager to have good leadership and selected them as the best candidates. Together these women's various campaigns indicate that black women had decided by the mid-1930s that they could make effective, if not successful, forays into electoral politics. They could raise issues and shine a spotlight on problems that plagued African American communities. In the process, not incidentally, they advanced their own careers.

Educational access and professional status marked an important class boundary that set most of these women apart from the majority of poor and working-class African American women in the city. Although they represented an expanding group, professional women were still a fraction of the African American population in New York.[2] As they responded to the public's needs, which were greatly exacerbated by the economic and wartime upheavals of the 1930s and 1940s, this cadre of black women increasingly challenged gendered and racialized assumptions about who should appropriately fill public leadership roles. Electoral politics remained a male preserve, mainly, though not exclusively a white male preserve, a decade after the Nineteenth Amendment's passage. The fact that its association with masculinity began to change at all in the public's mind was the result of countless women of all races engaging in political forums in whatever capacities they could. Although frustrations like Whaley's periodically made it into the press, black women tended to demonstrate their belief in women's rights through their actions rather than argue for them publically in words. Additionally, black women's concerns about gender equality were always more complicated than simply about women's rights. Their determination to eliminate racism and its insidious machinations was a centerpiece of their activism. Still, nuanced gendered appeals found their way into black women's public discourse. While the women who ran for elected office in the 1930s and 1940s did not necessarily *justify* their public roles with gendered, particularly maternalist language such as that used by Progressive Era activists, they did make specific appeals to other black women for support nonetheless.

The changes African American women helped bring about in the distribution of economic resources and political influence in the 1930s and 1940s through their new levels of engagement with the state and as political candidates were uneven at best; the gains they made were exceedingly fragile. By the time the economy had stabilized and the guns of World War II fell silent, however, a number of black women in New York City had attained an impressive level of political experience. They understood that it was very difficult to translate new access to political circles into power and resources for the community, but they also appreciated that their total absence from these circles meant that black women's social, economic, and political concerns would otherwise not be addressed and would not change. They were determined to see that this was not the case. The upheavals in New York City during the Great Depression and World War II gave them unprecedented opportunities for change.

New Struggles and New Opportunities

By 1932 the nation was in the full throes of an unprecedented economic crisis. Unemployment approached 25 percent, and the gross domestic product had plummeted from \$103.6 billion in 1929 to \$56.4 billion.[3] Although African Americans had long faced economic discrimination in the North as they had in the South, the depression created even greater and, at times, desperate challenges. In New York City's black communities, the focus on race work and cultural expression that had burgeoned during the Harlem Renaissance gave way to struggles for survival as unemployment for men and women topped 50 percent.[4] The strategies African Americans had learned to deftly employ during the prior two decades were adapted to the crisis at hand as the Depression proved resistant to the Hoover administration's anemic efforts to alleviate the disaster. Intellectual leaders like W. E. B. Du Bois wrote thought-provoking articles in *The Crisis* on a monthly basis; labor activists, liberals, and leftists forged new alliances that yielded the Popular Front and the American Labor Party; and local politicos like Fred Moore, a Republican, and Whaley, a Democrat, put their respective parties on notice that black voters could not be taken for granted.

Depression-era and later wartime struggles for safe and affordable housing, decent jobs, community safety, and political leadership in cities like Detroit, Chicago, Philadelphia, and most dramatically in Harlem, were foundational elements in what has become known as the Northern civil rights movement. Black women were often central actors and at times leaders in these battles. Some of their important efforts, especially those in Detroit and Chicago, have begun to be told.[5] Like their sisters who had migrated to other Northern cities, black women in New York were heavily involved in campaigns for economic, social, and political justice. In Harlem and in Brooklyn, their activism helped sustain communities in need; it also provided these women with skills and leadership capacities that would later launch a number of them into national political and organizational leadership.

Pushing Through the First Barrier— Black Women in New Deal Jobs

Economic stability remained an aspiration rather than a reality for a majority of African Americans because racial discrimination continued to exclude black men and women from steady, well-paying work. With the election of former New York Governor Franklin D. Roosevelt to the U.S. presidency in 1932, however, the government's approach to the economic crisis, the New Deal, with its aggressive use of federal funds to create city, state, and federal government jobs and social programs promised new possibilities for economic change. While most African American women toiled in underpaid, onerous domestic labor, a handful of well-educated, middle-class women made noteworthy progress in government employment, and they often used those positions to fight for social and economic justice.

In the spring of 1931 Carita Roane was appointed by Frances Perkins, former Progressive Era activist and now New York State Commissioner (and soon to be U.S. Secretary of Labor), to head the Harlem office of the State Labor Department. A black woman with plenty of experience in trying to find Harlem residents employment through the Dunbar Vocational Placement Service, Roane seemed positioned to allocate jobs to Harlem's unemployed in unprecedented ways.[6] But the potential that her job promised versus the reality of the bureaucracy in which she functioned, laden with gender-biased and racist assumptions, meant that few white collar jobs were offered to African American job seekers.[7] Of the three thousand women and two thousand men who came through the Harlem office of the State Employment Service office each week, 80 percent of the placements for women were in domestic work, and 88 percent of placements for men were in unskilled and semi-skilled jobs.[8] Despite her efforts, Roane, one of the first black women appointed to a state position, was unable to effectively pressure employers to hire black workers for skilled and better-paying jobs. Businesses would only change their hiring practices when forced to, and Roane, a novice in the field, could not compel that change alone.[9] This was the problem Whaley raised in 1931 when she stated that women in the professions lacked influential allies.

Despite its limitations, Roane's appointment represented a considerable advancement for black women in the administrative state. A handful of black men had benefited from political patronage, but black women had made no notable advances in government work. Once in the Labor Department, she found few, if any, African American women whose path she could follow, but she was determined to change that. One of the indispensable things she did was to help build an avenue of opportunity for other black women. In 1934, for example, Roane hired Anna Arnold Hedgeman, the former YWCA executive, as a social worker. She was "a fabulous executive," Hedgeman asserted, yet she further emphasized that up to that point, African Americans had been all but excluded from civil service jobs.[10] Roane also helped single black women find housing. And finally Roane's work with Mary McLeod Bethune to found the National Council of Negro Women (NCNW) in 1935 was vitally important. Working with a small cadre of other leaders Roane helped create in the NCNW a tremendous network and a vehicle with which black women could raise their collective concerns to political, civic, and church leaders more effectively.[11] Her efforts inside the state and in women's organizations helped advance incremental but critical changes for black women in public leadership roles and for Harlem residents.

From her job with Roane, Hedgeman moved into the Emergency Relief Bureau as part of the organization's "experiment with Negro supervisors," as she referred to it. Because of her effective work in the Brownsville section of Brooklyn (an area as poor in Hedgeman's determination as the desperate pocket of Mississippi she had taught in during the early 1920s), Charlotte Carr, a white trade unionist and now the director of the Emergency Relief Bureau in New York City, appointed Hedgeman to be the Consultant on Racial Problems. In her new position, Hedgeman organized young black women in Brooklyn to fight for jobs. Noting their success, Hedgeman said, "It was no accident that we secured the first 150 provisional appointments the city had ever given the Negro community."[12] Among her other responsibilities, she worked with trade unions to organize workers when the New Deal leadership opened up opportunities for labor organizing with the Wagner Act and the Fair Labor Standards Act. This experience further sharpened her belief in the need for unions that protected female workers.

Finally, Mayor LaGuardia asked Hedgeman as the Consultant on Racial Problems to investigate the Bronx "slave markets" in response to complaints he received from angry taxpayers about women who allegedly received public assistance but refused work. Working undercover, Hedgeman confronted a reality sharply at odds with the taxpayers' accusations. She spoke with women who were desperate for work. The underground labor market they populated, where many bartered or sold their domestic or sexual labor for appallingly low wages under wholly unequal circumstances, underscored their economic vulnerability as little else could. Hedgeman's report to the mayor, in which she emphatically argued that "too many women would take any kind of job rather than accept welfare," challenged racist, gendered accusations about black women and public assistance in the 1930s that would repeatedly surface throughout the twentieth century.[13] She also demonstrated a keen sensitivity to the problems that poor and working-class black women faced, and she used every position she held to try to alleviate them.

Hedgeman's work in the Welfare Administration reached beyond the poor and working class. Dorothy Height, another emerging leader in the city's welfare relief efforts, asserted, "More than once I thanked God for Anna Hedgeman."[14] Born in Virginia and raised in a small town outside of Pittsburgh, Height moved to New York City in 1929 to attend Barnard College; but when she arrived, she was denied entrance because of the school's racist acceptance policy. Distressed but undeterred, she was able to use her Elks scholarship elsewhere and instead attended New York University where she received a bachelor's *and* a master's degree in four years.[15] A steady A-student, Height found the invitations sent to her to join sororities revoked when she arrived at meetings and the young white members realized she was black. Instead, she and other African American students formed their own club called the Ramses Club, even as she regularly socialized and studied in interracial groups. She soaked up the richness of cultural life in Harlem, where her neighbors included the Mills Brothers, a popular jazz quartet, and W. C. Handy, who, as Height warmly recalled, "would take several of us under his wing and go out to the clubs to hear the great jazz players."[16]

Shortly after she graduated, Height became a leader in the United Christian Youth Movement and strived to embody the organization's slogan, "Christian Youth Building a New World." When, in 1935, the Popular Front formed in response to the growing international threats of fascism in Spain, Germany, and Italy and as a vehicle for leftist organizations to work with liberals in the New Deal, Height served as the Harlem Christian Youth Council representative. The broad coalition movement took various forms across the nation from San Francisco to Minneapolis to Detroit. In New York City, it included members of the Communist Party (CPUSA), which was the Popular Front's driving force; progressive religious organizations (such as the one Height represented) and religious leaders like Rev. Adam Clayton Powell Jr. of the Abyssinian Baptist Church; cultural artists like Paul Robeson, Marc Blitzstein, and Martha Graham; and Socialists and labor leaders like Frank Crosswaith of the Negro Labor Committee and A. Philip Randolph of the BSCP and first president of the newly formed National Negro Congress. During an interview years later, Height remarked on her Popular Front colleagues from the Young Communist League. "I learned so much from the Communists," she maintained. "Those were some of the best minds that I ever came upon . . . the tactics I learned."[17] She elaborated on the excitement and commitment that she felt as part of the youth movement in the 1930s: "We really believed that in these little meetings we had, we were building a new world. We were making it piece by piece. . . . When I went to work with the YWCA, that's how I got into the whole thing about the domestic workers."[18]

At the same time that she relished her late-night meetings with progressive activists and her participation on picket lines as part of the "Don't Buy Where You Can't Work" campaigns, Height made great strides in advancing her professional career. Even before she had finished graduate school, she began work as a social worker in the Brownsville section of Brooklyn, a community buckling under the weight of the Depression. Height's deft abilities with the unemployed led Charlotte Carr to offer her a position in the New York City Welfare Administration. Height, already attuned to the challenges people in utter poverty faced, now learned about the ways government support could benefit but also disrespect its needy recipients. She observed, "I grew to appreciate some of the difficulties faced by welfare recipients—the constant surveillance, the loss of control over your life, and at the bottom, the loss of self-esteem, . . . I came to realize that the way we gave the help was more important than what was given."[19] It was also at this time that she forged a treasured friendship with Hedgeman. Together the two strategized to hold "the gains we'd made in minority recruitment." Height understood fully, as her friend and colleague did, that "without a conscious and deliberate effort to place or promote workers of color, little or no progress would be made."[20]

In 1937, Height shifted professional gears and moved fully onto the path that became her life's work. Sought after for her leadership skills by a number of organizations, she accepted Cecelia Cabaniss Saunders' request that she join the administration of the Harlem YWCA. Daily, she heard heartbreaking stories of women seeking work in the Bronx "slave markets." Her mind sharpened by her left-wing friends and progressive Christian activists and her already impressive level of experience with the city's poor, Height ventured to the city council to advocate on behalf of unemployed, poor black women.[21] Though unable to move the government body that day, Height would find herself trying to influence policy makers in various ways for the rest of her life, even as she became a fixture in black women's organizations.

The New Deal agencies in New York City proved fertile ground for yet two other future leaders in the fight for racial justice and human rights—namely, Ella Baker and Pauli Murray. Baker was a native of Virginia but had spent her youth and college years in North Carolina. Upon graduation from Shaw University in 1927, she migrated north to Harlem. As the weaknesses of unregulated capitalism fell into starkest relief in the early 1930s, Baker joined with George Schulyer, a columnist at the *Pittsburgh Courier*, to form a consumer cooperative organization, the Young Negroes' Cooperative League (YNCL), where she served as its executive director. Despite her impassioned efforts and although the cooperative movement had some pockets of support across the country, especially in African American communities, it never had the mass appeal or access to resources it needed to fully take root and flourish.

A woman concerned with the countless manifestations of racialized economic injustice, Baker, like Hedgeman and Height, turned her sharp mind and political skills to the crisis many poor black women in New York faced. Together with Marvel Cooke, a Communist and W. E. B. Du Bois's secretary, Baker documented details of the Bronx "slave markets" in a powerful exposé in the November 1935 issue of *The Crisis*, underscoring the role of economic desperation that sent black women, old and young, to the streets for work.[22] Shortly after the article was published Baker was hired by the New York City division of the Workers Education Project (WEP) of the Works Progress Administration (WPA). According to Conrad Lynd, one of Baker's co-workers and a lawyer for the Young Communist League, the WEP staff was composed of men and women who were "committed to the cause of labor."[23]

Baker biographer Barbara Ransby notes how important Baker's work with the NYCL and the WEP were to her political and intellectual development. While at the government agency, Baker routinely exchanged ideas with leftists of many stripes from Socialists, to anarchists, Lovestoneites, Trotskyites, and orthodox Communists. Not aligned with any particular leftist ideology, Baker instead was driven by her commitment to educating people for their own empowerment.[24] It was in this light that she understood her cooperative work and her consumer education efforts.

Pauli Murray was born in Baltimore, Maryland, in 1910. She was three when her mother died, and Murray was sent to North Carolina to live with her mother's family. Eager to leave the segregated South and segregated environments more generally when she finished high school, Murray turned down a scholarship to Wilberforce University to attend college in New York City. She aspired to attend Columbia University or Barnard but was unable to afford it (and would likely have confronted the same discrimination Height did had she applied, given that it was the same period.) Instead, Murray went to Hunter College, an all-women's school in midtown Manhattan. Upon graduation in 1933 she worked briefly for the Urban League's *Opportunity* magazine. She then landed a position with the Works Progress Administration (WPA), first as a remedial reading teacher and then with the Workers Education Project (WEP). She remarked that the WEP "was a tremendous intellectual experience for me, because it brought me into contact with the young, radical intellectuals of that period, young Communists, young Socialists, young Trotskyites, young Republicans, young Democrats, it was a highly politicized project."[25]

Harlem and her WEP work provided Murray with friends like Baker, mentors like Ruth Whitehead Whaley, professional experience, and intellectual stimulation.[26] The sense of interracial solidarity within "the radical-liberal part of the population" inspired and politicized her. Not only did she participate as a volunteer labor organizer and march on picket lines in the neighborhood, but she also took time off from the WEP to attend Brookwood Labor College just outside of New York City in 1937. While there, Murray studied about the political economy and worked with classmates to publish strike newspapers. She also recalled her final farewells to a number of compatriots who volunteered to fight fascism in Spain with the Abraham Lincoln Brigade. Upon her return to Harlem, Murray used her position at the New Deal agency to educate people about the relationships between labor, consumption, the economy, and the social order and at the same time she began to think about a career in law.

The government-agency work that Roane, Hedgeman, Height, Baker, Murray, and others did helped a city in crisis, especially some of its most underserved and resource-poor communities. It also helped each of them sharpen their political worldviews, which increasingly included the possibility that the state could be a vehicle for social, political, and economic transformation for the historically dispossessed. Some of these women took government jobs after working as grassroots activists; others came via their work in women's organizations, especially the Harlem YWCA. Regardless of these women's paths in, New Deal agencies became new sites of political education and activism for all of them. The work was important, but the legacy of racialized gender discrimination meant that they had to negotiate a social and political landscape hostile to them as African Americans living in a white-dominated society and as women living in a patriarchal one. They worked unflinchingly to change it. At the beginning of the decade, Ruth Whaley had underscored both the barriers to progress and the glimmers of possibility that professional women would likely find in public life. The others were living proof of Whaley's assessment. As the Depression wore on, yet more black women sought a path into the government. Less inclined to administrative or social work, they sought access through electoral politics. They hoped that as candidates and elected officials they could come closer to the levers of power in the city and the state than they could as community activists and government workers.

New Candidates for Office

It was more than cliché in the early 1930s to note that politics was "an old boys' club": it was a reality. Women's suffrage was more than a decade old, but in New York City not a single woman was elected to the state legislature between 1920, when Marguerite Smith won in Harlem, and 1933, when Doris Byrne, a white woman from the Bronx achieved the same. But by the early 1930s some small stress signs began to appear in the walls of resistance to women in electoral politics. Women's concerted efforts within political clubhouses and the changing New Deal context created some new possibilities. In 1933 Julia Coleman, who had served as president of the Professional Women's Republican Club in the 1920s, spearheaded an effort get a black woman elected to Congress. Noting that Harlem had close to fifty thousand potential black female voters, Coleman wanted to mobilize them "into a concrete militant body, free of party bias and devoted to the single idea of electing one of their own group to represent the district at Washington."[27] Although she could not know that it would take two generations of women's efforts for her goal to be attained, Coleman had to look no further than the seasonal election roster with its dearth of African American female candidates to appreciate the challenge before her. This reality, combined with more positive forces—namely, the prominence of many African American women in community activism and the increase of women on voter registration rolls—led a number of black women, including Layle Lane, Eunice Carter, Jane Bolin, Ruth Whaley and Sara Pelham Speaks, to run for elected office in Harlem during the 1930s. They each hoped to gain access to the fruits of political power to help their struggling community.

Socialist Efforts

Layle Lane was born in Georgia in 1893 and moved north to New Jersey with her parents while still in school. She received degrees from Hunter College, Howard University, and Columbia University. Like Coleman, she felt that a black woman should serve in the U.S. Congress. Contrary to Coleman, however, Lane decided to run for office herself. A teacher by profession, Lane was a civil rights activist who later served on the executive board of the 1941 March on Washington movement, a labor leader who worked with Southern tenant farmers and served as vice president of the American Federation of Teachers, and a Socialist who believed deeply in the centrality of the state to the alleviation of poverty and racial discrimination.[28] She concluded that grassroots efforts alone were insufficient to address the racist problems African Americans in Harlem faced with housing, in jobs, and in education, so she turned her sights to politics. By the mid-1930s the political landscape had broadened to make room for candidates on leftist party ballots, specifically the Socialist Party, the newly formed American Labor Party (ALP), and Communist Party tickets.[29] The hostility that Socialist candidates like Grace Campbell and A. Philip Randolph faced in the early 1920s had dissipated somewhat during the unprecedented global financial crisis. While it was not popular among the majority, the Socialist Party fielded an increasing number of candidates throughout the 1930s and 1940s, including (as they did in the late 1910s and early 1920s) a number of women.

Lane's political beliefs and her vision for society were evident in her campaign literature, but even more with regard to the way she engaged her work as an educator, labor organizer, and community activist. She was explicit about the need for government to step in aggressively to address injustices. "I believe housing and slum clearance are major obligations of government and should be provided for adequately," she wrote on a questionnaire about her political positions. She also favored state planning and argued that state aid was necessary to eliminate inequality in education for young people in cities and rural areas alike. As with many other leftists, she favored price controls and government-supported full-employment programs.[30] Her activism inspired pan-Africanist labor leader Maida Springer to write Lane in appreciation for the work she did in pursuit of freedom and racial equality, noting poignantly that, "Whenever I feel particularly despondent at the weaknesses of we humans, including my own, you stand out like a beacon in the darkness."[31]

In her 1934 campaign for the U.S. Congress, Lane tried to advance her concerns about racial justice, housing access, and socialism simultaneously, arguing that the housing crisis could be "a sufficient wedge for Socialism" within the black community. At the same time, her advocacy of socialism was not naïve. She was aware that some leaders could be elitist and racist, which made the party less appealing to working-class and poor African Americans. In one case, Lane penned a letter of rebuke to Socialist leader Charles Solomon in reaction to a speech he gave in Harlem. Charging that it denigrated Harlem and its residents, Lane argued that racial discrimination in education, housing, and especially in trade unions made it all but impossible for African Americans to improve their collective economic plight. She endeavored to change that by running for office, but she also held the party leadership accountable for making statements that "presented no incentive to spread Socialism beyond a small group of workers of intellectual interests." She concluded by reminding Solomon that "'Workingmen of the world, unite' was meant especially to free those whose chains are heaviest."[32]

Despite her critiques, Lane received strong party support in her campaign. August Claessens, a party organizer, wanted to let Lane know that the party was going to make an extra effort, stating that "special publicity will be given to our women comrades who are candidates for public office."[33] To that end, a series of events were organized, including a music and tea social with the Parent-Teacher Association. It was possible in this era of economic upheaval and progressive activism for a mainstream organization like the PTA to host an event for three black female Socialist candidates. Lane, Alma Crosswaith, and Jane P. Morgan ran together in Harlem on the Socialist ticket for various legislative offices, and their campaign targets included local parents. Crosswaith, wife of the labor activist Frank Crosswaith, ran for a state assembly seat, and Morgan, a British immigrant of African descent, ran for state senate.[34] Despite proven records of fighting for racial equality and their outreach efforts, Lane and her fellow Socialists lost in the November elections.

In 1936 Lane ran for U.S. Congress but lost that election by a landslide. Democratic incumbent Sol Bloom won 73,853 votes, Republican W. S. Bennett garnered 24,720, and Lane, the Socialist, had 2,125. Roosevelt's—and by association, the Democratic Party's—popularity and the creation of the American Labor Party (ALP) posed formidable challenges to those with electoral aspirations on the left end of the political spectrum.[35] Nevertheless, Lane forged on, running for the state assembly in 1937 and 1938. In the 1940s, she ran five more times, for offices at the local level, including city council and city controller, the state level, and again for the U.S. Congress. In spite of her successive defeats, Lane maintained that "political democracy is meaningless unless accompanied by economic democracy." She believed that problems in poor communities like Harlem would only end when there was "economic security for all."[36]

A few insights can be drawn from Lane's campaigns. How important was her racial identity for Harlem voters? Clearly, the fact that she was a black woman did not motivate a majority of black voters to support her. Racial identity was not a singular or, in this case, determinant factor; if it had been, she would have fared much better in the elections. Was the fact that she was a woman a significant factor in her losses? Lane's repeated defeats were proportional to that of Socialists in other districts across the city, suggesting that her sex was not necessarily a distinct problem for voters. Her leftist platform that situated the government at the center of solutions to housing, employment, and labor problems did not appeal to the masses. Yet despite her losses, Lane's campaigns did something important nonetheless.[37] She helped voters acclimate to seeing a woman's name on the ballot and to dislodge even a little bit their very strong association between politics and masculinity. So did a handful of other black women who turned to electoral politics to try to bring about economic, social, and political improvements for African Americans in New York City.

The Republicans and the Democrats
Give a Little Ground—Very Little

Breaking with their deeply held traditions that understood politics as primarily a white male domain, the Republicans and Democrats fielded black female candidates in the 1930s. Sometimes the party clubhouses did so strategically, and sometimes women asserted themselves into primary campaigns despite the lack of party support. The Republican Party machine in Harlem gave ground first. Fifteen years earlier it had started to run black male candidates in Harlem and had met with some success; in the mid-1930s the Party leadership began to rethink their resistance to black female candidates.

Eunice Hunton Carter was born in 1899 in Atlanta, Georgia. Her family left the South after the 1906 race riots and settled in Brooklyn. She graduated with a bachelor's and a master's degree from Smith College and moved back to New York in the early years of the Harlem Renaissance. Eight years after Ruth Whaley paved the way, Carter received her law degree from Fordham University. In 1934, she ran for the state assembly on the Republican Party ticket, the first black woman to do so. One of Carter's opponents was Socialist Party candidate Alma Crosswaith. Despite the election's historic dimensions, black newspapers ignored the fact that these two African American women were running against each other. This was predictable in part because the *New York Age* and the *New York Amsterdam News* gave Socialists and Communists minimal and generally hostile coverage. Not only that, they had given women's political issues, including the struggle for suffrage, little attention. Carter's election helped change that.

Carter, a highly respected attorney, came from an impressive lineage of race activists. Her mother, Addie W. Hunton, was not only one of the founding members of the NACW and National Council of Negro Women (NCNW), she was also an ardent suffragist and a peace activist who addressed the Pan-African Congress in Paris in 1919. Also an organizational leader, she served in numerous offices in the YWCA and the NAACP, and as the president of the International Council of the Women of Darker Races. Addie Hunton brought Eunice along on many of her travels and to countless Women's International League for Peace and Freedom (WILPF) and YWCA meetings, and to the Pan-African conference in New York City in 1927. Eunice's father, William Hunton, was an international leader in the YMCA, a practicing attorney, and a one-time candidate for the assembly seat she was now running for. Her brother, Alphaeus

Hunton, was a prominent Pan-Africanist, a Marxist, and a leader of the anti-colonialist Council on African Affairs (CAA). From childhood, Eunice Carter was raised with an awareness of racial injustices, the importance of women's independence, and a commitment to fighting for a better society.

In that fall 1934 campaign, Carter faced James Stephens, a Democrat, an African American, and, posing the greatest challenge, the four-term incumbent for the Nineteenth State Assembly District seat. The last and in fact only assemblywoman to have served the district was Marguerite Smith, a white woman. But Carter had impressive qualifications that gave her credibility with people across the community. Not only had she been a social worker in Harlem since her graduation from Smith in 1921, she worked at the city's Home Relief Bureau during the Depression. Moreover, she was active in race work, writing articles for *Opportunity* and serving on the Board of Directors of the Urban League.[38] Like her mother, Carter was involved with the YWCA and was also a member of the Advisory Committee of the New York County Republican Committee—instrumental in helping her secure strong party support. With many African Americans still committed to the party of Lincoln in 1934, she had at least a fighting chance in the election.

Given her upbringing, Carter's campaign held out particular appeal to middle-class, educated black women. Carter had been raised in a world of women's club meetings and surrounded by some of the most dynamic black women in early twentieth-century history, including her own mother. Moreover, as an active member of the Harlem YWCA, Carter was connected to an impressive network of women including the highly respected and influential Cecelia Cabaniss Saunders, Anna Hedgeman, Ella Baker, and Dorothy Height. In a dramatic change from the past, the *New York Age* gave Carter's campaign coverage—positive coverage at that. They proclaimed her "exceptionally well qualified for the position," and the editors formally endorsed her.[39] Confidently they projected that "with certainty for the first time a Negro woman will be elected to the Assembly."[40] While their hope was justified given Carter's many strengths, it was also ultimately overblown. She lost to Stephens in November, but it was an instructive loss. The vote was 7,582 to 6,005. That a female Republican won almost 45 percent of the vote in a year when Democrats won their local elections across the board suggests that Carter's biggest liability—her sex—seemed less important to voters than the gendered nature of electoral politics would suggest.[41] Her party affiliation, in this very Democratic city, was likely at least as problematic or even more so.

Carter lost the election, but she caught Mayor LaGuardia's attention. A year after her failed campaign, the mayor asked Carter to serve on an interracial commission charged to study the causes of the 1935 Harlem riot and make recommendations to alleviate them. Of the twenty-two members appointed, Carter was the sole woman. The group determined that economic inequality was the primary cause of the riot, a conclusion that would not have surprised any of the black women who had worked in Harlem's grassroots organizations or New Deal agencies.

At the end of its lengthy report, the commission began its recommendations with the acknowledgment that "the economic and social ills of Harlem, which are deeply rooted in the very nature of our economic and social system," cannot be cured by any single administration. Nonetheless, the members determined that there was a great deal that the municipal government of New York City could do to alleviate racial discrimination. The commission proposed the creation of employment, housing, education, and health policies designed to redress the profoundly unequal system. They also advocated for changing civil service practices, hiring African Americans in public utility jobs, and improving schools, community playgrounds, and hospitals.[42] Harlem's infrastructure was in a state of decay despite the best efforts of its residents. Poverty, intentional municipal neglect, and racism were a devastating combination that no single individual or group of community volunteers could effectively undermine. According to the commission, government action was necessary to generate structural progress.

Carter's positive contributions brought her further notice. The commission's chair, Charles Roberts, designated her to lobby the state legislature for housing legislation. Shortly after that she was hired by the New York district attorney and became the first black woman in that position. At the same time and as evidence of the multidimensional ways these African American women engaged in activism, she worked closely with Mary McLeod Bethune to build the largest organization of African American women in U.S. history, the NCNW.[43]

Two years later Jane Bolin decided to run for office. Born in Poughkeepsie, New York, in 1908, Bolin graduated from Wellesley College in 1928 and from Yale Law School in 1931, the first African American woman to do so. Like Carter, her father was a lawyer and she was a Republican. She fought for racial justice through the NAACP, the Urban League, and the Harlem Lawyers Association, of which Ruth Whaley was also a member. These networks played a vital role in connecting this small, talented group of women together. As a lawyer practicing in Harlem, Bolin came face to face with the economic inequalities that ultimately led to the 1935 uprising, and she used her professional talents to address them. In 1936, she added a run for elected office to her list of strategies.

For anyone running for office on the Republican Party ticket in 1936, the challenge was particularly daunting. The head of the Democratic Party, Franklin D. Roosevelt, was an immensely popular president running for reelection. Bolin found herself with an uphill battle against the incumbent of the Nineteenth District, Assemblyman Robert Justice, a black man and a Democrat.[44] Despite Bolin's sterling credentials, the challenge proved too much. In the 1936 election African American voters underwent a dramatic sea change. Many in Harlem and Brooklyn had steadily decamped to the Democratic Party over the past twenty years; now the rest of the nation's black voters outside the Jim Crow South joined them. Roosevelt's victory was "one of the biggest Democratic landslides in American history."[45] Even popular Republicans in Harlem went down in defeat. Bolin lost by a four-to-one ratio.[46] Although hers was no more a defeat than many Republican candidates in the city experienced, it meant that there would still be no black women in the state house come January. On the other hand, Bolin's career, just like Carter's, scored continued successes after her electoral defeat. In 1939 Mayor LaGuardia appointed Bolin to serve as a judge on the Municipal Domestic Relations Court. She was the first black woman to achieve that legal height.[47] While not known for his feminist sensibilities, LaGuardia was an astute politician who helped advance black women's public leadership through appointments of women like Hedgeman, Carter, and now Bolin.

The Republican Party hemorrhaged black voters after 1936. Would a black female candidate running on the Democratic Party ticket succeed where Carter and Bolin had failed? Was there any way to know if they lost because of their membership in a party in decline, or did the fact that they were women work against them more than seemed immediately apparent? The 1937 Democratic Party primary campaign for the Nineteenth State Assembly District seat suggests that when party affiliation was a potential positive factor, discrimination against African American women was likely still at work, at least in the deeply masculine bastion of Tammany Hall.

Harlem attorney Ruth Whitehead Whaley made history as the first black woman to practice law in New York. Born in Goldsboro, North Carolina, in 1901, Whaley was also the first African American woman admitted to the bar in her home state of North Carolina.[48] Abandoning the party of Lincoln ahead of most African Americans, Whaley was active in the Democratic Party by 1924. She defended her decision, arguing that the New York Democrats "were offering more toward the advancement of colored citizens." She was committed to civic and organizational work at the same time that she pursued political goals. Whaley was the first president of the New York City National Association of Negro Business and Professional Women (NANBPW), chair of the Council of Democratic Women, an active member of the NCNW after its 1935 founding, and counsel for the New York City Colored Women's Federation.[49]

Like most African American women who ventured into public life, Whaley was very familiar with the challenges of negotiating an arena that was crafted by and expected to be run by white men. This reality had not prevented her from trailblazing in law school and in her legal practice, however, and it was not stopping her now. In 1937, she entered the Democratic primary election.[50] In the crowded field of contestants, Whaley had great difficulty garnering attention as a serious candidate. Despite her longstanding loyalty to Tammany Hall, she had neither party backing nor support from Harlem's African American leadership, and so her first run for office failed. Nonetheless, she pushed the door open ajar by being the first black woman to run as a Democrat. New York City was such a strongly Democratic city that without that party's backing, electoral victories would be extremely hard to come by. In order for a true shift in access to political power to occur for black women, Democrats were going to have to come around to supporting black female candidates.

Whaley may have had a hard time getting the Democratic Party's attention in 1937, but Sara Pelham Speaks did not. Born in 1902, Speaks was a graduate of the prestigious Dunbar High School in Washington, D.C., the University of Michigan, and New York University law school. Like Carter, Speaks came from an impressive family of race leaders. Her father, Robert A. Pelham, was the former editor and publisher of the *Washington Tribune* (a black newspaper); her mother, Gabrielle Lewis Pelham, was the first honorary member of the Delta Sigma Theta sorority; and her sister, Dorothy Pelham Beckley, was the sorority's second president. Speaks assisted her father in organizing the Capital News Service, a black news agency in Washington in the late 1920s. In New York, she was active in a number of civic and women's groups, including the Urban League and the Deltas.[51] A lifelong Republican, Speaks decided in 1937 that the time was right for her to move from being a campaign supporter to a candidate, so she accepted the Square Deal Republican Club's request that she run in the Twenty-first Assembly District primary. She had already demonstrated her political acumen when she served on the Republican state committee and helped wrest control of the Twenty-second Assembly District from the old political machine. She had also worked tirelessly on behalf of GOP presidential candidates.[52]

In 1937 her party's local figurehead, Mayor LaGuardia, was up for reelection. The liberal Republican mayor remained popular across the political spectrum, not just because he was having some success bringing Tammany's influence to heel but also because of his New Deal programs. Additionally, after 1936 the Republicans and all minor parties benefited from a significant change in the way city council members were elected. Gotham's voters decided to implement proportional representation, which helped weaken, even slightly, the Democrats' iron grip on power locally. While this did not affect Speaks's campaign directly, it helped create a climate of political openness and possibility.

Once her candidacy was announced, Speaks faced an immediate backlash. Her Republican rival, Ed Watts, petitioned to have her name removed from the ballot on the grounds that she had not lived in the district long enough. The Board of Elections agreed and invalidated her candidacy.[53] Speaks fought back, appealing to the State Supreme Court; the court found in her favor. With her name restored on the ballot, women rushed to support her campaign. Speaks remarked with delight, "I have my opponents to thank for thousands of dollars of free publicity. Hundreds of Republicans have learned of my candidacy through the Board's ridiculous action who might otherwise have taken my workers a long time to reach."[54] The primary campaign was a bruising introduction to electoral politics, but when the votes were counted it was Speaks who was left standing. She beat Watts by a handful of votes in a nail-biting recount. With one victory under her belt she turned her sights on Assemblyman William T. Andrews, a black man and the popular Tammany Democratic incumbent from her district.[55] Speaks lost precious resources and time on the primary vote recount and therefore came late to the general campaign, but like Carter and Bolin, she received the *New York Age*'s endorsement, and as the Republican-Fusion Progressive candidate, her political agenda was in line with the mayor's.[56]

According to the *New York Age*, Andrews's political club, the Beavers-Ramapo Democratic Club, was concerned enough about the threat Speaks represented that they circulated a rumor that she was a white woman "in an effort to fool the Negro voters of the district."[57] The rumor exposed certain racialized gender calculations Andrews made, at the same time that it exposed the ways race shaped politics in Harlem. Given Carter's strong showing three years earlier, Andrews may have expected black women to support a black female candidate. But he also believed, the rumor suggests, that it was the combination of Speaks's race and her gender, and not just her gender identification alone, that would attract black female voters. In other words, black women would vote for a *black* woman but not a *white* woman. Racial identification would trump gender identification, Andrews believed, but a candidate who embodied the two could be trouble.

But hundreds of women were not fooled, and they worked frenetically to get Speaks elected. It was more than time, they felt, for a black woman to serve in Albany. When the votes were counted, Speaks carried the majority of the African American districts, including the Forty-eighth District, where the Beavers-Ramapo club was located. But that was not enough. She lost by fewer than three hundred votes.[58] The *Chicago Defender* noted, "Against most any other candidate except the most popular local candidate in Harlem [William Andrews], she might have won despite the fact that she is a Republican, the minority group in New York City."[59] Speaks's campaign suggested that the 1936 election, which saw wholesale support of the Democratic Party at the national level, was less determinant of the local political disposition. It also reinforced the message from Carter's campaign that a significant number of Harlem voters were more than willing to vote for a black woman.

By the time the decade drew to a close, a handful of highly educated African American women, almost all of whom were lawyers by profession, had run for office and familiarized Harlem voters with the idea that black women belonged on electoral ballots. Carter and Speaks convinced a sizable minority that they even belonged *in* office. The close calls of the 1930s gave others reason to hope that the world of electoral politics was opening up—even a little bit. But how would the impending global crisis affect African American women at the polls?

Harlem in the 1940s

The war in Europe and Asia arrived on the nation's shores on a quiet Sunday morning in Pearl Harbor, Hawaii. After that "day that will live in infamy," December 7, 1941, neither the nation nor the world would be the same. A strategic peacetime draft started a year earlier by President Roosevelt rapidly expanded and millions of American men went off to battle. With an equal commitment to military victory, women on the home front moved into public life at an even greater pace. Not only did they plant victory gardens in backyards across the country that met more than 40 percent of the nation's produce needs, nearly two million women became the "hidden army" that helped keep munitions flowing out of factories. These "Rosie the Riveters" have been brought out of obscurity over the past two decades by scholars and filmmakers.[60] Less recognized are the women who advanced in politics. They also eagerly filled the gaps and embraced the opportunities created by men who departed for war.

African Americans were focused on the international task at hand—defeating the Central Powers in Europe and Asia—but they wanted a "Double V," a victory against fascism overseas and a victory on the home front, one which gave them true democracy and which would finally put an end to the hateful system of Jim Crow. The former goal, ending fascism overseas, would ultimately prove easier than the latter, bringing the full rights of citizenship to *all* Americans.

Local politics was eclipsed by these national and international events, and then was transformed by them. In New York City, reverberations from World War II were felt in every neighborhood. After the Hitler-Stalin pact in 1939, the New Deal Popular Front, the dynamic coalition of liberal and leftist activists, lost some support. Yet as historian Martha Biondi has demonstrated, progressive forces remained very active and scored some important successes in New York City in the 1940s.[61] The ALP and the CPUSA, for example, continued to find favor among a substantial number of New York voters. This was most evident in the election of two Communist City Council members, Peter V. Cacchione, a son of Italian immigrants who was elected in Brooklyn in 1941, and Ben Davis, an African American native of Georgia who was elected in Harlem in 1943, and the election of Vito Marcantonio from east Harlem to the U.S. House of Representatives, where he served as a member of the American Labor Party from 1939 until1951.

But it was also apparent in the activism that has come to be known as the Northern civil rights movement. Leaders of this surging movement for racial equality, well underway since at least the 1910s, were joined by labor activists and progressive New Dealers. Together they capitalized on the abundant need for wartime labor, the federal requirement for defense industries not to discriminate, government price controls, New Yorkers' general openness to progressive politicians, and the second massive migration of African Americans to Northern cities like New York to push for new and expansive employment, housing, and education policies that supported the goals of racial, social, and economic justice.[62]

African American women, many of whom had been very active in the 1930s, were also part of these efforts in direct and indirect ways. In Harlem and for the first time in Bedford-Stuyvesant, a rapidly growing black community in Brooklyn, they seized the openings generated by the war and its aftermath to further their pursuits of racial and economic justice, and political opportunity. Prominent women, including Layle Lane and Anna Arnold Hedgeman, joined with A. Philip Randolph to pressure the president to open up defense jobs to

African Americans through the 1941 March on Washington movement. Their efforts yielded the Fair Employment Practices Commission (FEPC). Ella Baker fought against racial discrimination during the war years, first as an NAACP field secretary then as Director of Branches. During that time, the organization's membership swelled from fifty thousand to over four hundred thousand. Pauli Murray, now at Howard University law school, led a group of students in a lunch-counter sit-in in the nation's capital to challenge the color line.[63] Brooklyn women like Ada B. Jackson and Maude Richardson led struggles against racist press coverage of predominantly black neighborhoods, as well as discriminatory rent and job hiring practices.

At the same time, electoral politics attracted those who were growing tired of the limited, temporary results that protests seemed to yield. Some of the candidates' names were familiar. Layle Lane, Sara Speaks, and Ruth Whaley had already tested their political mettle in the 1930s and were ready to try again. But there were also new names on party ballots. In particular, Ada B. Jackson and Maude Richardson captivated Brooklyn's Seventeenth District's residents. Pauli Murray also made her one and only foray into electoral politics in the 1940s. The ideas that each of these women had about the organization of society and the government's role in it, their relationships to the political parties, and their own professional aspirations shaped the ways and the frequency with which they pursued office.

In 1943, the New York legislature reapportioned U.S. congressional districts creating new boundaries for the Twenty-second District, which was centered in Harlem. African Americans finally had the potential to elect a black leader to serve in the U.S. Congress along with William Dawson of Chicago, the only African American there. Adam Clayton Powell Jr., the popular pastor of Harlem's Abyssinian Baptist Church and a driving force in the "Don't Buy Where You Can't Work" campaigns in the 1930s, saw the seat as his. Fiercely independent, Powell easily won a City Council seat in 1941 without Democratic or Republican party support. Co-owner of the left-leaning weekly paper, the *People's Voice*, Powell garnered a good deal of leftist support among the ALP, Communists, labor leaders, and other progressive activists in New York City.[64] Always more pragmatic than ideological, Tammany Hall also backed Powell in his bid for the new congressional seat. When he secured the nomination, Powell became the first black man in New York City to run for Congress on the Democratic Party ticket. This was a significant victory for African Americans, who were slowly overcoming the racial barriers that had historically kept them out of elected office.[65] With such broad support Powell felt confident of victory.

The Republican Party knew it had to be strategic if it wanted a shot at winning the new congressional seat. There was at least a window of opportunity because, after twelve years of Republican Mayor LaGuardia, local Democrats had lost some power in the city, and New York Governor Thomas Dewey, a Republican, was challenging the aging President Roosevelt in the presidential race. In addition, the party had done surprisingly well in a special congressional election in March 1944 in the Twenty-first Congressional District, which was just adjacent to the new seat. Moreover, despite Powell's mass appeal, there were a number of Harlem leaders who did not like his independence or his style. Finally, the Republicans hoped that gender would be a factor in the campaign. With so many men in the military, women outnumbered men on Republican, Democratic, and American Labor Party voter registration rolls in 1944.[66] Republicans felt that they had a fighting chance to capture the seat, and they chose a black woman with years of GOP experience and a near miss in her last election to challenge Powell.

Despite her opponent's popularity, Sara Pelham Speaks embraced the challenge ahead of her. After her 1937 campaign, she worked for the GOP on the 1940 presidential campaign as Director of Women's Activities for the Eastern Colored Division of the Republican National Committee. Even as she maintained a busy law practice, Speaks worked with the New York Urban League and she served as president of the New York State Federation of Business and Professional Women's Club and chaired its anti-discrimination committee.[67] During the 1944 campaign, she promised to fight for abolition of the poll tax, legislation to make lynching a federal crime, and effective enforcement of anti–Jim Crow laws. But these were standard issues for African American candidates in New York City. Powell, a political progressive, was equally committed to fighting for these changes. Speaks ran against this towering community figure for the same reasons she ran against the popular incumbent, William Andrews, in 1937. She believed she had a better message, a better approach to politics, and a better delivery system—the Republican Party.

Speaks and Powell had dramatically different campaign styles. He aggressively pursued the Harlem spotlight from the pulpit of Abyssinian Baptist Church and on the streets. Speaks publically critiqued what she called his "emotional and inflammatory approach." A number of influential African Americans, including Herbert Bruce, a Tammany Hall district leader in Harlem; Eardlie John, chairman of the labor and industry committee of the NAACP; Frank R. Crosswaith, chair of the Harlem Labor Committee and a Socialist; B. F. McLaurin, international organizer with the Brotherhood of Sleeping Car Porters and chairman of Harlem Unity Liberal party; and William T. Andrews, a Harlem assemblyman and Speaks's opponent in 1937, all had serious reservations about Powell.[68] When Powell first announced his candidacy, he promised that he would "represent the Negro people first," a comment that upset some Tammany Hall operatives nervous about running their first black congressional candidate.[69] Although he recanted his statement, Powell was considered a loose cannon.

Speaks attacked Powell personally, questioning his integrity, his reliability, and his ambitions.[70] She also tried unsuccessfully to exploit the fact that he had Communist Party support.[71] Charging that Powell was a "rabble rouser," Speaks offered an alternative. She embodied reliability and trustworthiness. She also promised that she would be a team player in Congress. "Cooperative activity within the framework of an established political party will lead to the improvement of the position of the Negro in America," Speaks argued. "You can't pass bills with one vote. A Representative must work through friendships and party associations."[72] If people in Harlem were looking for differences in style and approaches to leadership, they could not have found sharper distinctions than those between Speaks and Powell. He promised to be a renegade; she pledged not to be.

Just as she had in her 1937 campaign, Speaks made direct appeals to women in Harlem, and many responded. Prominent leaders, including Lucille Randolph (A. Philip Randolph's wife), Bertha Diggs (New York State Secretary of Labor), and Gertrude Ayer (the only African American principal in New York City's public schools), backed her campaign. More than two hundred neighborhood women organized a non-partisan committee to elect her.[73] At the same time, she did not necessarily advance a specifically gendered platform, although her effort to cast herself as a team player suggests an appeal to certain gendered stereotypes. However she did not claim legitimacy as a maternalist, promising to clean up the public sphere and she did not justify her campaign on the basis of her sex. She was a political party activist who wanted to advance her own ideas about civil rights and Harlem's needs in general, and she said as much.

The *Amsterdam News* continued its tendency to favor Republican candidates into the 1940s. Its editors enthusiastically endorsed Speaks' campaign, which was not surprising considering Powell owned a competing paper, the politically left-leaning *People's Voice*. But when the *Amsterdam News* endorsed Speaks, it did more than challenge a competitor. The paper's editors underscored the potential opportunity Speaks' campaign represented to make right a historical injustice in the same way that the *New York Age* did during Carter's campaign. They stated "At long last the recognition rightly due Negro women from political leaders in the major parties has been given in the designation by the Republicans of Sara Speaks as a candidate for Congress."[74] Speaks recognized the changes in the political environment that the war created and again made herself an appealing candidate to the GOP. The *Amsterdam News* congratulated the party on its judgment "in the light of increasing interest of the masses of women in political affairs," and they predicted that women would turn out in large numbers for the 1944 election.

Progressive leaders in Harlem were less excited about Speaks, although no one expressed reservations on the basis of sex. Congressman Marcantonio, the representative from neighboring East Harlem, believed that Speaks "could be counted upon to support all progressive legislation."[75] However, he refused to endorse any candidate who opposed Roosevelt, which Speaks did. She was a dedicated Republican and spoke against FDR because he had failed to repeal the poll tax and had not pushed for an anti-lynching bill.[76] Benjamin Davis, the Communist City Council member who Powell backed as his successor when he decided to run for Congress, expressed reservations about Speaks as well. An African American radical, Davis praised Speaks for "her day to day struggle with the masses," but he worried that she had never been "on the firing line on the issue of the poll tax, the Fair Employment Practices Commission, jobs, housing and other such mass issues." He also suggested that the Republican Party was trying to exploit the gender issue for its own benefit and he charged that the party was masking its "reactionary tracks behind the skirts of an intelligent woman."[77] Speaks did not see herself as a party dupe, and more, she herself tried to capitalize on the gender split of the voter registration rolls. If Harlem leaders or voters were worried about Speaks being a woman, they did not say so in public. Her Republican affiliation, her promise of pragmatism in Congress, and her lack of front-line experience seemed to concern them far more.

Speaks presented herself as the more responsible candidate, the one who was most likely to work effectively with other members of Congress, and she may very well have been. However, she was not a grassroots fighter in the same way that Powell was. Though she was an ardent advocate for racial equality, she very much wanted to conduct her battles in the traditional political establishment, in conventional ways. But with the war still waging, and the "Double-V" campaign far from won, her desire to collaborate with fellow Congressional representatives did not win over the majority of residents in the Twenty-second Congressional District. They had just closed a decade that began with "Don't Buy Where You Can't Work" boycotts. They had lived through the Harlem riots of 1935 and 1943. Political decorum was not what they wanted.

The *Amsterdam News* engaged in a bout of wishful thinking when it predicted a landslide vote for Speaks in the August primary. In fact, it was a landslide, but Speaks did not win. A number of prominent Harlemites who were uncomfortable sending Powell to Congress supported Speaks, but she did not have mass appeal. The vote tally (4,755 for Powell and 1,772 for Speaks) on August 1, 1944, confirmed Powell's popularity.

Speaks's campaign exposes the complicated political landscape in New York City in the 1940s. She and the GOP attempted to exploit the political openings created by World War II. As the minority party, the Republicans remained more willing than the Tammany Hall Democrats to back a black female candidate. They had less to lose, and more than that, they hoped that Speaks could be an asset and pull in female voters. With more women than men registered to vote, it was not a bad strategy. Furthermore, the campaign illuminates some of the differences of political opinion within the African American community in New York. The candidates appealed to different constituents who had their own complex set of reasons for choosing one candidate over the other that included ideology, style, and likely gender as well. For one out of every four voters in Harlem, Speaks was the better choice. Finally, Speaks's campaign is an example of the opportunities that were opening up for women in the war era. Her very presence in the congressional campaign suggested that women were being taken seriously as candidates, at least among the parties vying to gain power in New York City, and this was an important step.

The Democrats, however, were still generally resistant to running African American women for office, although they made two modest efforts to explore black women's viability at the polls in the mid-1940s. In the first case, Tammany Hall decided to field a challenger to the popular Democratic/ALP incumbent, William T. Andrews, in the primary campaign in August 1944. Out of favor with the Tiger, Andrews faced Twelfth District co-leader Ruth Brown Price at the polls. All assembly districts were structured to have a leader (by tradition a man), a co-leader (by tradition a woman), and an assemblyman (who could also be the district leader but was not automatically so). Although she gave Andrews a good fight, Price lost the primary race and Andrews went on to hold his seat handily in the November election.[78]

A year later, another Harlem lawyer threw her hat into the ring for a second try at elected office. By 1945, Ruth Whitehead Whaley was a veteran of clubhouse politics. For more than twenty years, she had fought to eradicate the gender and race biases inherent in Tammany and in public life more generally. In 1941 she had served as a campaign manager for William O'Dwyer when he ran for mayor against Fiorello LaGuardia.[79] Though O'Dwyer lost, he and Whaley maintained a political relationship that would pay off for both of them over time. Whaley was a smart and pragmatic politico. This was particularly apparent in the way she made the most of an unfavorable situation in the 1945 city council elections. That summer, Tammany Hall split over the controversial decision to endorse Ben Davis, an avowed Communist, for New York City Council. The Democrats initially threw their support behind Davis. He had first made his name as a lawyer in the early 1930s defending Angelo Herndon, an African American Communist labor organizer in Georgia. Influenced by his experiences defending Herndon, Davis moved to New York and became a radical crusader for racial justice, taking on such explosive issues as police brutality and discrimination in housing, the military, and prisons.[80] He was very popular in Harlem and had won his first election for the city council.

Tammany's mayoral candidate William O'Dwyer, a World War II veteran, insisted that Davis be removed from the Democratic ticket and ordered the party to "designate in his stead another Negro of indisputable faith in the Democratic Party and its principles."[81] The Tammany leadership complied and sought a likely sacrificial lamb to run against the well-liked Communist activist. Whaley, O'Dwyer's political ally, was the chosen candidate "of indisputable faith."[82] Neither Whaley nor Tammany leaders could have expected a victory although the *New York Age* called Whaley "formidable opposition." She publically framed her nomination "as symbolic . . . it's a recognition of Negro women by the Democratic Party."[83] Even this was a stretch when many Harlem leaders in her Party supported her opponent.[84] Its importance lay elsewhere. It proved a strategic career move. She subsequently garnered increased access to the mayor and later a civil service job that gave her both power and a lifelong position. In 1947, for example, Mayor O'Dwyer called a meeting of Harlem leaders to discuss the community's grievances. Whaley was one of the few women he asked to attend. In a fashion reminiscent of the mayor's commission in the wake of the 1935 riot, the group delineated a damning list of indictments against the city—"dirty streets, fire trap houses, and price-gauging landlords, crime-producing slums, numbers racket, poor police protection, Jim Crow schools, and inadequate health facilities."[85] Little had changed in twelve years. Whaley offered a slate of proposals to alleviate some of Harlem's most urgent problems. As a result of their meeting with the mayor, the group established the Citizens Planning Council of Harlem and elected Whaley as the vice-chair. Among her priorities were better health facilities, welfare, and jobs for Harlem's residents.

Although unsuccessful at the polls, Whaley had found another way to fight for the beleaguered community.

Three years later acting-mayor Vincent Impellitteri, a long-time Tammany politician who was elevated from city council president to mayor when President Truman appointed O'Dwyer ambassador to Mexico, ran for reelection. The Tiger, fading in significance after years of scandal and LaGuardia rule, was unhappy with Impellitteri and refused to back him. Whaley defied Tammany and became one of his most active campaigners in Harlem.[86] After his victory, Impellitteri appointed Whaley, his former Fordham law classmate and loyal ally, to serve as secretary of the board of estimate. Members of the board, including Whaley, helped decide on the city budget and approved all major capital projects. The board was considered a "full-time participant with the mayor in governing the city."[87] Although the Democrats failed to support her two campaigns for office, through years of effort and by putting herself in line for party patronage Whaley attained a position of considerable power in the largest city in the United States.

In addition to her fiscal responsibilities, Whaley spoke to women's groups throughout the city and received awards and honors for her work, including the Sojourner Truth Award for outstanding community service.[88] Speaking at the annual Empire State Federation of Women's Clubs in 1956, Whaley urged the audience to use their right to vote "to gain greater benefits from the democratic system of government." Recalling the hard-won victories of African American women in the past, she warned, "We should not allow the priceless heritage which they left us and our children to slip away by a lackadaisical attitude toward voting." As a mayoral appointee, Whaley understood that votes could be used as political leverage if enough people went to the polls. "Those who don't vote, don't get counted by those who make and administer the law."[89] Northern black women had an important political resource in the ballot that their Southern sisters still did not. Whaley frequently urged them to use it.

Brooklyn Battles in the 1940s

African American women across the East River in Brooklyn also took advantage of the openings created by World War II and waged their own political battles. The Democrats were no more willing to support a black female candidate in Brooklyn than they were in Harlem, but African American women found strong support among the GOP, ALP, and the Liberal Party, which was formed in 1944 when a group of political leaders broke off from the ALP.[90] Brooklynites Ada B. Jackson and Maude Richardson vied to become the first black women elected to office in New York City. These two women ran against men and they ran against each other. Their campaigns together tell a story of competition over political ideals and expose the ways African Americans gained ground in New York City's various political parties.

Both women had migrated to New York from the Jim Crow South. Jackson was from Georgia; Richardson was a native of Arkansas. They had similar backgrounds—both were highly respected citizens in Brooklyn and active in their churches and community. Each had worked with grassroots organizations to fight for racial equality and led numerous endeavors to improve the area's quality of life. They shared the distinction of polling in the top ten of the *Amsterdam News*'s "10 Leading Brooklynites" annual contest. Jackson and Richardson even shared party affiliation. In 1944, both were registered Republicans and pursued their first campaigns on the GOP ticket. For Richardson, the party affiliation was a lifelong commitment; for Jackson, it was a strained relationship whose days were numbered.

No woman in Brooklyn tried to win elected office more often in the 1940s than Ada B. Jackson. This daughter of a former slave had not only witnessed a lynching in her home state but had escaped a lynch mob herself. She was an ardent, progressive activist for racial equality and social justice.[91] At the time of her first campaign, Jackson was thoroughly involved in civic activism. She served on the PTA and the YWCA, was the president of the Bedford Stuyvesant Women's Voluntary Services, and the *Brooklyn Eagle*, a local paper, voted her one of the borough's four "Fighting Ladies" for her war work. She was also a leader in the Brooklyn Interracial Assembly, a coalition of sixty-five organizations forged to challenge racist representations of Bedford-Stuyvesant in the city's mainstream newspapers.[92] The assembly was a piece of the broader civil rights movement underway in New York, which was led, in large part, by progressive labor leaders, leftists, and black activists—a coalition that Biondi has termed the Black Popular Front.[93] Under Jackson's direction, the Interracial Assembly conducted a detailed study of living and working conditions in Bedford-Stuyvesant and proposed ways to improve race relations and circumstances in the neighborhood. It exposed connections between problems in the community with the countless expressions of racism in the job market, in housing, and in a lack of city services. The assembly's recommendations included an extension of policies administered by the wartime Office of Price Administration Board (OPA) to combat the discriminatory pricing system that plagued black shoppers and renters.[94] They insisted that until systemic racism was rooted out, the poor living conditions and limited opportunities for New York City's black residents would continue.

In 1944 a Citizens' Non-Partisan Committee nominated Jackson to run for state assembly, the same year Speaks ran against Powell. Jackson understood the importance of grassroots activism but was also painfully aware of its limitations. So when the request for her to run for office was made, she accepted. She entered the Republican and ALP primary races. She lost the Republican primary to Louis Warner, an African American GOP leader, but she beat him on the ALP ticket. After defeating her in the Republican primary, Warner asked Jackson to withdraw from the race on the ALP ballot as well. He proposed that "all Negroes combine in the community to defeat the 'white Democratic' candidate."[95] But the committee that had nominated Jackson urged her to remain in the race on the ALP ticket, arguing that she was the best candidate for the job. Jackson complied but felt she had to defend her decision. A woman of strong ideals, she argued: "Negro people have cast their votes on the basis of issues, not party labels. . . . If my Republican opponent and I stood for the same things . . . it would be unwise for us to be competing for the same office. . . . It is an insult to the intelligence of the voters to speak as though they had only to choose between one or another Negro."[96] As with the Speaks-Powell campaign, two African American candidates faced off against each other. But a critical difference in this campaign was that Jackson remained in the race on a third-party ticket. This meant she had the potential to divide the loyalties of voters who wanted to advance the community's black leadership. If Warner's only opponent were the white Democratic incumbent, he likely would have won more votes. For Jackson, however, this was not a good reason to drop out. She persisted because of her commitment to progressive ideas, which included a postwar full-employment program and expanded social security.

During a Brooklyn voter registration rally a month before the 1944 general election First Lady Eleanor Roosevelt addressed an enthusiastic crowd of two thousand women. Jackson was also a featured speaker, and when she took the stage she highlighted the "importance of the woman's ballot" as Speaks did in her campaign. With so many men off to war, women in Brooklyn had new opportunities as candidates and new influence as voters. Like Speaks, however, Jackson made her appeals on more than gendered grounds. She had a demonstrated record of fighting for racial equality, and she had fervent ALP support. As the *People's Voice* noted, Jackson had "a knowledge of what her district needs . . . to an extent seldom matched by professional politicians," and the paper suggested that her name was synonymous with progressive activity.[97]

Gender analyses did not escape the press altogether, however. Even as it celebrated Jackson's activism, the *People's Voice* remarked on her maternal sensibilities. The editors implied that her leadership "arose naturally from her primary occupations of being a mother and housewife." Concern for her children's education led her to the PTA, where she served as president from 1940 to 1944, they said. And in case any readers feared that Jackson's household fell apart while she tended to civic needs, they reassured them that "despite her varied outside activities, Mrs. Jackson still runs a large house, does her own housework, cooking, and baking, and spends time with her four children."[98] Jackson, represented in the article as a wonder woman of sorts, had seemingly conquered the tensions within the double shift of home work and work outside it. The focus on Jackson's maternal sensibilities is noteworthy in part because it indicates that the newspaper expected readers to question a woman's ability to be both a successful politician and a responsible mother, even though more women worked outside the home during the war. Gender norms evinced some flexibility in the workforce and in the larger society, though less than the Rosie the Riveter propaganda suggested.[99] But in politics the male ideal seemed fixed despite the fact that increasing numbers of women were in party politics and ran for elected office. The *People's Voice* wanted to show that Jackson effectively balanced the two. In fact, they claimed her motivation for political activism stemmed from her role as mother, not from any kind of personal ambition or political convictions. At the same time, her most celebrated attribute was her activism, and that was what the papers commented on most frequently.

Despite their best efforts, both Jackson and Warner were defeated in the November election. Jackson was blamed for splitting the black vote and causing Warner's loss, a charge that would be leveled at her more than once. Her decision to remain in the race against another African American candidate indicates her deep-seated commitment to political ideology over racial identity. It also suggests her awareness of the limits of grassroots activism to bring about sustained and meaningful changes for the relatively poor black community in Bedford-Stuyvesant. She wanted a seat in some arena of government to fight for those changes, and so she continued her pursuits of political power.

Maude Richardson, the other black female candidate who ran a number of times in the 1940s, came within arm's reach of a historic victory. A prominent civic leader and champion of racial equality, Richardson was vice president of the Brooklyn NAACP, chair of the wartime Four Freedoms Committee of Brooklyn, vice-chair of the Negro Republicans of Kings County, and staff writer for the *Amsterdam News* and the *People's Voice*. In 1945, Bedford-Stuyvesant residents formed a nonpartisan committee to pick a viable candidate for city council. Thirty-five candidates vied for the nine open seats in Brooklyn. Council members were still elected by proportional representation, which meant that one council member was elected for every seventy-five thousand voters in the borough, rather than on a district-by-district basis. After two months of meetings the Bedford-Stuyvesant committee announced their chosen candidate—someone they expected to serve them well in office and who could garner wide public support: Maude Richardson. Before entering the race, Richardson checked with Bertram Baker, the black Democratic spokesperson of Kings County, to see if he was going to run. He had run once before for city council in 1941 and lost.[100] Richardson was concerned that if he ran, the votes from Bedford-Stuyvesant would be divided. Baker assured her that he was staying out of the race, and Richardson launched her campaign. A party leader, Richardson easily secured the GOP's backing, but she hoped to win the ALP's blessings as well, given the nature of the nonpartisan committee that asked her to run. The Progressive Party, however, held back its support.

A few weeks into her campaign, Richardson was taken by surprise when Baker reneged on his promise and entered the city council race as a Democratic and ALP candidate. The Democrats in Brooklyn had not, to date, demonstrated any commitment to ensuring that a black candidate won elected office in Brooklyn. The *Amsterdam News* speculated that the Democrats intentionally entered Baker in the race to divide the black vote. According to the paper, "in order for a Negro candidate to be elected in the City Council from Brooklyn, he or she must receive approximately 85 percent of the Negro vote, plus a goodly portion of support from the white."[101] With Baker in the race, there was a strong likelihood of a divided vote.

Nevertheless Richardson waged an aggressive campaign to win voters' loyalties in Bedford-Stuyvesant. She emphasized the poor state of race relations in New York and argued that the city was "sitting on an atomic bomb of race hatred." Only two years earlier, Harlem had exploded in fatally violent frustration. She promised to outlaw the "preaching of racial intolerance and discrimination," an early proposal of hate speech legislation that would only emerge fifty years later.[102] Additionally, with the war just over, job and housing conditions became an ever-greater concern, particularly for the city's largest minority group.

The *Amsterdam News* enthusiastically backed Richardson, defining her as "a hundred per cent race woman."[103] They argued that she would be an effective voice for Brooklyn in the city council. The *People's Voice* endorsed Baker. But when the votes were tallied, neither Baker nor Richardson won enough votes to secure a city council seat. In the borough-wide election, Baker garnered just over ten thousand votes and Richardson nearly six thousand. Even in defeat, Richardson claimed one victory; she "held a majority in the Negro-inhabited districts," just as Speaks had done eight years earlier against Andrews.[104] Voters in Bedford-Stuyvesant showed that they were willing to give a black female candidate their support if they liked her platform. Richardson was well known, respected, and supported because of her grassroots activism. She exploited the openings created by the proportional representation structure and aggressively pursued the seat for which her community nominated her. To many people in Bedford-Stuyvesant, Richardson's experience, commitment, and message mattered. While it is impossible to measure gender bias for or against her, it is clear that a majority of Bed-Sty voters had no problem voting for a woman.

When the 1946 election season rolled around, there were only two women among the sixteen African American candidates running for office in all of New York City. They were the only black candidates from Brooklyn, and they were both vying for the Seventeenth District seat, centered in Bedford-Stuyvesant. Maude Richardson faced Ada B. Jackson in the Republican primary. The Democrats failed to nominate a black candidate, which the editors at the *Amsterdam News* underscored for their readers. "This brings the age-worn Brooklyn difficulty of having the Negro vote split wide open," they argued, "with Negroes running on both the ALP and Republican tickets, splitting the votes so that the white Democrats will have an easy time romping on to victory."[105] If the Democrats had also fielded a black candidate, Bedford-Stuyvesant would have ended up with a black representative in Albany, regardless of who won.

A *People's Voice* questionnaire circulated to the candidates revealed many similarities between Richardson's and Jackson's agendas, especially regarding their commitment to the fight for racial equality. Their paths diverged though over the question of organized labor's role in the government. Richardson was opposed to it; Jackson favored it. During the campaign Richardson complained that "Communists and American Laborites had poured money and workers into the district in a campaign against her nomination."[106] She was anti-Communist and was becoming more explicitly so over time as the wartime alliance between the United States and the Soviet Union rapidly devolved into an ideological standoff that reordered much of the world into oppositional camps, and that simultaneously reconfigured the home front in ways that generated rapid, far-reaching, and often viscous attacks on progressive coalitions like those fighting for racial and economic rights in New York City.[107]

As primary day approached, the campaign grew heated, but Richardson, more active with the GOP in Brooklyn, was predicted to win. The papers reported that "no other fight has caused such furor in the uptown [Bedford-Stuyvesant] area." More than a hundred women gathered to formally endorse Richardson. The *Amsterdam News* enthusiastically championed her candidacy as well. Jackson, however, had impressive backing from the Left and labor. Progressive leader Henry Wallace campaigned in Brooklyn for Jackson and the rest of the ALP slate. The *People's Voice* gave her their endorsement, and the Transport Workers Union defended Jackson, stating, "She is an outstanding leader, fighting for the welfare of the people."[108] The Congress of American Women, a Left-leaning organization founded in the wake of the war, also eagerly backed her campaign.[109] Although both candidates shared a deep commitment to racial justice and had spent much of their public life fighting for it, it was clear that they had some ideological differences. Jackson was very much a part of the progressive movement with anchors in the trade unions and the American Labor Party.[110] Richardson represented a decidedly different view.

In the Republican primary election in 1946, the progressive coalition was unable to stem support for the regular GOP candidate. Richardson defeated Jackson by a vote of 1,024 to 729. After her victory in the primary, Richardson faced the white Democratic incumbent John Walsh—and Jackson again. At the urging of progressive ALP leaders, Jackson, a long-time Republican, finally abandoned the party and remained in the race on the ALP ticket. Earlier she had criticized the GOP for maintaining segregated political clubs.[111] After this loss, she never ran as a Republican again.

Walsh, backed by the powerful Democratic machine, thought he had little cause for concern, particularly with Jackson remaining in the race. He expected the two women to split black voters' loyalties in Bedford-Stuyvesant. Brooklyn's 125,000 black residents had yet to see an African American elected to office. It appeared that with these two popular grassroots activists wooing the same voters, the situation would persist.

In September 1946, Jackson offered Richardson conditional support. Although it was legally too late to take her name off the ballot, she pledged not to campaign. ALP leaders suggested that only a collaborative effort between the Republicans and the ALP could topple the Democratic incumbent. Richardson was initially hesitant to accept Jackson's endorsement, but she eventually signed a statement welcoming the ALP's backing. Before Richardson went public with the news, however, she reversed her decision. Jackson accused the GOP leadership of pressuring Richardson to reject the ALP support and ultimately undermining the possibility of an African American victory. It is unclear whether Richardson followed the party's dictates, as Jackson suggested, or decided on her own to reject the ALP. In any case, she declined the endorsement.[112]

In the November election, the vote was so close that a recount was necessary. But when the final tally was reached, Richardson had lost to the Democratic incumbent by seventy-seven votes. The warnings in the *Amsterdam News* had proved prescient. With Jackson polling 4,397 votes, the black vote was divided again, and Richardson was denied what would have been a remarkable victory. She tried to put a positive spin on the outcome, stating, "I am happy at the results of the unprecedented effort made by the voters in the 17th A.D. to place a Negro in the State Assembly."[113] Nevertheless, Richardson had to have been very disappointed.

When the dust settled, Bedford-Stuyvesant leaders hurled criticism at Jackson for dividing the vote. At the same time, they had harsh words for the Democrats: "The Democrats had better get wise and nominate Negroes in the 17th from now on, or they will be dead ducks."[114] In reality, there was plenty of blame to go around. The Democratic Party generally resisted running black candidates for state-level offices. In a city where that single party dominated, this hurt African American political aspirants significantly. At the same time, the Republicans undermined their own candidate by insisting that she reject the ALP's support. Jackson claimed they did so to divide the "Negro vote." Because she held to the party line, Richardson lost an unprecedented opportunity to serve her community in the state house, and she undermined the hopes of black residents in Bedford-Stuyvesant to send an African American to office. One could also question Jackson's motives. The African American community of Bedford-Stuyvesant was positioned to make history in 1946. However, Jackson was ideologically committed to the liberal-left coalition and agreed to run in the general election on the ALP ticket. She could have said no. Yet, her offer to throw her support to Richardson suggests that she and the ALP were more flexible than the GOP. In the end, the political parties as much as the candidates themselves thwarted a black victory. African Americans in Brooklyn would have to wait for another election to realize their goal of having a black elected official.

But a Republican black woman had come remarkably close to winning this election. How should we understand Richardson's near upset of a white, male, Democratic incumbent who had the backing of the powerful local political machine? She likely benefited from the national political mood swing to the right in 1946. For the first time in at least sixteen years, New Yorkers sent more

Republicans than Democrats to Congress. However, New York City was still a heavily Democratic city. Richardson's near victory sounded a clear warning to the Party bosses. Bedford-Stuyvesant wanted an African American elected to office, and at least in 1946, the candidates' race seemed to factor as significantly to voters as their party affiliation. The fact that Richardson was a woman, it appears, was not a problem for enough voters that she came within striking distance of a victory.

Despite being labeled a spoiler among certain discontented voters and the major black newspapers, Jackson continued to inspire many community residents and the city's Left-leaning activists. She ran unsuccessfully for city council in 1947. In 1948, they asked her to run for office yet again. During the presidential campaign that year, Henry A. Wallace, the Progressive Party candidate, crisscrossed the nation seeking votes. The Bedford-Stuyvesant Wallace for President Committee endorsed ALP candidate Ada Jackson for Congress. Jackson became the first African American to run for U.S. Congress from Brooklyn, and she ran against two white men for the office.

As the election grew near, Jackson appealed to black voters to support the Progressive Party on racial grounds, stating that, "For the Negro people this is no political disagreement; this is a matter of survival." Promise after promise had been broken, Jackson charged. "This has been the lot of the Negro people faced with a Democratic Party dominated by Southern racists and a Republican Party that has conveniently forgotten Abraham Lincoln."[115] But by 1948, the political climate was becoming far less tolerant. The diminishing but enthusiastic supporters could not prevent the impending defeat. Jackson lost by more than a three-to-one margin to her Democratic opponent. At the top of the ticket, Henry Wallace won fewer votes than Strom Thurmond, who ran for president on the Dixiecrat ticket in response to the Democrats' civil rights platform. The tide was clearly turning even in New York City; the days were numbered for self-identified Leftists in electoral politics. Not one to give up easily, Jackson ran on the ALP ticket one last time in 1949, this time for Brooklyn borough president. She won nearly eighty thousand votes, an impressive number in its own right but in terms of the election, she was soundly defeated, even losing in the Seventeenth State Assembly District, the heart of Bedford-Stuyvesant.[116] This was more than a defeat; it was an unmistakable message that Jackson and her politically progressive message had lost favor even in her own community.

On the other side of the political fence, Maude Richardson was as determined as Jackson to win elected office. In 1948 she and Bertram Baker had a rematch. Their 1945 face-off had been for City Council; this time they competed for a seat in the state assembly. Richardson ran on the Republican ticket, Baker on the Democratic ballot. With the two major parties fielding black candidates, it was certain that Brooklyn would finally have its first black elected official. The Democrats had learned their lesson. However, they were not ready to break completely with their clubhouse traditions; they ran Baker, a black man, although there were many black women involved in Democratic Party politics. Maude Richardson was a formidable contender and a smart choice for the Republicans. The party hoped that Governor Dewey's campaign for president on the Republican ticket and Richardson's near victory over Walsh meant that they had a better-than-usual chance to win this typically Democratic seat.

In the immediate postwar years, New York City campaigns reflected the contested political climate of the nation at large. Anti-Communism was becoming more palpable even in local elections. Evidence of the growing conservative temperament was obvious in Richardson's campaign. She was no longer interested in garnering ALP support. Instead, groups like the Negro Elks of New York used Richardson's election to make anti-Communist pronouncements. Elks leader J. Finley Wilson referred to Richardson when he said, "With such assistance from Negro leadership our efforts in Brooklyn will be redoubled to drive Communist influences out of the 17th A. D."[117] Her campaign was held up as proof that African American citizens were "loyal to the philosophy of American traditions" and avowedly anti-Communist.

Still, progressive elements were not completely silenced. Baker benefited from the ALP backing even though he drew most of his support on the Democratic Party ticket. For the third time in four years, Richardson lost her election. In the presidential election year of 1948, the Seventeenth Assembly District voted heavily in favor of the Democratic candidate as it usually did. Baker beat Richardson by a two-to-one margin to become the first African American elected to political office in Brooklyn. Bedford-Stuyvesant residents wanted a black representative. Richardson had come dangerously close to beating John Walsh in 1946, and the Democratic leadership heeded the warnings. They would not risk losing the seat by running a white candidate against Richardson again. As in Harlem, when the Democrats first decided to run a black candidate, they ran a man, not a woman. Despite her unwavering work for racial equality and community betterment, the political climate did not sustain this vocally pro-Dewey Republican. Richardson had run—and lost—her last political race.

The 1948 campaign for the Seventeenth District raises questions about race, gender, and political identity. How much did gender matter when both candidates were African American? The answer is unclear, but it had not kept

Richardson from near victory in 1946 when the candidates' race was of significant interest to voters. Yet thcy seemed most often concerned about party affiliation and the issues. Richardson was a holdout despite the fact that most African Americans had left the party of Lincoln twelve years earlier and showed no serious signs of returning. In a city as Democratic as New York, she was fighting a losing battle. It was increasingly clear that black women could only get so far in political races on third-party and Republican tickets.

The decade closed with a campaign effort by a rising star among black female leaders. When she left Harlem and her WPA work with Ella Baker, Pauli Murray moved to Washington, D.C., where she pursued her law degree at Howard University and led a successful sit-in to desegregate a popular luncheonette. She graduated in 1944 and immediately after that completed an L.L.M. (Master of Laws) at the University of California. Murray made her one and only bid for office in 1949, when she ran for city council in Brooklyn. She had developed a keen sensitivity to race and gender-based injustices challenging, unsuccessfully, the Jim Crow admissions policy at University of North Carolina and the sexist admissions policy at Harvard.[118] In addition, she demonstrated her willingness to put herself in physical danger, first helping defend Odell Waller, a black sharecropper convicted of murder, and later in the lunch counter sit-ins and pickets. More than any of the black female candidates before her, Murray articulated black women's oppression in terms of sexual discrimination as well as racism.[119]

Of the 102 candidates seeking office in the city, Murray was the only African American woman and the only black candidate from Brooklyn running for city council.[120] Not evidently driven by an ideology, Murray ran on the Liberal Party ballot. Her campaign embodied many of the issues that grassroots activists had been fighting for—more and better schools, safe streets, and quality-of-life issues.[121] When it was formed in 1944, the Liberal Party espoused three principles that likely appealed to Murray: equal access to jobs, homes, medical and social welfare facilities; integrated schools; and an end to segregation in the military. It believed in civil rights and political equality. And it believed in the equal treatment for immigrants of all backgrounds.[122] Herbert Lehman, candidate for the U.S. Senate, and Robert F. Wagner Jr., candidate for the Manhattan borough presidency, headed the ticket. Significantly, these two white men ran on the Democratic Party ballot at the same time. Murray did not. Without Democratic support, her battle was much more difficult, but she explained her decision to run in her autobiography. "As a budding feminist I recognized the importance of women actively seeking public office, . . . especially Negro women, who were then virtually invisible in politics."[123] The Panamanian native and union activist Maida Springer was her friend and campaign director. Springer recalled that she and Murray "passed out copies of her platform at busy intersections and shouted themselves hoarse." Despite Murray's underfunded campaign, Democratic incumbent Sam Curtis saw her as a threat. In an effort to undermine her legitimacy, he used class-based rather than race- or gender-based attacks. Ignoring her college education and law degrees, he accused her of being "unqualified to hold office because of her occupational background as a waitress and a dishwasher."[124] The *New York Post* came to Murray's defense, calling her a "witty and a penetratingly earthy speaker." Murray believed that her past experiences and connection with the community were an asset, not a liability, which the *Post* quoted. "It is more important to the people," Murray explained in the interview, "that I worked longer as a dishwasher, waitress, elevator operator, . . . than as a practicing attorney."[125] She understood the needs of her community on an intimate level. Empathy, however, was not enough.

In the end, Murray was no more successful in winning elected office than Speaks, Whaley, Richardson, or Jackson. She finished third out of four candidates, beating out only the ALP candidate, Helen Wishnofsky. Proportional representation, approved in 1936, had been voted out in 1947. The Democrats had a lock on politics, winning twenty-four of the twenty-five available seats, and they refused to run black women. After the election, Springer sent out thank-you letters to supporters, claiming a silver lining in the defeat. "Although we did not elect our candidate," Springer wrote, "we demonstrated that independent liberals can arouse and activize [sic] citizens who have never before participated in political affairs."[126] Such was the plight of black female candidates in the 1930s and 1940s; they had to find the victorious elements embedded in their defeats. Murray, who had benefited from Ruth Whaley's professional mentoring, forged a path forward outside organized politics, seeking as she went to open further the cracks in the system Whaley had pointed to. Her activism during the Depression and as a political candidate, like that of the other women documented here, was part of the larger Northern civil rights movement that fought to open up the world of electoral politics to black candidates, including black women, and also to break down racist barriers in the labor force, in housing, and in schools.

Conclusion

In her 1931 interview with the *Afro-American* Ruth Whitehead Whaley had delineated some of the challenges professional black women had to contend with, but she also believed that there were potential windows of opportunity to be opened. African American women who engaged in public life were well versed in the indignities that racism and sexism yielded on a personal level and the daunting challenges they created on a professional level. But in the face of adversity these women of action only embraced the struggles for justice more firmly. As part of the larger struggle for racial equality and social justice underway in cities across the nation, especially New York, they seized the possibilities born of economic and wartime crises to fight for their communities in new ways. The women who ran for office in the 1930s and 1940s lost their elections but they, as had the women who worked for municipal-level New Deal agencies, frequently advanced their careers in various branches of government and within the African American community as a result of their efforts. For Carter, it was on the mayor's commission and then as a legal advocate; for Bolin, it was as a judge. Lane and Hedgeman helped A. Philip Randolph launch a major effort for African Americans' access to wartime jobs through the March on Washington movement. In 1944, Randolph asked Hedgeman to be executive secretary of the National Council for a Permanent Fair Employment Practices Commission. In that capacity, she spoke at FEPC rallies and led strategy meetings on how to get the legislation through Congress.[127] Once the war started, Baker, an administrator with the NAACP, grew the organization's membership tenfold and in the process educated vast numbers of people about the struggles for racial justice on the home front. Murray fought to desegregate the nation's capital, the University of North Carolina, and the ultimate bastion of elite male privilege, Harvard University. Then she moved to New York City and ran for city council. And Whaley parlayed her political activism into an appointment on the New York City Board of Estimates, which oversaw the city's finances. These women showed that they were willing to challenge existing social mores and political structures that had historically excluded black women from the centers of power.

But electoral victories remained frustratingly out of reach. More than a dozen black women had run on the Republican, ALP, Liberal, and Socialist Party tickets over a fifteen-year period. They ran against each other, and they ran against black men as well as white men and women. Even though they lost their elections, the sizable number of votes that women like Carter, Speaks, and Richardson won demonstrated that they deserved a greater voice and more influence in New York City politics and policymaking. Their numerous unsuccessful campaigns confirmed that the workings of racialized gender discrimination posed a significant hurdle in at least one crucial way. The Democratic Party dominated politics, and it resisted running black women for office in any serious way. That the party's token experiments with Price and Whaley, if hers can even be described as such, rather than its full throated support of black female candidates, meant that an electoral victory would likely remain a goal rather than a reality until the Democrats could be convinced to rethink their strategy. When the party let down its resistance to running black men, black men started winning. Long active in Democratic Party politics, black women were slowly chipping away at Tammany's resistance. But when and how would change finally come?

CHAPTER THREE

Pushing Through the Doors
of Resistance in the 1950s

"Women form the majority of voters in Harlem, and it is time they took a stand in the political affairs of the community," Bessie Buchanan declared in July 1954.[1] At the time of her pronouncement, Buchanan was the Democratic Party candidate for the twelfth district of the New York State Assembly located in the Harlem section of Manhattan. As she spoke, she echoed the sentiments of two prior generations of African American women who had fought for a foothold in electoral politics. The time had come indeed, because in the wake of the May 1954 *Brown v. Board of Education* decision, communities and political leaders across the nation were, to varying degrees, assessing their commitment to the legally sanctioned Jim Crow way of life in the South and the de facto Jim Crow way of life in the North. Additionally, the time had come because women outnumbered men on voter registration rolls in Harlem, and they showed they were unafraid to make use of the right to vote that was still denied their Southern sisters. And finally the time had come because the Democratic Party decided to actively support a black woman for office. The white, male-dominated political network that had grudgingly made room for black men when Harlem became a majority-black district thirty years earlier was compelled to lower its customary resistance to running black women—and in a city dominated by Democrats, this change was critical.

By the time Buchanan took her oath of office, Anna Arnold Hedgeman had already served her first year in New York City Mayor Wagner's cabinet. African American women were changing the political landscape in New York City, haltingly but unmistakably. The meaning of the changes, the ideas about equality and justice that these women, historical "firsts," were able to raise once they were in office, and the power they were or were not able to clutch as the rewards of their hard-won positions—all were shaped significantly by international, national, and local dynamics beyond their control. The Cold War cast a long, dissent-stifling shadow across the nation, including on the progressive, interracial coalitions made up of leftists, labor leaders, and reformists in New York City.[2] Moreover, as the newest members of their respective political domains in Albany and city hall, these lone black women had no role models to follow and few if any networks to tap into inside the walls of the government they had just scaled.

Despite these challenges, Buchanan, Hedgeman, and scores of other African Americans nevertheless continued to wage battles for social, economic, and political equality in New York City. Activists frequently engaged in grassroots struggles for decent jobs, affordable housing, political representation, good schools, and against police brutality.[3] But, as was the case in the past decades, the repeated need to fight for these vitally important issues exposed the weakness of piecemeal, grassroots struggle. Advocates who fought on multiple fronts against racism and injustice understood that permanent structural change would only come through government action, specifically the creation and enforcement of new laws and policies. Like their predecessors, a number of women, including Shirley Chisholm, Bessie Buchanan, Ella Baker, Anna Hedgeman, and Constance Baker Motley understood that the state was an obstacle to racial and gender equality, but it was also a necessary advocate. They fought to tip the balance so that the government and civil society would work more fairly for African Americans and increasingly for women. Although most progressive alliances had been all but shut down when the Cold War took its toll on domestic debates, by the mid-1950s these women had nevertheless helped nudge the scales in their favor, opening new pathways for action.

As they did in the 1930s and 1940s, African American women in the 1950s who ventured into public life in New York City embodied and embraced new models of leadership that collectively broaden our understanding of the history of women's activism in the public sphere. Their efforts helped expand the space for women's voices, including those of black and poor women, in policy debates. Not only that, as women of color speaking out in the political domain that was stubbornly gendered male despite years of women's activism, and in a society still widely steeped in notions of white supremacy, they challenged racist and gendered assumptions about who could legitimately serve as a public leader. They did this by inviting media attention when they led community groups, spoke out against injustices, lobbied for housing and education reform, ran for office, and argued for civil rights in courtrooms.

To make the situation more complicated for women in public life, there were highly charged gender dynamics at play in the postwar era. The progress "Rosie the Riveters" made in expanding gender norms in the war years all but evaporated when battle-worn men came home from the front. In the 1950s, public women of all races had to navigate a social landscape that rigidly defined femininity and prescribed heavy doses of domesticity. Female candidates and government appointees found their clothes, their houses, and their marriages fair game for journalists. While aspects of this kind of coverage were prevalent right after women won the right to vote, the amount and depth of coverage given to the management of women's domestic lives in the 1950s and 1960s was new.

Not only that, women who actually made it through the layers of resistance and secured a political position had to contend with sexism from male colleagues. African American women were doubly burdened in this environment. Whereas white women benefited from race privilege that enabled them to move to neighborhoods of their choosing, send their children to schools with better resources, and be assumed sexually moral, most black women had none of those racialized benefits—and they had to work within the parameters of a sexist society. More than half a century after the first black women's clubs were formed to defend black womanhood, these various public figures subtly but undeniably adhered to models of respectability. Through their carefully constructed public performances, they simultaneously advanced their political agendas and represented models of black womanhood that helped undermine negative stereotypes of black women.[4] They also embodied, with their college and post-baccalaureate degrees, a challenge to racially misogynist assumptions that conflated racism, gender, and poverty and that decades later would rear its ugly head most obviously in the epithet "welfare queen."

Despite the numerous limitations they faced and the pervasive sense that the 1950s was a decade of quiescence for feminist activism, Chisholm, Baker, Buchanan, Hedgeman, and Motley demonstrate that black women who were committed to creating a more just society through formal politics were extremely busy. They succeeded in introducing new issues into the political discourse as elected officials and government administrators, they pressured political leaders through protests, and they effectively used the courts. With increasing frequency they helped to bring change to laws, policies, and political party practices. They also, through their examples of leadership and methods of organizing, encouraged historically disempowered people, especially black women, to engage in politics of all kinds and to demand change from state actors and politicians to judges, police chiefs, school administrators, and municipal and state bureaucrats. These women made meaningful and hitherto underappreciated contributions to the larger processes of change that were underway in the United States from the end of World War II through the 1960s—a period shaped significantly by Cold War politics as well as civil rights and women's activism.

The Cold War Context in New York City

The postwar struggles for social, political, and economic justice were waged against a national backdrop of McCarthyism. For many women in Brooklyn and Harlem who had connections to radical or left-leaning organizations, the change in the political climate limited what forms of protest would be tolerated and what coalitions could survive.[5] Anti-Communism took its toll on labor unions, nationally prominent race-specific organizations like the NAACP and the NCNW, and grassroots activists. Dramatic evidence of the narrowing ideological space for political dialogue and community activism played out when Harlem radicals Ben Davis and Claudia Jones were jailed under the Smith Act. After release from federal prison, Davis remained active in the Communist Party, but Jones, an immigrant from Trinidad, was deported to England.[6] Political repression had less spectacular but similarly destructive manifestations for other African American leftists, including the longstanding Brooklyn leader Ada B. Jackson who fell victim to red-baiting in the early 1950s. Jackson had fought for economic, political, and social equality in countless ways. She had led the interracial alliance of organizations that had formed in 1943 to fight against biased media coverage of Bedford-Stuyvesant. She was a member of the progressive Congress of American Women (CAW) and a five-time candidate for political office on the American Labor Party ticket.[7] She served on church and local school committees. She was also president of the Brooklyn chapter of the NCNW. Accused of being a Communist sympathizer in 1953, Jackson was asked to resign as head of the board of directors of the Brooklyn Home for Aged Colored People. Other board members feared the allegations against her would hamper their fundraising ability. The charges against Jackson stemmed from an announcement in the *Daily Worker*, the Communist Party's official paper that listed her as a speaker at a National Council for American-Soviet Friendship gathering. She told the Associated Negro Press that "I am not and never have been and never dealt with people at the Communist level." On the defensive, she said the Communist paper had incorrectly reported that she would appear at the American-Soviet Friendship meeting and purported instead that she was "being persecuted for her activities with the American Labor Party and her trip to the International Peace Conference in Bucharest, Romania in 1948."[8] Jackson had cause to worry. Leftists were being purged from labor and civil rights organizations across the board. In her many associations with trade unions, the ALP, the CAW, and on a visit to the Soviet Union in 1949, which received positive press coverage at the time, Jackson had certainly met "people at the Communist level."[9] But to acknowledge that risked public silencing and civic and political exile.

Years of activism had not left Jackson bereft of supporters, however. Prominent Brooklyn leaders protested her removal publically: "We believe such an allegation . . . far underestimates the intelligence of the public, its confidence and respect for one who has given so much of her time and energy for the betterment of our city. Mrs. Jackson's work and devotion have been of the highest caliber, equaled by few and excelled by none."[10] Jackson held her ground at the same time, refusing to resign. In a close vote, the board reconsidered its decision, but their willingness to silence a woman who had given so much to the community demonstrated how precarious the situation was for African American leaders with progressive affiliations. Despite the board's reversal, Jackson fell out of the news completely. Her commitment to racial equality and her untiring efforts to improve the quality of life and the dignity of African Americans in Brooklyn for more than twenty years meant little in the face of anti-Communist witch hunts.

The coexistence of the Cold War and civil rights struggles, which were by the early 1950s beginning to garner national attention created a number of tensions for other black female leaders as well. Dorothy Height returned to New York after five years in Washington, D.C., to become the YWCA's secretary for interracial education. In an interview she gave years later, she recalled the effects of anti-Communist repression on African Americans. "I was very active in the National Negro Congress, and McCarthy held that anything that was dealing with the issues that we were dealing with had to be Communist," she explained.[11] In a cautious attempt to fight back, she helped organize a collaborative public outreach event between the YWCA and the National Council of Jewish Women titled "Speak Up, Your Rights Are in Danger."[12] But McCarthyism generated so much fear that a number of black women's organizations lost members.

According to Height, "The National Council of Negro Women underwent a very rough time. . . . Vivian C. Mason (the NCNW president 1953–57) . . . had been accused by the HUAC of being a Communist. . . . Outstanding women, particularly those who were in teaching jobs [in the South], and that's where most black women were—just got absolutely frightened."[13] The impact was dramatic as many women steered clear of the NCNW.

With women like Jackson stifled in the North and black women avoiding even the moderate and nonpartisan NCNW in the South, advocates of racial equality faced new and daunting challenges. Yet despite the purges of leftists and the silencing of many moderates, a number of committed activists forced their way into Cold War liberals' debates to paradoxically open up new conversations about inequality even as the boundaries of those debates contracted dramatically. As a result, a small but growing number of black women moved closer to the centers of political power and brought with them ideas about the ways American society should be organized, and despite risks of red-baiting, they said so. One such example played out in the Bedford-Stuyvesant section of Brooklyn.

Anatomy of a Political Insurgency in Bedford-Stuyvesant

Wesley "Mac" Holder, a former editor of the *New York Amsterdam News*, was widely known as the "Dean" of Brooklyn politics in the 1950s and 1960s. Committed to increasing African American political representation in Brooklyn, Holder had organized against the Democratic machine bosses first in the 1930s.[14] When, in 1953, Judge Edward Wynn of the Second Municipal Court (in the Bedford-Stuyvesant area of Brooklyn), died suddenly, Mayor Vincent Impellitteri had the opportunity to rectify an obvious racial inequality in filling the vacancy. Harlem could boast a number of black judges on the municipal courts, but Brooklyn had none. The mayor, however, dismissed requests from black leaders and instead appointed Benjamin Schor, a white judge from another part of the city, to fill the position. Community residents protested. Louis Flagg Jr., a black civic leader, lawyer, and longstanding resident of the Bedford-Stuyvesant, had run for the state assembly more than twenty years earlier, and also for a judgeship in 1949.[15] He was well qualified and eager for the job, but Schor got the temporary appointment and the Democrats' backing for the seat in the September primary election.[16]

Flagg, however, had substantial support from an expanding contingent of Brooklyn professionals and activists who were ready to fight for the seat. Under Holder's leadership, Flagg, Thomas R. Jones, and Shirley Chisholm formed an ad hoc committee to get the Bedford-Stuyvesant local elected in a direct challenge to the Brooklyn Democratic machine. The Democratic Party tried to undermine Flagg's campaign at every turn. The September primary race was close, but Flagg won, beating Schor by fewer than three hundred votes.[17] With help from the American Labor Party, the insurgents had scored a coup. In the November election, Flagg defeated William Staves, a black man put forward by the Republican Party, and Schor again ran on the Liberal Party ticket. With this victory he became the first African American elected to the judiciary in Brooklyn.[18] Flagg's triumph suggested that, in the face of collective action, the old guard was not invincible. The fight for political representation, however, was only beginning. One judgeship had been attained, but, with the exception of Bertram Baker's assembly seat in the Sixth District, the door to elected office was closed to African Americans and to the growing Puerto Rican population.

In the wake of the victory, Holder turned the election committee into the Bedford Stuyvesant Political League (BSPL) with Chisholm's help. The BSPL pushed for civil rights commitments from political candidates and for economic opportunities and improved services for members of the community.[19] It also challenged racial discrimination in the housing market, taking local residents by the busloads to city hall and to the state capitol in Albany to demand change.[20] But internal dissent soon sapped the league's strength. Holder and Chisholm had a standoff over control of the organization in 1958. According to Ruth Goring, a Bed-Sty activist, "Women were doing the work and wanted input into the decision-making."[21] Chisholm lost the struggle and ultimately left the group, which itself eventually faded out of existence.[22]

Chisholm departed the BSPL in 1958, but her absence from grassroots activism did not last long. The community she lived in was one of the poorest in the city and needed advocates with access to political power and economic resources. Between 1950 and 1960, the black population in the borough had increased by over 50 percent as white Brooklynites, unhindered by racial covenants and red-lining that literally kept African Americans hemmed into certain neighborhoods, moved to new suburban communities to reap the benefits of government subsidies in the form of GI Bill mortgages and business start-up loans. [23] Outnumbering Manhattan by nearly a million people, Brooklyn had 2.6 million residents, including more than 370,000 African Americans by 1960.[24]

In addition to the seismic demographic shift underway, Brooklyn suffered a dramatic loss of factory jobs in the postwar era, including at the Brooklyn Navy Yard, the largest industry in the borough. The privatization of military contracts undermined the yard's ability to compete.[25] Although African Americans benefited only minimally from the city's industrial sector jobs because of racial discrimination, these disappearances were a severe blow to Brooklyn's economic base nonetheless.[26] The factory closings added injury to a town smarting from the 1957 loss of its hometown pride, the Brooklyn Dodgers, to California.

Bedford-Stuyvesant, Brooklyn's largest neighborhood, was densely populated. A substantial majority of Brooklyn's black population lived in the district. Health and crime indicators underscored the neglect and resource starvation the area suffered. Its infant mortality rate and juvenile delinquency figures were many times higher than the rest of Brooklyn and the city. Economic indicators illustrate the disparities most clearly. Bedford-Stuyvesant's unemployment rate was 100 percent above the city's average.[27] Compounding the problem, the median annual income for Brooklyn's nonwhite families was $2,000 less than for New York City families generally.[28] The racialized sexual division of labor resulted in an even bleaker picture. Black men's unemployment rate was nearly twice as high as black women's, and with nonwhite women earning 40 percent less than nonwhite men, the depths of the crisis and the urgent need for action could not have been more clear.[29] Disproportionately poor district residents fought the problems as best they could; however, the biggest aggravating factor was that the city's financial commitment to the community was grossly inadequate to deal with the problems. Well aware of the desperate plight of too many African Americans, insurgents organized again, this time with the goal of bringing permanent change to Brooklyn's political structures.

Raising Consciousness, Taking Action

In 1960, Thomas R. Jones from the "Elect Flagg" committee led the effort to create the Unity Democratic Club (UDC), a new community-based organization. Shirley Chisholm was on board from the start. The club's goal was to take over the Seventeenth Assembly District and put the white Democratic machine out of business. A number of those who helped launch the new organization spoke of their own experiences with racism. For example, Jones, who had moved to Bedford-Stuyvesant with his family in 1930, recalled trying to go into Child's Restaurant on Nostrand Avenue. Not only was he barred from entering, he had glasses thrown at his head.[30] After fighting for his country in Europe during

World War II, the Brooklynite said that he and fellow African American service-men "were determined to have a better life . . . and to take [their] proper places politically" when they got home.[31] Yet their drive for change was more than personal. For Jones and others like Ruth Goring and Jocelyn Cooper, it was at root the poor conditions in the community, and the anger over the intentional political neglect that drove them to the UDC.

Goring had lived in Bedford-Stuyvesant since the 1940s. The first president of the UDC, she was asked by an *Amsterdam News* reporter why she entered politics. She responded, "Walk through the streets of Bedford-Stuyvesant and see why. Look at our youth, the unemployment, the young adults and the el-derly, and see why. Look at the political structure. They gave us nothing." She channeled her anger into the UDC, no longer able to "just sit by and watch the community go to pot."[32] Goring blamed assemblyman and district leader Sam Berman for the abysmal conditions in the district.[33] Moreover, she felt that the white ethnic groups that controlled the Democratic Party in Brooklyn intentionally kept African Americans out of power. She explained that they had "cut out the one Black district and given it to Bertram Baker and that District was supposed to contain the Blacks." "But," she went on, "we were aware that our people were moving throughout Brooklyn and were disenfranchised by this specific gerrymander. Anytime you made a bid for political power, or political input, they would say, 'well you've got the Sixth [Assembly District], what more do you want?'"[34] Goring joined the reform organization to unseat Berman, both a symbolic and real obstacle to political advancement. If access to political power and government resources were improved, she expected that it would help African Americans. It was not an unreasonable assumption in a city that historically saw white politicos share the benefits of patronage widely in their own ethnic groups. In a district where racism significantly undermined the chance to compete for power, the opportunity to launch a serious challenge to the establishment promised progress.

Jocelyn Cooper expressed sentiments similar to Goring's as she reflected on her introduction to community activism and politics. Born in the 1930s and raised in Jersey City, she made her way to Brooklyn and married Andrew (Andy) Cooper, a Brooklyn native from a middle-class, civil-servant family. The couple's lawyer, Tom Jones (Unity's founder), invited them to a meeting. Jocelyn accepted the offer. Although at the time she knew little about the local political structure or the ways its power flowed, she stated, "I knew the things that I saw around were puzzling to me. . . . I needed to do something about my community, and that's what motivated me."[35] The frustration level reached a boiling point for people like Goring and Jocelyn Cooper. When the opportunity presented itself to become involved in community betterment, both women seized it and put their energies into the young organization.

In the 1960 election Jones challenged Berman, the incumbent and a veteran political operative, for the district's assembly seat and leadership. If elected, Jones promised, he would address the list of concerns familiar to most people living in Bedford-Stuyvesant, including improvements in "education, housing, sanitation, transportation and . . . health and hospital facilities . . . and upping of wages of low income residents."[36] Although he lost the race, he made a respectable showing against the incumbent, and thereafter the UDC redoubled its efforts to organize and educate the community. It also forged alliances with other organizations in a campaign for jobs.

Unity was considered a politically progressive club by some of its members because Jones had been active in the American Labor Party and a member of the radical National Lawyers Guild. But in reality it was a reform organization, part of the Committee for Democratic Voters, a citywide reform organization.[37] Although the UDC did not draw many of the working poor into its ranks— members most often hailed from the middle class—it was racially integrated. [38] Jones saw the interracial membership and mission of the club as a strength. "We had an amazing combination of people—black and white—who came together for the first time under black leadership," he recalled. "And this of course shook up the politicians all over the state, because if white people could accept black leadership, there was no telling how far this campaign could reach."[39] Not only that, African American women like Shirley Chisholm, Ruth Goring, and Jocelyn Cooper were important leaders in the grassroots political education efforts in Brooklyn. Like Septima Clark, the courageous trailblazer in the citizenship education movement in the South, these Brooklynites understood the importance of simultaneously demystifying an intentionally opaque and often hostile political machine and empowering people who had historically been excluded by law or by custom from it.[40] It was disappointing to find, however, that even in this new organization, women had to fight for respect and authority. In fact, Goring, UDC's first president, stated that she left the organization because of gender discrimination.[41]

The political insurgents faced a daunting challenge to undo the deep level of disillusionment that generations of racial discrimination and intentional political neglect had generated.[42] For too long, racism and cronyism shut African Americans out of the political decision-making process. Politicians and city administrators were both part of the oppressive system and also potential allies; and grassroots activists tried to shift the balance from one to the other. But before it could woo voters, UDC had to get people registered to vote and interested in the political process.[43] Chisholm, Goring, Cooper, and other members pounded the pavement and knocked on doors across the district in an effort to defeat the all-white, all-male Seventeenth Assembly District regular club. Chisholm recounted, "I walked these streets until I almost went crazy."[44] Cooper emphasized the importance of interpersonal contact in the political education process: "By climbing those steps and ringing those bells, inevitably people lived on the top floor, . . . when they think that you have an interest in asking them, they respond."[45]

Andy Cooper, Jocelyn's husband, described the process of bringing people into the political system. He and Pat Carter, both UDC members, spent Saturday mornings in front of grocery stores distributing information about voter registration procedures. Not only did they encourage people to register, they also recruited people to attend weekly meetings. They taught people about politics on a local level—who was a district leader and who was an assemblyman, and what were they supposed to do. Andy Cooper remarked that he would encourage residents to assert their individual political rights and, collectively, their political power. "First," he had told them, "you ask people who are in office to do something for you . . . and when they don't respond, you work against them. You vote them out of office. . . . You may not win the first time around, but you can scare the hell out of them."[46]

Employment discrimination had plagued African American workers in New York City throughout the twentieth century. Protests and acts of resistance were commonplace, but most African Americans still had difficulty getting work in Brooklyn's factories, on construction sites, and in stores and restaurants, despite their steady patronage and heavy demographic majority.[47] The UDC coordinated with members of the Brooklyn chapter of CORE and with church ministers to fight employment discrimination. In addition to populating picket lines, UDC's Tom Jones provided legal representation when protesters were jailed.[48] The effort further demonstrated the UDC's commitment to economic justice and helped break down justified skepticism to organized politics, and it also earned them critical support.

In 1962, with a far broader base established, the Unity Democratic Club again set its sights on the regular political machine. Jones ran for the assembly seat and district leader, and Goring ran for the district co-leadership position, which was the standard gender breakdown. (All districts had male leaders and female co-leaders.) The traditional Democratic machine realized its vulnerability. They were forced into action by changing political realities rather than by any kind of ideological commitment to racial equality. Fearing defeat if they continued to run white candidates in the heavily African American community, district leader Berman and his cronies made a strategic substitution shortly before the primary. Berman came off the ballot for the assembly seat, the public face of the political machine, and they put Wesley Holder in his place. Holder had challenged the white-dominated political machine a decade earlier by founding the BSPL. In 1962, he had seemingly become part of it. At the same time, Berman maintained his candidacy for district leader, the position of power. Jones insisted that the switch was a desperate effort to maintain the status quo by buying off African Americans' votes with Holder's candidacy. As cynical and calculated as Berman's move was, it did not work. Jones defeated Holder for the assembly and Berman for the district leadership in the September primary.[49] The UDC had struck a decisive blow.

In the November election, Jones faced off against two black female candidates. The Republicans had frequently run black women and men for public office. But in a city as thoroughly dominated by the Democratic Party as New York, their efforts were futile. Jones defeated both women easily.[50] He and Goring were now in charge. Nearly fifteen years after Baker made his successful bid for the office against Maude Richardson, Brooklyn finally had its second African American state assemblyman and district leader. The racism embedded in the system, reinforced by generations of exclusionary political maneuvering, began to show signs of weakening as a result of local pressure and the changing national civil rights context.

With three African American candidates in the general election—including on both major party tickets—the race issue was effectively neutralized even as it remained central to the concerns of candidates and voters. Among voters' priorities, the candidate's race was clearly important; that the Democrats finally started to field black candidates like Bertram Baker in 1948 and Bessie Buchanan in 1954 illustrates that point. Party affiliation, not race, however, was the main determinant of voters' decisions. There were plenty of unsuccessful black candidates who ran on Republican, American Labor Party, and Liberal tickets who could attest to that. After 1936, when black New Yorkers made their switch to the Democratic Party, with the exception of Maude Richardson's near victory in 1946, nothing dislodged that loyalty.[51]

Despite UDC's success, racism and cronyism continued to shape the way political spoils were distributed in the city. Mayor Robert Wagner Jr. denied

Unity what he gave to white-led clubs. In an interview with scholar-activist Carlos Russell of Brooklyn, Goring explained the rules of local politics. "Usually," she said, "the patronage goes with the leadership. . . . Tom [Jones] and I met with Wagner. . . . He said as district leaders, 'you will be part of the process.' Even though we were sitting there nodding, we knew it was not going to happen, because Tom and I have been Black all of our lives and we knew how the political structures deal with Blacks."[52] Jones made the same point. He stated bluntly that "The politicians who gave out the jobs . . . withheld from me the jobs and other embellishments of office. I was starved out."[53]

The Jones-Goring victory was just a first step for the UDC. African American communities had much further to go before elected office yielded any direct political or economic benefits. Jones' fight for change was genuine, but his expectations seemed almost naive. He came to realize what Shirley Chisholm perhaps already knew—that in order to get anything done, one had to stay connected to the old power structure. Her time to rise up the political ladder was to come soon enough. But in the meantime, across the river in Harlem, other African American women long active in struggles for justice were making slow but real headway of their own.

Postwar Harlem and Black Women's Activism

The NAACP's membership grew robustly between 1940 and 1946 from fifty thousand to more than four hundred thousand, in no small part because of Ella Baker's untiring efforts.[54] Working as a field secretary, Baker regularly traveled deep into the South to recruit new members, and even more to help people realize their capacity to be change agents in their own lives and in their neighborhoods. As historian Barbara Ransby notes, Baker's was a "profoundly political and deeply human" process of organizing.[55] Three years into her post, as the nation remained ensnared in a global battle against fascism and African Americans remained simultaneously in a fight against racial discrimination at home, Baker became the director of the NAACP's branches. She was committed to empowering regular, everyday folk, often to the dismay of the organization's leadership. A year after the war ended she determined that her philosophical differences about organizing and working with people were too much at odds with the NAACP's elitist leadership to remain in her position, so she tendered her resignation. Returning full time to New York City, the adopted home of all the women in this story save the handful who were born within its borders, Baker unexpectedly became a mother. In 1946 she adopted her sister's nine-year-old daughter, Jackie. As the young girl made her way from North Carolina to start her new life, Baker, married but childless, was in equally unfamiliar territory. [56]

Domestic responsibilities and her need and desire to do meaningful work compelled Baker's job search. She took an organizing and fundraising position with the Harlem Branch Cancer Committee. [57] Though important to the community, the position did not allow for the kinds of transformative politics Baker was committed to. Unwilling to abandon her fight for economic justice even as labor unions and organizations like the NAACP were scared into exorcising leftist members, she spoke in Harlem about the importance of cooperative buying. She made the case to her audience of small business owners, arguing that "the only effective way for independent merchants to compete with the larger chains is by pooling their resources and buying collectively."[58] Baker's critique of capitalism, with its unbridled pursuit of profit, remained as sharp in the face of McCarthyism as it was in the height of the Great Depression's progressive years. The FBI took note, although the government had no case to make against her.[59]

Baker returned to the NAACP in 1952, eager to be more fully part of an activist civil rights organization again. This time, however, she eschewed the national office and assumed the presidency of the New York City branch, becoming its first female leader. But even as she marched headlong into local struggles against police brutality and school reform, Baker diverted from her path of grassroots activism to explore the possibility of an elected office. In September 1953 she resigned from her post to run for city council on the Liberal Party ticket.[60] She followed in the footsteps of numerous African American female activists in New York City before her, including radical and progressive women like Layle Lane, Ada B. Jackson, and Pauli Murray, but also liberal women like Sara Speaks, Ruth Whitehead Whaley, and Maude Richardson, who chafed at the ways racism, class inequality, and gender discrimination were abetted by elected leaders and administrative bureaucrats alike. The government was most often an obstacle, but on rare occasion it could also be an ally in the struggles for justice. She, like a growing number of political aspirants (including seven black women in 1952), used their campaigns—if not the elected offices themselves—as ways to raise issues and push change forward slowly but steadily.[61]

The odds for an electoral victory were against her. Living for more than twenty years in a city long dominated by the Democratic Party, Baker knew that. Yet as head of the largest civil rights organization in New York and garnering positive press coverage for her ongoing efforts to stop police brutality, she could hope that her chances were better than others who had run in the past on third party tickets. And more than that, the campaign meant another public platform from which to speak about issues she felt were important in the fight for social, political, and economic justice. Together with Rev. James Robinson, a popular Harlem pastor and civic activist who ran on the Liberal Party ticket for Manhattan borough president, she attended a number of events and campaigned on issues of importance to their community: housing, daycare funding, police brutality, schools, and slum clearance. Because they ran on the Liberal Party ticket, they also advocated for one of its top priorities, eliminating government corruption.[62]

James Robinson, who shared the Liberal Party ticket with Baker, had stepped into a fierce political power struggle far more complicated than Baker's. While Tammany leaders deliberated about who would run on their slate for borough president along with mayor-designate Robert Wagner Jr., anti-Wagner forces within the Democratic Party, including Mayor Impellitteri, nominated Chauncey Hooper, a black lawyer, to run in the Democratic primary. At the same time, the Republicans recruited Elmer Carter, an African American man and commissioner of the State Commission Against Discrimination to run for the same office on their ticket.[63] Tammany risked losing the position if it too did not field a black candidate. That was the message that came loud and clear from its black leadership in Harlem. Four black assemblymen demanded that Wagner name an African American to his ballot for the borough presidency slot or risk losing black voters. With three other black candidates already running for the position, the threat was more than an idle one. White Tammany Democrats gave ground under duress.[64] Weeks before the September primary they put Hulan Jack, long-time assemblyman from Harlem, on Wagner's ticket and in so doing guaranteed that the city of New York would have its first borough-wide black political leader. Robinson's chances for victory diminished dramatically with two black men backed by Democrats.

The Democrats had been forced to attend to voters' concerns about the race of their candidates in Brooklyn and in Harlem. The Liberal Party, on the other hand, had been open to running African Americans and women for office since its founding ten years earlier. For example, in the prior city council election in 1949, Baker's New Deal colleague and friend, Pauli Murray, had also run for city council on the Liberal Party ticket. Like other third parties, it had nothing to lose and perhaps something to gain by running a popular black female activist in a district where women outnumbered men on voter registration rolls. Baker was, after all, the president of the New York City NAACP. She likely had as good a chance as anyone against a Democrat.

Baker's opponent was the incumbent councilman, Earl Brown, a Harlem Democrat who also secured the nomination on the Republican ticket in the absence of any competition. Brown was a civil rights advocate in his own right who used his position on the city council to push for a plan to end police brutality. He and Baker had worked together on the issue during the past year.[65] With Tammany backing, the benefit of incumbency, and a record of civil rights legislative action, Brown proved an indomitable opponent. Baker (and Robinson) went down in defeat in the November election.[66]

The fight for integrated schools, which gripped the nation in the wake of the seminal *Brown v. Board of Education* decision, had local iterations as well. A masterful organizer and consummate people's advocate, Baker returned to the New York City NAACP branch leadership after the election and turned her energies to New York City's school reform. Two years after *Brown*, an *Amsterdam News* editorial exposed persistent patterns of segregation in New York City's schools, arguing, "While we condemn the lily white school at Mansfield, Texas, we must also condemn the all-Negro schools in New York. . . . And we would remind . . . city officials, that it is just as much a violation of the law to operate a Jim Crow school in New York City as it is to operate one in Clinton, Tennessee."[67] Harlem and Brooklyn parents, especially the mothers, stood ready to take on the intransigent city officials under Baker's orchestration.

Women swelled the protest ranks in large part because of their traditional parenting role. Many wrote letters, boarded buses to city hall, and carried placards demanding change for the first time in their lives. Baker led more than one hundred women to a city planning commission meeting in downtown Manhattan. Predominantly black schools were in terrible condition compared with schools in white neighborhoods because of de facto segregation and discrimination, and the group demanded action. "It is morally wrong to continue to give 'hand-me-downs' to children who have had to put up with slum conditions most of their lives," parents charged.[68] Their outrage and frustration were palpable. The language used and the arguments made by hundreds of women, who were legitimized in the public debates as *mothers*, were designed to appeal to policymakers' consciences. These conventional gendered strategies represented a narrowing of social discourse from the more fluid gendered landscape of the 1940s and harkened back to the maternalist rhetoric of the Progressive Era.

Despite their justified indignation, the Harlem women found it extremely difficult to wrangle concrete action from the city government. So in September 1957, Baker ratcheted up the pressure. With five hundred African American and Puerto Rican parents in tow, she organized a picket line around city hall, some carrying placards that read, "Is Brooklyn, New York Above the Mason Dixon Line?" and "Rezone for Integration." When Mayor Wagner finally agreed to talk with a selected delegation, he found himself in an unpleasant position. The city had "reneged on its promise to desegregate its public schools," Baker asserted. No political novice, she forcefully reminded Wagner weeks before the election, "We know the ballot has speaking power and parents are concerned with what happens to their children."[69] With a thinly veiled threat on the part of African Americans and Puerto Ricans to decamp the Democratic Party in November, she managed to wrest a number of verbal commitments from the mayor. Nonetheless, Baker knew the pressure had to be kept on. The fight over funding, integration, and control of the schools would not be solved so easily. That was obvious in Little Rock, Arkansas, where it took the U.S. 101st Airborne to keep nine teens alive as they integrated Central High School, and in Prince Edward County, Virginia, where the board of supervisors closed the public schools for five years rather than comply with the *Brown* decision. It was also distressingly evident in New York City where, in 1968, the struggle finally exploded in a dramatic confrontation between parents who wanted control of their local schools and the city's teachers' union.[70]

As committed as she was to the New York struggles, Baker increasingly focused on the dramatic events unfolding in Montgomery, Alabama. She knew E. D. Nixon and Rosa Parks from her work with the NAACP national office. Now they had sparked a grassroots battle for racial justice that she had done so much to prepare the masses for. Keen to be part of the final Southern battles to destroy Jim Crow—and just as important to her, to cultivate within the movement the commitment to participatory democracy—Baker left New York and headed south. Other African American women in New York, however, remained in the city to dismantle the subtler, though equally poisonous, manifestations of racism and increasingly of gender discrimination as well. Their forty-year struggle to scale the fortress guarding New York City's political spoils was about to come to an end.

History Making in Harlem

For political activists keeping a ledger of domestic policy gains and losses, 1954 was a promising year in at least two key respects. Senator Joseph McCarthy, the public face of Cold War hysteria, had turned his witch hunt on the U.S. Army— and by standards of even the most cowed senators—went too far; his colleagues proceeded to censure him. Moreover, despite the years of violent struggle that still awaited those who believed in racial justice, there was no mistaking the seismic shift in the nation's social landscape that the *Brown* decision generated. Black New Yorkers contributed their own blow to the walls of segregation and inequality that year. With a record number of African American women registered as Democrats in Harlem, the Party was made to realize that black women were an important and active constituency. A dedicated and recognized civic activist, Bessie Buchanan was well known and loved in the Harlem community. Her husband, Charles Buchanan, published the left-leaning Harlem weekly, the *People's Voice*, with Adam Clayton Powell Jr. in the 1940s. Bessie had a column in the paper. Charles also owned the famous Savoy Ballroom. A former dancer and screen star, Bessie Buchanan was a close friend and associate of Josephine Baker's.[71] Just as important, Buchanan was a loyal Democrat who, over the years, had proved herself to the Tammany Hall leadership in Harlem.[72] Having long paid her dues in the local political machine, in 1954 she was ready to reap the benefits.

Buchanan seized the opportunity created by an internecine struggle in Tammany's ranks to make her bid for office. She had become the party favorite after the Democratic incumbent, an African American man named Leslie Turner, found himself on the losing side of a political power play. Black women outnumbered black men on voter registration lists in the predominantly African American assembly districts from 1944 onward, and Buchanan actively courted them.[73] She likely used this as a reason to compel Tammany to run her in the first place. Tammany's endorsement was critical to Buchanan's victory, and she made the most of it. It had been hard for black women to get Democratic support because of racial barriers and gender discrimination, but she turned her two biggest potential liabilities to her advantage when pursuing voters. The Democratic Party finally backed a black woman, and Buchanan won the primary. In assessing her victory, Buchanan recognized the importance of Tammany's sponsorship, but she also underscored the centrality of women's votes. She expressed hope that her victory signaled a breakthrough in party politics through which other women could follow.[74]

Buchanan's success in the primary pitted her against the Republican candidate Lucille Pickett in the general election. Pickett faced a significant challenge; the Twelfth Assembly District had not voted for a Republican in well over a decade. In addition, Buchanan got the upper hand and made gendered appeals to voters, explicitly calling attention to the need for black women in politics. Her campaign platform included something for African Americans in general and something for black women in particular. She pledged to fight for "stronger anti-discrimination laws, more daycare centers and increased unemployment and workmen's compensation benefits," demonstrating a concern for race, gender, and class issues.[75]

Buchanan's campaign provides further evidence that gender dynamics had changed from the 1940s in some significant ways. In the immediate postwar years, Richardson and Jackson had functioned in a social and political context that was somewhat fluid regarding women's roles in the public sphere. By 1954 the national rhetoric had largely returned to promoting traditional gender norms. Yet as historian Joanne Meyerowitz has argued, in the postwar era "allusions to femininity and domesticity probably helped legitimate women's public achievements."[76] Coverage of the campaign reflected the complexity. The press approached the election through a female-gendered lens and implied that Buchanan and Pickett were appropriately feminine, but it is important to note that they also acknowledged their experience. An *Amsterdam News* headline, for example, noted that the campaign was a "Battle of Brains [and] Beauty." A second marked shift was the expansion of the candidate's platform to include explicitly women's issues. Buchanan appealed to female voters by promising gender-specific legislation. Speaks, Jackson, Richardson, and Murray years earlier had not done this.

Buchanan's local popularity, the Democratic Party's support, the record number of women on voter registration rolls, and the trend for African Americans to vote Democratic all worked in her favor. She soundly defeated her opponent and made history as the first black woman elected to office in New York. She headed to the state capitol, where she made good on her promise to fight against all forms of discrimination.[77] The first bills Buchanan introduced addressed pay inequities based on sex, and discrimination in banking, education, and insurance based on race. She teamed up with a few liberal colleagues and reintroduced these and other civil rights bills every year but made no progress in seeing them translated into law. Although she succeeded in getting only three of her bills passed into law in her eight years in the state assembly, she helped bring a new level of attention to both women's issues and civil rights issues.[78] This was significant insofar as it forced members of the state assembly to respond to issues that had rarely if ever entered the legislative debates before. It also helped build momentum for important changes that transpired in the 1960s. While Buchanan broke down one important barrier for black women in 1954, Anna Arnold Hedgeman broke down another.

Hedgeman's Path to City Hall

In January 1944, Anna Arnold Hedgeman became the executive secretary of the National Council for a Permanent Fair Employment Practices Commission (FEPC) at A. Philip Randolph's request. In that capacity, she spoke at FEPC rallies and led strategy meetings on how to get the legislation through Congress. She believed that only a groundswell of grassroots pressure across the nation would override resistance from the Southern bloc, particularly Senators James Eastland and Theodore Bilbo of Mississippi.[79] Despite hers and others' efforts, in the emerging Cold War context where many government programs were labeled as Communist to kill them, the FEPC budget was slashed in half and then eliminated completely in 1946. Nevertheless, her determined efforts and great skill as a public speaker attracted national attention. Congressman William Dawson of Chicago brought her on board the national committee to reelect President Truman. In the first presidential election after Roosevelt's twelve-year, party-realigning reign, Hedgeman received a high-level federal post for her work on behalf of the Democratic Party. She was appointed to the Federal Security Agency (later the Department of Health, Education, and Welfare) as an assistant director to Oscar Ewing, the department's head.[80] India Edwards, executive director of the Women's Division of the Democratic National Committee, had maintained a list of women for whom she sought high-level government appointments. Hedgeman's name topped the list; her reputation had spread far beyond the borders of the predominantly black communities of Harlem and Brooklyn that had nurtured her and within which she had honed her political skills.[81]

Even as the Cold War escalated to a national level of hysteria, with the Truman Doctrine, Federal Employee Loyalty Program, and HUAC hearings defining the boundaries of politically safe activity, writings, and speech, Hedgeman used her position on Ewing's staff to advocate for socialized medicine, arguing that it was the "only way to improve the health and living conditions of minority groups."[82] This was not out of keeping with the president's own unsuccessful goals for a national health care system, although he explicitly asserted that his plan was not Socialist. But it did demonstrate her belief in a strong, activist state that should work on behalf of the people's well-being.[83] At the same time, as an ardent proponent of organized labor, she met with teachers unions and farm unions, and addressed the United Automobile Workers annual convention, the first woman to do so.[84] Like Baker, Hedgeman's activities attracted attention from McCarthyites. During an investigation she was asked, not surprisingly, if she was a Communist. Hedgeman responded, "I'd had so much difficulty trying to secure my part of American democracy that I had no time to study Communism."[85] Regardless of the government's suspicions, Hedgeman was not a radical or Communist sympathizer but a Cold War liberal who simultaneously embraced American capitalist democracy and committed her professional life to making it much more expansive, inclusive, and fair.

In 1953 the Republicans took over the White House and Congress for the first time in twenty years, and Hedgeman, a Democratic appointee, returned to New York, by this point her emotional and physical home. A group of Harlem citizens welcomed her back to the North by requesting that she run for the Manhattan borough presidency on the ticket with mayoral candidate Robert Wagner Jr., son of the towering New Dealer, Senator Robert Wagner.[86] This was the same campaign in which Baker and Robinson had run as Liberal Party candidates. Although she was open to the idea and briefly explored the possibility, Hedgeman knew clubhouse politics and decided against challenging Hulan Jack, an African American Tammany leader in Harlem. Reflecting on the persistence of gender biases in party politics, Hedgeman wrote in an autobiography that "Jack was vehement about the fact that a woman would not be acceptable as Borough President."[87] Accustomed to navigating complex social and political dynamics, Hedgeman campaigned for the Democrats nonetheless. This proved more than her loyalties; it also demonstrated her savvy and her ambition.[88]

When the Tammany slate won, speculation began in Harlem about who would represent the black community in Wagner's new administration. According to the *Amsterdam News*, several influential Democrats, including Oscar Ewing, Averell Harriman, Eleanor Roosevelt, and Senator Herbert Lehman, urged the mayor to name Hedgeman to the city's $15,000-a-year Commissioner of Welfare post. Alerting its readers to the near total absence of black representation in the city administration, the article noted that "Negroes are in policy-making positions in only two of the city's 42 departments and these are only token appointments."[89]

The mayor was disappointingly slow in making the appointment. White Tammany leaders gave no ground without a struggle. Only after intense pressure from the black community, Wagner named Hedgeman as one of the eleven members in his cabinet. With this post, she became the highest positioned African American in City Hall.[90] Although the appointment was rightly celebrated as political progress for the black community, the victory was not without its blemishes. Edward Lewis of the New York Urban League wrote to the mayor in anger. "The published salary for this job [Hedgeman's]," he argued, "raises some questions as to whether or not this is really a top policy-making position."[91] Rather than a $15,000-a-year post, Hedgeman was given a vaguely defined position at $8,000 annually, which looked a lot more like tokenism than a serious commitment on the mayor's part to bringing meaningful racial and gender representation into city government.

Hedgeman understood racism, sexism, and party politics too well to have been terribly surprised. But she was determined to make the most of her position in any case. She had been a popular speaker at civic, labor, and women's events before she took her new job. Once on Wagner's staff, she was in greater demand than ever. Yet at the height of McCarthyism, she was careful to balance criticisms of U.S. inequalities with celebrations of its ideals. Attentive to the liberation struggles unfolding in Africa, for example, Hedgeman stated during a speech to a women's group in Harlem that "American Negroes . . . understand the world's cry for freedom and equality of opportunity, which it is difficult for other Americans to comprehend. . . . We should be determined that the world will not be run by men who do not understand that people who live in mud huts will be looking for a way out, and we hope that way will be democracy. To be sure that it will be, the best way is by example."[92] In this presentation and on other occasions, she linked the oppression of colonized peoples around the world to those in the United States. As part of a state department mission in 1952 she had travelled to India to help blunt criticism of the U.S. racial inequality that circulated in foreign presses. She was willing to speak for and defend the nation, but she also believed it had to be held accountable for its serious faults and it had to change.[93] Full democracy in the United States, which required real racial and economic justice, would win the nation support overseas, she argued. She fought for it, and she wanted her audiences to as well.

Hedgeman often doled out to her audiences self-help advice along with appeals for race pride. At an Alpha Kappa Mu Honor Society dinner in Baltimore she urged faculty and students to "help the Negro love himself." She recognized the struggle to maintain race pride "in a society which emphasizes in every possible fashion that White is beautiful, efficient, honorable, clever, significant, important and born to lead." Giving voice to her own and her audiences' frustrations, she insisted that "these affirmations of superiority have left no margin for persons of color; worse than that, they have insisted that emphasis on the inferiority of color is an essential to their superiority."[94] Yet in spite of the social, economic, and political barriers African Americans continued to face in 1956, Hedgeman's call for her audience to "help all of our communities become 'open' communities where people may find housing, occupation and education freely" seemed increasingly tame when the memory of young Emmett Till's murdered and mutilated body refused to fade and when ordinary people in Montgomery were walking to work to change the system of apartheid.[95] Hedgeman was now part of the municipal government that Ella Baker's picketers had demanded justice from. She issued muted calls to action even as she poignantly elucidated the devastating consequences of white supremacy.

As cautious as her call to arms was in the fight against racism, her plea for recognition of black women's contributions to society were bold. Hedgeman used her positions in women's organizations like the YWCA and NCNW, as well as her government jobs in the 1930s and now in Wagner's administration in the 1950s, to raise awareness about women's contributions to the struggles for racial advancement, which were often eclipsed by the workings of men or forgotten altogether. In a *New York Age* series, "Negro Women Fought Hard for Recognition," she wrote, "One must pay tribute to the Negro women who in the last 75 years have given such magnificent leadership . . . [t]hese women who, with faith in their husbands and children, washed and ironed, scrubbed and cooked, took endless insults, saved nickels and dimes for tuition because there was often not even a grade school in the home community, are truly significant pioneers."[96] Governor Harriman subsequently appointed her and Ruth Whitehead Whaley to an advisory group that was tasked to review the Woman's Program of the New York State Department of Commerce. Between 1956 and 1958 they analyzed details of women's employment across the state. In their final report they emphasized that although the state's work program was intended to support women's home-based businesses, in fact more than two million women were already in the waged labor force. Moreover, they noted that women wanted to work when their family responsibilities had abated.[97] The labor market review that was done by Whaley, Hedgeman, and their fellow advisory board members exposed some of the issues that President Kennedy's Commission on the Status of Women (PCSW) report, *American Women*, would publicize a few years later. Though rarely an explicit part of her political agenda, Hedgeman's actions, like those of other black women in public life, demonstrate her strong commitment to gender equality and women's economic and political opportunity.

As a public speaker, Hedgeman inspired audiences. She was successful in charting a new path for black women into city government. She raised issues—access to affordable housing, better schools, and health care for poor and working people—at cabinet meetings and spoke about them publically. However, she was unable to influence the mayor, the city's black leadership, or the city council. She ultimately found her limited capacity to bring about change from within the government frustrating.[98] In 1958 she left city hall, disappointed not only in the mayor but also in the black community's leadership, which she felt did not support her efforts.[99]

Yet Hedgeman was unable to abandon organized politics fully. She was tempted back three more times, suggesting her belief in the power of the government to help redress social, economic, and political injustices as well as her own ambition. In 1960, the same year that the Unity Democratic Club was trying to unseat the old "bosses" of Brooklyn's Seventeenth Assembly District, the East Bronx Committee for Democratic Reform, an insurgent organization formed by African American and Puerto Rican community leaders, consulted Hedgeman about their lack of access to political power.[100] Charles Buckley, a white Bronx congressman and the borough's Democratic leader, had told the black and Puerto Rican activists, "You aren't ready" for political recognition or support.[101] In their search for a skilled candidate to challenge the Democrats' regular candidate for the Twenty-third U.S. Congressional District, the East Bronx Committee chose Hedgeman.[102] Troubled by the ways Buckley and the political old guard dismissed the concerns of the rapidly growing Puerto Rican and African American constituencies, Hedgeman agreed to run. A reform organization founded by Senator Herbert Lehman and Eleanor Roosevelt, designed to eradicate boss politics in New York, endorsed her.[103] The campaign evinced some of the increasing racial tensions between African Americans, Puerto Ricans, and Jews in New York City. In the June primary Hedgeman faced Jacob Gilbert, a five-time elected official, the incumbent, and part of the Buckley Democratic Party machine. Gilbert was also Jewish, but the district that had once been 75 percent Jewish was, by the spring of 1960, 50 percent African American and Puerto Rican.[104] Six weeks before the election, Buckley created a committee of five Puerto Rican members to bring out the vote and "consult" with the county Democratic organization on "matters pertaining to Puerto Rican voters."[105] It is hard to know how threatened Buckley felt. He had set up the committee to stave off Puerto Rican support for the insurgents, suggesting at least minor concern. But against a powerful political machine and with little financial support, Hedgeman and the East Bronx Committee were no more able to tackle the old-guard Democrats than the UDC was in 1960. Power brokers were not going to give that quickly.

A bright spot for Hedgeman during the campaign was that Lucille Dreher, wife of one of the prominent black ministers in the Bronx, organized a group of women who traveled around the district with her to distribute campaign literature. Days before the primary, Hedgeman told reporters, "This is a movement of all people in the district who find themselves neglected in their attempts to be an integral part of the total political machinery."[106] Able to be more of a grassroots catalyst in the Bronx than when she worked for the mayor, Hedgeman shared Baker's commitment to ordinary people. She straddled the line between insider and outsider. She demonstrated the passion and vision that oppositional politics allowed for. But she also wanted to be back in the government. Ambition was likely one of her motivations. On this point she differed from Baker. But more than personal drive, Hedgeman believed that the government was the best hope for economic, social, and political resource redistribution for African Americans and other disempowered groups, and she wanted one of the levers of power to dispense it.

In the end, Hedgeman's political fate mirrored that of most of the black women who had run for office in the 1930s and 1940s. She lost to Gilbert, the incumbent, in the June 1960 Democratic primary.[107] The Democratic old guard was not going to disappear without a fight. In reaction to the outcome, Hedgeman sounded remarkably similar to Ruth Whaley, Maude Richardson, and Pauli Murray, reaching for the silver lining in a disappointing defeat. "I am pleased with the results," she declared. "I think this is pretty terrific. . . . We've just begun to fight, because you don't kill corruption in ten minutes."[108] As a former party insider, Hedgeman knew what she was talking about. But her thoughts went beyond the immediate election to the larger racial dynamics at work in the city. In her 1964 autobiography, *The Trumpet Sounds*, Hedgeman outlined three lessons from the campaign. First she noted that the white political elite saw coordinated efforts by African Americans and Puerto Ricans through a lens of race, not of a desire to be part of the system. Moreover, when African Americans selected candidates from their own communities, Hedgeman maintained that the Democratic Party leadership rarely supported them. The regulars wanted to make the decisions about who ran. And finally, Hedgeman argued that "the power structure fears any unified action between Negroes and Puerto Ricans."[109] Time and again, her insights proved true. Two years after Hedgeman's 1960 campaign, for example, Mayor Wagner's party leadership in the Bronx made minor concessions to the insurgency by creating a committee to select candidates, but they controlled who was on the committee and what candidates were chosen.[110] Small steps forward, wrested from the power structure only after intense pressure, compelled the Democratic Party to change its ways, but the changes were often so small that one could understand the local communities' frustrations and cynicism.

One illuminating dimension of Hedgeman's 1960 campaign for Congress was found on the pages of the *New York Citizen-Call*, a local paper. Exhibiting the narrow parameters of gender ideology that dominated in the 1950s and early 1960s, Rhea Calloway, a journalist for the paper, wrote a feature article on Hedgeman days before the June election. Rather than delving into the issues that Hedgeman and the insurgency championed, including better housing, hospitals, parks, schools, and political representation, which the *New York Times* focused on,[111] Calloway's article reinforced conventional ideas about femininity, which had, ironically, excluded black women throughout U.S. history. She focused disproportionately on aspects of Hedgeman's private life, especially her appearance and her home. Hedgeman "was wearing a lovely cotton and Dacron dress in which she was very becoming," she remarked, and added approvingly that her sleeveless frock was appropriate for the warm weather. Hedgeman's first comment in the interview suggested both her familiarity with this kind of coverage and her disdain for it. "I frankly don't want this kind of interview," she declared, "because what'll you ask me, can I cook?" Instead the veteran activist volunteered her view of modern marriage, stating that "cooking ought to be a part of a man's capabilities as every woman's duty," because "the economic situation being what is, wives must work, therefore this means that a couple must share responsibilities for making the home." A fairly progressive view of marriage at the time, Hedgeman's comment elicited no response. Undeterred, Calloway circled back to personal issues and remarked that the candidate's apartment "fairly sparkled." Although she mentioned Hedgeman's political accomplishments, Calloway dedicated far more space to her home décor and clothing.[112] For women who ventured into the public life and found the media spotlight upon them, there was increasingly no escaping the demeaning coverage that reduced them to clean houses and proper, attractive grooming. While all of the women in this story valued and, in fact, took refuge in their homes and families, they were far more complicated than their ironed pleats, polished floors, and well-fed families. Even a 1965 *New York Times* feature article that focused primarily on Hedgeman's professional achievements could not resist leading with a stereotypically gendered and patronizing comment, "A handsome, soft-voiced woman with a perky little hat on the side of her head. . . ."[113] One would not have surmised from the article's lead that Hedgeman was a life-long civil rights, labor rights, and increasingly women's rights advocate. For women with years of dedicated activism and impressive accomplishments, the reductionist media representations had to have been maddening.

Although Hedgeman turned her energies to the Southern struggle for the next few pivotal years, she did not abandon the possibility of elected office in the future. So in 1965 when William Ryan, a congressional representative from Manhattan, urged her to join his ticket, she agreed. He was running for mayor as a reform Democrat against the regular Party candidate, and he wanted Hedgeman to run with him for city council president.[114] But a few transformative changes in the women's movement had transpired since Hedgeman's 1960 campaign. In the wake of the PCSW and Betty Friedan's book *The Feminine Mystique*, women in public life had to evaluate and often address their relationship to the burgeoning feminist movement. Hedgeman equivocated. She argued that women had been excluded from politics because they were "second-class citizens in this society."[115] At the same time, she stated, "I'm not a feminist but I'm for women."[116] She distanced herself from what she understood the evolving feminist movement to be, which was dominated by white middle-class women who, through her years of fighting for racial equality, had given her little reason to believe they were committed to African American women's advancements or that they wanted to eliminate racism. At the same time, Hedgeman wanted to advance women's cause in electoral politics, so she crafted her own position toward women's activism. Her reluctance to mobilize women *qua* women or from a feminist position, in any case, had little to do with her defeat at the polls. She and the rest of the Ryan ticket could not gain enough momentum in the four-way primary to take the election.[117] She suffered the same electoral fate in 1968 when she ran for office one last time, for the New York State Assembly. Her opponent, incumbent Charles Rangel, beat her in the primaries.[118]

History had shown that when the right hands were on the levers of power, positive change—the expansion of rights, a more fair redistribution of resources—could happen through the government, and so Hedgeman endeavored repeatedly to get inside. As a federal appointee, on Mayor Wagner's cabinet, as a candidate, and in her civil rights work, she used the state to try to further equality and access, particularly on issues of healthcare, housing, and women's employment. She believed in the ideals of government even if its reality, including her years in Wagner's cabinet, continued to disappoint her. Her political acumen and passion led insurgents and reformers to select Hedgeman as their candidate. But for all her years of civic activism and political engagement, she could not break through the barriers to elected office. Bessie Buchanan had also been a local activist, but two of the keys to her victory were Democratic Party support, which Hedgeman never secured, and prominence as a screen star.

Constance Baker Motley was about to learn that those two ingredients, party support and professional fame, could also launch a political outsider into the very center of power, suggesting that for black women traditional paths through party politics may not have been the most effective ways to attain elected office.

Motley's Path to Albany via the U.S. Supreme Court

A native of New Haven, Connecticut, Constance Baker Motley was born in 1921. Her parents, Willoughby Alva Baker and Rachel Keziah Huggins were immigrants from the Caribbean island of Nevis. Motley's father remained a loyal Republican throughout his life, but her mother supported Franklin D. Roosevelt and the New Deal. The ninth of twelve children, Motley grew up in a strict household that strongly emphasized education and religion. During high school she decided that she wanted to be a lawyer. Sara Lee Fleming, founder of the Women's Civic League, a group of influential black New Haven women, encouraged young Constance to attend meetings. It was through Fleming that Motley first met Dorothy Height. Motley took note, even as a teenager, that Mayor La Guardia appointed Jane Bolin, a 1931 black Yale Law School graduate, to the New York City domestic-relations court after her failed election campaign. As she contemplated her future, Motley wrote that poverty, rather than racial or gender discrimination, was her biggest worry. In December 1940, she met Charles W. Blakeslee, a philanthropist who sponsored her through college and law school. In 1941, she headed for the first time into the Jim Crow South to attend Fisk University in Nashville, Tennessee. After spending a summer in New York City, however, Motley transferred to New York University and graduated from there in 1943. Like the generation of women before her, Motley's intellectually and politically formative years were forged in Harlem. While living at the YWCA on 137th Street, a hub of social, intellectual, and political activity, she met many prominent leaders, including the outspoken radical activist and politician Benjamin Davis. In 1944 she took an important step toward her career goals and entered Columbia University Law School. Bella Abzug, a future politician and national feminist leader, was one of her classmates.[119] Upon graduation, she joined a small, elite cadre of women, including her teenage inspiration Judge Jane Bolin, as well as Pauli Murray, Ruth Whitehead Whaley, Sara Speaks, and Edith Sampson, all of whom had overcome the racial and gendered barriers to become lawyers.

Motley started working at the NAACP Legal Defense and Educational Fund (LDF) in 1945, even before she finished law school. As an example of how little civil rights history there was in the schools, she wrote in her autobiography that she had not heard of the *Plessy v. Ferguson* case until 1945 when she went to work for the LDF.[120] In 1949, she argued a case involving racial segregation in Hempstead, New York, schools.[121] As her first solo victory, it marked the beginning of a brilliant law career. The same year, Motley ventured into a Mississippi courtroom on behalf of Gladys Noel Bates to fight the first teacher salary equalization case. Although she worried for her safety, Motley persisted, the lone black female lawyer in the Mississippi court. The *Chicago Defender* celebrated Motley's achievement, remarking that "her appearance in the Deep South courtroom proved something of a triumph for women."[122]

Motley quickly became accustomed to being the only black female lawyer in any given situation. Few black women had been able to overcome the innumerable hurdles necessary to get to the point Motley had. It was not only courtrooms where she found herself the only black female lawyer, but on the NAACP legal staff as well. Throughout her years with the LDF, Motley worked with Robert Carter and Thurgood Marshall as part of the *Brown* legal team and on numerous other civil rights cases. In the course of her life as a litigator, Motley fought segregation and racial discrimination in schools, in housing (including in Levittown, New York), and in voter rights.[123] She traveled from Harlem to the heart of Dixie on a regular basis to help break the Jim Crow system. Together with Marshall, she prepared the Autherine Lucy case to desegregate the University of Alabama in 1956, an effort that, though legally successful, was ultimately undermined by white backlash and mob rule on campus.[124] She fought to dismantle Mississippi's voter registration laws, arguing in 1958 before the three-judge federal panel that "she wanted to prove the policy, custom and usage in Mississippi was to limit Negro voting."[125] Before she ended her tenure with the LDF, Motley had argued ten civil rights cases before the U.S. Supreme Court. She won nine of them, including the case of James Meredith, which desegregated the University of Mississippi. Not only did these cases slowly change the lived experience of African Americans throughout the South, they also secured Motley's reputation across the country as a courageous and successful civil rights advocate. People in Harlem had been very attentive and particularly impressed.

In late 1963, New York State Senator James Watson approached Motley, his former college classmate and friend, about his imminent retirement from office. He planned to run for a judgeship and he wanted Motley to run for his senate seat, which covered Harlem and the upper west side of Manhattan. Although Motley responded that she "didn't have the stomach for it," in fact she was persuaded by a number of politically informed friends to run.[126] J. Raymond Jones, one of the most powerful Harlem leaders in city government, got behind Motley's election. So did Dorothy Height, who as president of the NCNW, contributor to the 1963 March on Washington effort, and former member of the President's Commission on the Status of Women, was one of the most respected and influential black women in the nation (see Chapter 4). In short order, Motley was elected to the New York State Senate in a special election in February 1964.[127] The life-threatening risks she had taken as she waged a legal war against racial discrimination and the public exposure those cases brought her all but paved Motley's path into elected office. Her victory was widely celebrated. When she received Bella Abzug's congratulatory letter, Motley responded by encouraging Abzug, "Please let me know if there [are] any bills you want me to introduce."[128] African American women also celebrated Motley's success, which they saw as an achievement beyond a personal victory. Geraldine Woods, president of the Delta Sigma Theta sorority remarked to Motley, "Your contribution will continue to make women everywhere proud." Motley responded in kind, suggesting, "I do hope my election to the NYS Senate will inspire other women to become more active in the political life of their communities."[129] Similarly, Mrs. Owens of the Girl Friends Inc. framed Motley's achievement in historic perspective, writing to her, "Through the years, the women of the world have been slowly striving to make inroads into professions, regarded, too long by the masculine sex, as their own private domain. Your recent election at the polls is another victory in this struggle. That you also happened to score another 'first' adds even greater prestige and stature in this office."[130] Motley had a lot of hopes and expectations riding on her new career as a legislator, but, given her battle-worn status, she was ready to take on the challenges.

Motley's success at the polls stood in marked contrast to the dozens of African American women who had tried, sometimes repeatedly, to win elected office and failed. Even she was understandably surprised by the ease with which she entered political office, writing in her autobiography, "I did not know my own strength. Certainly, I did not realize that all one needs to run for office is name recognition and political support. It seems that since I had represented James Meredith everybody in New York, thanks to the *New York Times*, 'knew my name.'"[131] In this brief admission, Motley identified the two ingredients most necessary to her success and which had been most difficult for African American women to secure: Democratic Party support and positive name recognition. Prior to her meteoric rise, only Bessie Buchanan had managed to win an elected seat, and she had done so by having the same powerful combination of dynamics. With these two women helping undermine the Democratic Party's resistance to running black women and with the national changes underway as a result of the civil rights movement and now the women's rights movement, perhaps the path would be easier for others in the future.

As soon as she was sworn in, Motley immediately set to work. She maintained a deep commitment to civil rights and social justice. In response to her constituents' requests for support of public housing, Motley sent letters to the Housing Authority pleading their cases.[132] She introduced legislation to remove the category of color on marriage licenses, to outlaw discrimination in volunteer fire departments and labor union apprenticeships, and to eliminate segregation in public schools.[133] She also fought on behalf of her constituents to check police abuse of power by voting against "Knock-Knock" and "Search-at-Will" legislation that would have given police increased access to people's homes.[134]

Motley's civil rights work brought her positive acclaim, but it also brought attempts to humiliate and intimidate her professionally, as well as frightening threats to her personal safety. For example, when she stood up to argue an appeal on the University of Alabama desegregation case, one of the Southern judges turned his chair around and refused to face her. Protesters routinely jeered at Motley and her plaintiffs when they walked into Southern courtrooms. And she received racist hate mail as a state senator and later as a judge.[135] Despite the personal risks to herself and her family, Motley fought on. She was successful in the state senate and was reelected in the general election in 1964.

Motley's time in Albany was cut short by New York City politicos, including J. Raymond Jones, who wanted her to fill the sudden vacancy in the Manhattan borough presidency. Jones oversaw the city council's special election in February 1965, six weeks into Motley's new senate term. The first black woman in the New York state senate was making history again, this time winning the borough presidency, the first woman to win that office. In November of that year, she ran for and handily won reelection on the Democratic, Republican, and Liberal Parties' tickets.

The borough president advocated for the borough's [county's] needs and balanced out the mayor's power in setting the city budget and land use. Motley was the most highly positioned black woman in politics up to that point. Even though she was responsible for the million and a half residents in Manhattan, she remained particularly committed to the people and the pressing needs in Harlem, which she stated explicitly in a speech she gave to the Harlem United Democratic Club in April 1965. "I consider it an important part of my function to advance the welfare of Harlem and its residents in any and all feasible ways . . . [s]o long as this is a depressed community, so long as its children do not have the maximum educational opportunities, so long as its residents do not obtain employment consistent with their abilities and ambitions the entire city suffers. Therefore the improvement of these and other conditions is of paramount importance."[136] Passionate and committed to justice, Motley proved a popular and effective politician.

The *New York Times* noted that Motley had been shaking up the status quo since she took office. They added that although "her smile is as warm as that of an old lady who has just been helped across the street, she has been one of the toughest civil rights lawyers in the country, . . . and as Borough President, a head-rattling questioner of city planners' favorite plans."[137] She was steadfast in whatever she put her mind to, but Motley's heart remained with the law. She wanted to be a judge. President Lyndon Johnson, who had learned about Motley from a number of civil rights leaders and politicians, including Ramsey Clark and U.S. Senator Robert Kennedy, was equally interested in her career and sought the right moment to appoint her to a federal judgeship.

Conclusion

The Cold War indisputably closed down certain avenues for collective organizing, protest, and change. At the same time, in evaluating some of the political activism African American women in New York City engaged in, we find layers of nuance to seemingly familiar Cold War, civil rights, and women's history narratives. There were many activists, including Chisholm, Hedgeman, Buchanan, and Motley, who supported American democracy and at the same time devoted their professional lives to making it live up to its promises and potential. They used the tools they had with grassroots organizations, in city and state government, and in the courts to advocate for racial and gender equality and for a more activist state to distribute resources more fairly. With the exception of Ella Baker, these women were not radicals looking to change the United States political economy, but in fact, had they succeeded in their goals of allocating housing, employment, education, and health resources justly, the United States would have been a fundamentally different country with all of its citizens truly able to pursue opportunities to the best of their abilities. But time and again, these women were reminded—even after they secured hard-won positions inside the state—that those with power never give it up easily. And so they began the next stages of activism, building networks inside and outside of government, and raising issues to their colleagues and the public and putting pressure on wherever they could.

For women like Buchanan and Hedgeman, few tangible victories resulted from their tenures in office during the 1950s, although their political participation meant that new issues were brought to the fore, and their public leadership helped give confidence to other women and inspired them to activism. Baker made a foray into electoral politics but believed in her heart that the way to create a more just society was by working with people in their communities, not in government. She never ran for office again. Chisholm had spent well over a decade as a Bedford-Stuyvesant activist, but when the UDC scored its victory in 1962 and overthrew the old guard, she was merely at the beginning of her historic political life. Her full story is told in chapter 5. And finally, Motley's exceptional political career starkly underscored the importance of Democratic Party support and public name recognition. She benefited from these dynamics as Bessie Buchanan had. At the same time, even her brief tenure in office also helped accustom voters and fellow politicians to seeing African American women in political leadership roles. Breaking down stereotypes was significant because it made the path easier for women coming after her.

These women's political lives—the issues they fought for, the coalitions they tried to form, and the concerns they managed to insert into public debates—suggest that while much criticism of the American political and economic structures had been stifled in the 1950s, there was more political activism than we often assume. These women managed to advocate for publically funded, universal health care, more accessible and affordable public housing, full and fair employment, an end to sexual discrimination in hiring and promotion, as well as the elimination of racial discrimination in all aspects of life. The arguments advanced, particularly by those women who had won positions inside the government, were often framed in terms of racial inequality, but they also raised concerns about class and gender inequality. In doing this, they forced their political colleagues to consider and take a stand on issues that had rarely, if ever, been raised. The changes they advocated for would have had the effect of reconfiguring social and economic relations had they come to pass in the 1950s. While they did not succeed in the McCarthy era, many of these issues became staples in discussions about equality and social justice, as well as elements of public policy in the 1960s. What is more, these women's stories further illuminate the complexities of the history of women in the 1950s. In addition to a tremendous amount of civil rights activism, African American women were engaged in trying to alter the nature of New York City politics in the 1950s and 1960s, including what got discussed and who got to participate. There was some noteworthy trailblazing done in the 1950s that made the changes of the 1960s more feasible.

Layle Lane, a teacher, civil rights activist, and labor leader, ran for elected office in Harlem numerous times on the Socialist Party ticket between 1934 and 1950. (Photographs and Prints Division, Schomburg Center for Research in Black Culture, The New York Public Library, Astor, Lenox and Tilden Foundations, 1945)

Eunice Hunton Carter, an attorney, NCNW leader, and one-time candidate for the New York State Assembly in Harlem, pictured here speaking at the microphone. Ruth Whitehead Whaley is on the far left; Maud Gadsen is next to Carter. (Photographs and Prints Division, Schomburg Center for Research in Black Culture, The New York Public Library, Astor, Lenox, and Tilden Foundations— James C. Campbell, photographer, undated)

Pauli Murray worked in the Works Progress Administration in New York City during the Great Depression, led a successful sit-in to desegregate a luncheonette while a law student at Howard University in the 1940s, and ran for city council on the Liberal Party ticket in Brooklyn in 1949. A legal scholar and feminist, Murray was a key participant in the Senate debate over the inclusion of "sex" amendment in the Civil Rights Act of 1964. (Photo of Murray, 1935–1945. Schlesinger Library, Radcliffe Institute, Harvard University)

Maude Richardson, a highly respected and consummate community activist in Brooklyn and a member of the Republican Party, ran for elected office three times in the 1940s. In 1946, she lost her campaign for the assembly to the Democratic incumbent by fewer than one hundred votes. (Brooklyn Public Library, Brooklyn Collection, undated)

Ada B. Jackson, a renowned Brooklyn activist and civil rights advocate, abandoned the Republican Party for the American Labor Party in 1946, when she ran against Maude Richardson for the New York State Assembly. Pictured here, Jackson (on the left) is giving an award to playwright Maxine Wood for "aiding oppressed minorities" with her Broadway play, *On Whitman Avenue*. Vivian Baber, star of Wood's award-winning drama, is standing next to Jackson; Milton Goell, president of the Brownsville Neighborhood Council, is on the far right. (Brooklyn Public Library, Brooklyn Collection, 1946)

Ruth Whitehead Whaley is being sworn in by Mayor Vincent Impellitteri to serve on the powerful New York City Board of Estimates. (Photographer—Nichols. Photographs and Prints Division, Schomburg Center for Research in Black Culture, The New York Public Library, Astor, Lenox and Tilden Foundations, 1951)

Honorable Bessie Buchanan was the first African American woman elected to the New York State Assembly in 1954. She represented the Twelfth Assembly District in Manhattan through 1962. (Photographs and Prints Division, Schomburg Center for Research in Black Culture, The New York Public Library, Astor, Lenox, and Tilden Foundations)

Constance Baker Motley, a former attorney with the NAACP LDF, is pictured here as the Manhattan borough president. She was the first woman to win this office. (Photographs and Prints Division, Schomburg Center for Research in Black Culture, The New York Public Library, Astor, Lenox and Tilden Foundations, Moss Photo Service, 1965)

Dorothy Height was a leading voice in African American women's organizations and for civil rights for more than seventy years. She served as the president of the Delta Sigma Theta Sorority (1947–1956) and president of the National Council of Negro Women (1957–1998). She was a member of the President's Commission on the Status of Women, 1961–63. (Delta Sigma Theta Sorority, Washington, D.C., undated)

Dr. Jeanne Noble served as president of the Delta Sigma Theta Sorority from 1958 to 1963. A professor of education at New York University, she was tapped by President Johnson in 1964 to create the Women's Job Corp, part of the War on Poverty. (Delta Sigma Theta Sorority, Washington, D.C, undated)

Anna Arnold Hedgeman, a member of Mayor Wagner Jr.'s cabinet (1954–58), three-time candidate for elected office, and one of the key organizers of the 1963 March on Washington, is pictured here with New York Governor Averell Harriman and Dr. Martin Luther King Jr. (Archives at the National Afro-American Museum and Cultural Center, Wilberforce, Ohio, undated)

Brooklyn Congresswoman and presidential candidate Shirley Chisholm on the campaign trail in California. Chisholm remained in the Democratic Party primary until the convention in Miami, Florida in July 1972. She served in the U.S. House of Representatives from 1969 through 1982. (Photo by Rose Greene)

CHAPTER FOUR

Feminism, Civil Rights, and Liberalism in the 1960s

"I look back on this experience [the President's Commission on the Status of Women] as an intensive consciousness-raising process leading directly to my involvement in the new women's movement that surfaced a few years later. . . . [U]pwards of two hundred able women (and a number of sympathetic men) from many professions and from all sections of the country were brought together . . . and out of these associations developed a new strength and increasing pride in being a woman. An important by-product of the Commission's existence was that like-minded women found one another, bonds developed through working together, and an informal feminist network emerged to act as a leaven in the broader movement that followed," Pauli Murray wrote in her 1987 autobiography.[1]

Racial discrimination and social injustices in jobs, housing, education, and politics—problems that women had been fighting for the past four decades— were now raised before leaders of the liberal political establishment at the national level. A select number of black women, most of whom had honed their organizing, leadership, and advocacy skills in New York City during the 1930s, 1940s, and 1950s, were explicitly asked for the first time to participate in the highest levels of policy debates on civil rights and increasingly on women's rights as well. Dorothy Height, president of the National Council of Negro Women (NCNW), Pauli Murray, a legal activist, and Jeanne Noble, president of the

Delta Sigma Theta sorority, all made important contributions to the President's Commission on the Status of Women (PCSW) meetings as well as the policy recommendations that resulted from them. Constance Baker Motley made history by attaining a federal-level judgeship. When time passed and many of the changes women hoped for were not forthcoming, they did what they had done in the past; they utilized outside pressure groups and organized constituents to demand change and hold leaders accountable. Sometimes they mobilized organizations they were already members of, like the NCNW, the Deltas, and the National Council of Churches (NCC), to support their political activism. At other times, they helped establish new ones as Ella Baker did with the Student Non-Violent Coordinating Committee (SNCC) and Pauli Murray and Anna Arnold Hedgeman did with the National Organization for Women (NOW).

Long engaged in struggles for racial equality and for human rights more broadly, these women found themselves at a historical moment when the politics of liberalism, civil rights, and feminism converged. Many of their efforts, including those they had engaged in Harlem and Brooklyn, contributed to bringing this moment about. Politically active in a society that was being compelled to reevaluate its policies and practices toward African Americans and women, they were well positioned, from their years of experience, to contribute substantively to policy decisions and to try to build coalitions to solidify meaningful social, economic, and political change.

Additionally, these women, who had always understood their struggles for justice and equality through a prism of race, had to determine their individual and collective relationships to the burgeoning feminist movement they were helping usher in, especially in the wake of the PCSW. Most of these women were engaged either directly or indirectly in the struggle for women's social, economic, and political rights. As the decade progressed, their awareness of gender discrimination was not only sharpened, but a number of them increasingly spoke about women's rights publicly including in male-dominated political forums.

Standing on the brink of momentous historical transformations, a number of African American female leaders pursued a politics of inclusion through the administrative, legislative, and judicial arms of the government at the national level. For decades they had fought to end many of the social and economic problems at the local level that the Great Society now promised to alleviate nationally, especially racial inequality and poverty. Significantly, for the first time, they were close to the centers of political power. Their capacity to influence changes, however, was often limited by subtle and overt manifestations of racialized gender discrimination that positioned black women as interlopers in these privileged circles. Frequently treated as tokens in national arenas, African American female leaders fought for legitimacy for themselves and for the causes and the people they championed. Their presence inside the state was only the beginning of the new round of activism. As the decade began, the question was whether African American women, new arrivals among the liberal elite, would be able to move power brokers and forge coalitions necessary to bring about meaningful social, economic, and political change in the areas most important to them.

An Unwitting Accomplice in the Women's Movement

In December 1961, President John F. Kennedy issued Executive Order 10980 establishing the President's Commission on the Status of Women, and he directed its members to evaluate the ways "prejudices and outmoded customs act as barriers to the full realization of women's basic rights" in the United States and to make recommendations for change.[2] The 1957 National Manpower Council had provided the justification for the president to turn his attention to women. The council's study, *Womanpower,* called women "essential" and "distinctive" workers. In the context of the Cold War, America needed to draw on all its resources.[3] Esther Peterson, a long-time trade unionist and the newly appointed head of the Women's Bureau; Katherine Ellickson of the AFL-CIO; and Secretary of Labor Arthur Goldberg were the driving engines behind the creation of the commission, and they were well versed in the consensus liberalism of the period, which was committed to the containment of Communism at home and abroad but also sought the balance of power between labor and management and the continuation of New Deal programs. Much in keeping with the new president's views, they envisioned using the apparatus of the state to bring about incremental social and economic changes for the good of society, especially for women.

The creation of the study represented a new window of opportunity at the national level that government leaders in New York had already begun to explore. Five years earlier, New York Governor Harriman had appointed a commission to review women's employment and economic activity. Two of the state's veteran black politicos, Anna Arnold Hedgeman and Ruth Whitehead Whaley, served on it. Completed in 1958, the final report emphasized that despite prevalent stereotypes to the contrary, millions of women were in the waged-labor force and wanted to be there.[4] In the case of the PCSW, the federal government sanctioned a full-scale evaluation of women in society, addressing elements that the New York study had examined, but also much more. It committed resources and executive support to the effort, and it promised policy changes based on the commission's recommendations. At the same time, the PCSW retained and reinforced deeply entrenched views that women should be, first and foremost, wives and mothers, not workers.[5] The president's executive order exemplified the nation's ambiguity about the appropriate role for women in American society. The traditional definition of gender went unchallenged; yet the commission was committed to eliminating discrimination on the basis of sex in the labor force and in the law.[6] While it was by no means radical, it had the potential to improve many women's lives, especially working women's lives, in concrete ways. Hence, the story of the PCSW must be read with an understanding of its place in time. It held great possibility for improving women's status in society, even as it operated in a political structure that rewarded moderation and caution. A small but influential cadre of African American women contributed to the process and influenced the Commission's potential to affect black women's lives.

Down to Business

The PCSW was in every way a top-down, elite structure. Eleanor Roosevelt served as chair. There were twenty-six members—fifteen women and eleven men. There were five members of the president's cabinet, four members of Congress, two college presidents, labor leaders, and presidents of four national women's organizations.[7] Dorothy Height, president of the National Council of Negro Women (NCNW), was the only African American woman on the commission. The commission members met together eight times over the course of two years. Most members also participated in one of the commission's seven committees, which were established to carry out in-depth studies on women's civil and political rights, the inequalities they faced in social insurance and tax structures, and their status in the home and community, in education, and in public- and private-sector employment. The detailed analyses these committees conducted over the life of the commission informed the final report. In addition to the seven committees, the commission sponsored four consultations, which addressed specific areas of concern: New Patterns in Volunteer Work; Private Employment Opportunities; Portrayal of Women by the Mass Media; and Problems of Negro Women. More than one hundred individuals representing women's organizations, the media, academia, business, labor, law, and government participated in the committees and consultations. In bringing representatives from these fields together, the PCSW facilitated the development of vital networks.

The commission created the space for national leaders to analyze the complex realities of women's lives and to advocate for changes when necessary. It also held the potential to influence the commitment of federal, state, and local resources, and to improve working conditions and educational opportunities for women. For African American women with hitherto few advocates in the federal government, this marked a potentially important shift. Moreover, it was the first time black women had been invited to a national-level policy discussion of this nature. Aware of the social, economic, and political challenges black women faced in American society, Dorothy Height asserted, "There needs to be some stimulation of women to recognizing the places within the local community where policies are made that affect their lives."[8] The forces that kept women, especially black women, oppressed were so numerous, she indicated, the women themselves were likely unaware of everything that was working against them. The commission presented an important occasion for women to gain transformative knowledge and to evaluate their own situations.

Committee Work

Although Height was the only black woman on the Commission, others, including Jeanne Noble, president of the Deltas and professor of human relations at New York University, and Pauli Murray, a legal scholar, human rights advocate, and one-time candidate for New York City Council, served on some of the seven committees.[9] Together these three and a handful of other black women sought to broaden discussions and raise matters of material economic, political, and social concern to African American women, while they rigorously explored issues of significance to women of all races and classes across the nation.

Jeanne Noble, author of an in-depth study on black college women, was appointed to serve on the Committee on Federal Employment, which was formed to analyze women in public sector employment. She and the other committee members compiled a trove of data establishing that in federal employment, women were heavily concentrated in lower-level jobs, and men were disproportionately concentrated in middle and upper-level posts. "Less than 2 percent of higher-level positions were found to be filled by women," the commission reported.[10] Although it was not included in the reports' findings, the public sector was a much more important avenue for African American women's economic advancements than the private sector had been because of pervasive racial discrimination. As historian Paula Giddings notes, "In 1965, in the Department of

Labor, 70 percent of Black employees, compared to 40 percent of Whites, were women. And in positions open to civil servants with modest credentials, Black women outnumbered men four to one."[11] The lopsided lack of opportunities for women to advance in public sector jobs, coupled with the fact that more than thirty percent of black women were still in low-paying domestic work, affected African American communities disproportionately. The commission's findings were compelling. Even before the conclusion of its work, the president issued a directive to federal agencies to hire and promote employees without regard to sex.[12] The actual impact varied greatly, however, especially when the recommendation failed to include strong compliance mechanisms.

The Committee on Civil and Political Rights was responsible for study-ing ways in which state laws discriminated against women in their exercise of citizenship rights, property rights, and in family relations, and it explored legal alternatives to an Equal Rights Amendment (ERA).[13] The PCSW's membership had been intentionally stacked against the ERA because Peterson and Ellick-son supported protective labor laws, and they feared the ERA would eliminate them. Only Marguerite Rawalt, an attorney and past president of the National Federation of Business and Professional Women's Clubs (BPW), actively sup-ported it.[14] But the amendment could not be ignored, as it had been introduced in Congress in every session since 1923 and was usually a part of national elec-tion platforms. The commission's leadership did not want to entertain in-depth and potentially divisive debates about it, so it charged this committee with the responsibility of finding a solution that could effectively quash consideration of an ERA and at the same time bolster women's political equality in society.

Dollie Robinson, a New York City labor activist and a colleague of Peterson's in the Women's Bureau, proposed that Pauli Murray, her friend and former neighbor from Brooklyn, serve on the committee. Murray had returned from teaching law in Ghana the prior year and was now a senior fellow at Yale Law School. In the thirty years preceding her work with the PCSW Murray had already demonstrated her commitments to fighting for social, economic, and political justice many times over. Frustrated by the realization that she "was a minority within a minority, with all the built-in disadvantages such status en-tailed," in the late 1940s Murray had run for a New York City Council seat. She saw the invitation to participate in the PCSW as yet another way to address the problem.[15] Murray was not ideologically opposed to the ERA, but she believed nevertheless that the U.S. Constitution already guaranteed women's equal rights and that a further amendment was unnecessary, at least at this time.

Murray was asked to prepare a legal memo examining the applicability of the Fourteenth Amendment as a tool to try sex discrimination cases. When Eleanor Roosevelt died in the summer of 1962, Murray worked with even greater determination, seeing her contribution as a memorial to Mrs. Roosevelt.[16] Having extensively analyzed legal decisions involving distinctions based on sex, Murray determined the time was right to seek out cases to demonstrate that women's equality was already guaranteed by the Fifth and Fourteenth Amendments of the Constitution. She and Mary Eastwood, a lawyer on loan from the Department of Justice, wrote the committee's recommendation, which was included almost verbatim in the PCSW's final report. It stated, "Equality of rights under the law for all persons, male or female, is so basic to democracy and its commitment to the ultimate value of the individual that it must be reflected in the fundamental law of the land. The Commission believes that this principle of equality is embodied in the 5th and 14th amendments to the Constitution of the United States."[17] With the debate over the ERA effectively sidetracked, Peterson had her way, but the committee had also left the door open to the possibility of the ERA at a future time by stating it was not needed *now*. The compromise was made for Rawalt's benefit, but neither she nor the others could imagine how soon the amendment would actually be voted on favorably by Congress and then sent to the states for ratification. In the interim, Murray and other feminist legal scholars pursued the strategy outlined in the report.[18]

The PCSW's Consultation on the Problems of Negro Women

Height, Noble, and Murray, and the handful of other African American women on the committees, offered valuable insights into the ways racism limited black women's opportunities, but they could not capture the enormity of the challenges that black women faced in American society. As a sign of the changing national context in the early 1960s regarding race relations, the White House urged Esther Peterson to hold a special consultation to discuss "Problems of Negro Women" as part of the PCSW's work.[19] Height chaired the one-day meeting in April 1963, held as the commission was finishing its work. It brought together twenty African American leaders, including a number of veteran New Yorkers who had fought for decades to break down racial discrimination in employment, housing, education, and the political system. They included Dollie Robinson, a labor and political activist, Ruth Whaley, a two-time electoral candidate and long-serving member of the New York City Board of Estimates, and Maud Gadsen, who in the 1940s had been part of an effort to break the racial barrier in the New York State Senate and who participated in the PCSW Consultation as the representative of the Beauty Owners Association. It also included Gerrie Major, active in the New York Democratic Party, the NCNW, and the NAACP, but who was most known as a seasoned journalist with the *New York Amsterdam News, Jet*, and *Ebony*, and Dr. Hilda Fortune, director of community services for the New York Urban League and who would soon be appointed to the Harlem antipoverty program, HARYOU-ACT (Harlem Youth Opportunities Unlimited).[20]

In her opening statement to the group, Height explained the commission's charge, some of its preliminary conclusions, and she elaborated on points she felt were particularly important to the consultation's work. Among them was the commission's goal to see that conditions were created across the nation to "assure the widest possible freedom of choice" to women, including the right to stay at home or to work. However, Height emphasized to her sympathetic audience, "I think for women in minority groups we are constantly aware of how little freedom of choice there often is around the things for which they care the most."[21] To underscore the persistent added burdens women of color faced in the United States in comparison to white women, Height quoted Mary Church Terrell who had written about the "double handicap of race and sex" sixty years earlier.[22]

Almost immediately after the meeting began, two participants raised issues that framed the rest of the discussion. Walter Davis of the civil rights department of the AFL-CIO observed that in talking about the problems black women faced, one could not ignore the central problem of racial discrimination that "permeates the entire thing, housing, education and so forth." The result, Davis maintained, is that "you can't isolate [black women's status] and put it in a vacuum and discuss it on that basis."[23] Racism, even more than sexism, he suggested, was the central problem for all African Americans, including black women. Cenoria Johnson of the National Urban League (NUL) raised a related and equally vexing point: "There has to be a basic concern that there be a united family [a husband and a wife] in whatever we are striving for." She asserted that too many African American families had historically been denied this normative ideal and that the comparative prevalence of female-headed families in African American communities was a problem for black women and a crisis for black families more generally.[24] Johnson indicated they were going to have to "deal with the male" and recognize the debilitating economic and social consequences of racial discrimination on black men, even more than focusing on black women and their problems. In making this argument she reinforced the mainstream gender ideal of men as providers and the family norm of a two-parent household, even though for decades African American families had constructed more expansive gender models and more flexible family norms as ways to contend with racial discrimination. Historian Alice Kessler-Harris has commented on the troubling consequences of this discussion. She argues, "[Whereas] the word *matriarchy* might have been conceived in a positive light ... [in] practice, it connoted disadvantage and rapidly became a code for what was wrong with the Negro family."[25] During the consultation, there was neither blame nor denigration directed at black women for the circumstances they faced, but there was a great deal of concern that the situation be rectified to bring African American families in line with conventional middle-class norms.

Proceeding from the assertions that "the problem of race discrimination permeates the whole life picture of the Negro" and that "[i]f the Negro woman has a major underlying concern, it is the status of the Negro man," the group analyzed a number of pressing problems for African American women.[26] These included black women's work in the waged-labor force and the need for and the challenges of getting more black women involved in local government agencies and civic organizations. And they analyzed the ways negative portrayals of African American women affected their interactions with white colleagues.

The discussion on work focused on the ways racism denied black women access to relevant job training, employment opportunities, and professional advancement. Paul Rilling, executive director of the D.C. Council on Human Relations explained that there were six secretarial schools in Washington, D.C., from which federal clerical workers were hired, but only one "makes any pretense at giving equal opportunity to Negroes." The foremost stenography school, he noted with frustration, "openly says it will not admit Negroes."[27] Other avenues for vocational training promised opportunity but often delivered disappointment. While the NUL was supportive of the Manpower Development and Training Act (first passed in 1962), Johnson cast light on its limitations, noting that it promised people training in technology fields but instead funneled workers into low-level jobs like service station operators and hospital attendants.[28] Unless the Urban League was willing to simultaneously fight for skilled jobs, she did not want it advocating for the training of domestic workers. At the same time, she tempered her critique, returning to the possibilities that government-sponsored job training held. Her recommendation, to have the manpower retraining program expanded, to have it reflect black women's economic needs, and "to let it be the vestibule through which Negro women go, whether for testing or job opportunities," was adopted as part of the final consultation report.[29]

Ruth Whaley, a lawyer by training, raised the problem of gaining access to skilled and professional jobs black women were routinely denied access to. "The college girl . . . can't get a job for which she is qualified and in which there is a vacancy, because she happens to look like me," she said wryly. These well-educated women did not need more training or education, she insisted: they needed "an open door." Both Whaley and Robinson contended, moreover, that it was not African Americans but rather white employers and white Americans more generally who needed the training and education to appreciate both the injustice of racist hiring practices and the loss of human potential when African Americans were excluded from good jobs.[30]

Consultation members recognized these areas of concern, but they also dealt with the reality that most African American women were neither in clerical training programs, nor were they college educated. Fifteen years after World War II ended large numbers of black women were still in domestic or household employment.[31] As a result, some participants, including Robinson, Whaley, and Alice Dunnigan, who was the first black female White House correspondent and a member of the PCSW Committee on Equal Employment, focused on opening up new opportunities and supporting black women's aspirations to move out of the "undesirable occupations," especially domestic work.[32] Gerri Major was more pragmatic, arguing that "it is going to be a long time before the bulk of the Negro working women can move into executive positions," and indicating that the consultation should craft proposals grounded in that reality.[33] One path to improved opportunity, the group determined, was to enable domestic workers to unionize so that they could fight for better wages, hours, and working conditions; a union could also help those who wanted more training or sought better job prospects.[34]

Women's paid labor took up much of the morning discussion, but the consultants also addressed the need to have more African American women in local government agencies and civic organizations so that they could contribute to decisions that were being made about their communities and to help those in need secure resources. Cenoria Johnson spoke up again. One public housing office she visited had no African Americans on the staff. She exposed a key source of the problem by asking, "How many Negroes sit in on the Commission that helped to design the regulations, how many Negroes had any chance to say anything about the operation of the public housing program, other than maybe to head a day-care center in the project." She wanted hiring mandates written into federal programs.[35] Her point was clear; whether or not the federal government was a proactive ally for black women, its programs were potential vehicles for pursuing valuable positions that they should tap into more.

But that was only the first step, others asserted. Grace Hewell of the U.S. Department of Health, Education, and Welfare for example, argued that it was not just a matter of getting the positions but making sure that thoughtful people concerned about racial justice and economic opportunity sat in those jobs. Too often, as the many examples shared at the meeting indicated, African Americans were selected by whatever group or organization they were on, as tokens or because they were perceived as "safe" and willing to say what the particular white-dominated organization wanted to hear.[36]

Similarly, in their discussion about the importance of African American women's increased participation in community service organizations and local policymaking boards, the consultants raised a number of related points. If communities were committed to incorporating black women's voices, then they had to recognize that most women worked during the day and that meetings should be scheduled with that in mind. Moreover, the group underscored the education and class gaps that often made African American women feel "socially uncomfortable" in these settings.[37] If the PCSW were serious about not only collecting information about the challenges black women faced but also about advancing solutions, then the consultants gathered under Height's leadership gave them plenty to work with, even if they did not challenge traditional assumptions about gender roles or family norms.

In her closing comments Dorothy Height summed up some of the key themes that emerged during the day. African American women had problems that were similar to other women's challenges, but they were also different in important ways. These differences, according to Height, included "the place that we are in the body-politic and in the economy, the impact of the racial factor and the role that the Negro woman has within the family." The problems demanded meaningful attention by the PCSW and society at large. Echoing the broader commission's premise that the focus on women had at least as much to do with families' and society's needs as women's needs as individuals, Height stressed the need for intervention "to improve family life." But in her final emotional appeal she focused in on black women. The differences in life that African American women faced, she concluded, "are quite major, in influencing the extent to which the sense of equitable participation in the democratic society can be realized and in which the sense of being personally fulfilled can ever be dreamed of as Negro women try to participate as members in our democratic society."[38] Height concluded with an unequivocal message: black women paid a terribly high and distinct price for being both black and female in a society that distributed the psychological and material benefits of political, social, and economic citizenship most heavily to others in the social order, but especially to white Americans.

Height worried that the consultation's efforts would not be reflected in the PCSW's final report and that this would leave readers "without having much understanding of how minority groups are affected."[39] When *American Women*, the commission's final report, was released on Eleanor Roosevelt's birthday in October 1963, Height could argue that her fears had been realized. There were but a handful of references woven through the document regarding the particular problems black women faced. But she could also glean that the consultation was not totally in vain. The final report included a statement on the discrimination of black women in the labor force and it directly incorporated one of the consultation's statements in relation to education and career counseling. Both points were made, however, with no context and with no recognition of the history of racialized gender discrimination that created their current circumstances.[40]

The PCSW made its most forceful statement about African American women in its introductory section, "Invitation to Action." "Discrimination based on color is morally wrong and a source of national weakness. Such discrimination currently places an oppressive dual burden on millions of Negro women," the report stated unequivocally.[41] Neither general readers nor policymakers could mistake this clear message and its implications. Even with few other explicit comments made in *American Women*, this assertion about black women's challenges was a noteworthy departure from the past. Moreover the final report, "Problems of Negro Women," was published and widely available (as were the findings from the "Consultation on the Portrayal of Women by the Mass Media," the only other published consultation report).

Black women's participation in the PCSW was significant for a number of reasons. In a departure from the past, it brought them right to the center of the national debate about women's roles in American society. The committees, which met a number of times, gave them a platform to address the multiple burdens of discrimination they faced in the workplace, the political sphere, and the community.[42] Their contributions informed both President Kennedy's and later President Johnson's liberal agendas. In addition, they challenged emerging feminists to think more broadly about the category "woman," and they focused policymakers' attention on the fact that black women faced different and often more complicated forms of gender discrimination than white women. And as evidence of their influence and importance to national conversations about gender and racial equality, Murray, Noble, and Height were not only brought into subsequent policy discussions and nongovernmental efforts focused on women's rights and gender discrimination, but they were understood as leaders in these conversations. Each one would find herself embroiled in further activism and program development inside and outside the state administrative structure very soon after the commission's conclusion.

The PCSW was a watershed insofar as it represented an unprecedented opportunity for women to use the state to improve their status in society. That the president and Congress responded with some immediate and meaningful changes (in civil service hiring practices, for example), the passage of the Equal Pay Act of 1963, the establishing the Citizens' Advisory Council on the Status of Women and the Interdepartmental Committee to monitor annual progress, and the encouragement of state-level commissions demonstrated that at least some of the potential was being realized. Further, it confirmed that women were finally able to make some headway in their pursuits of power by taking advantage of the political currents flowing as a result of the Cold War, the change in administration, and the civil rights movement. These savvy female leaders drew arguments from the National Manpower Council and used the president's executive order eliminating discrimination on the basis of race in government contracts as a model to tackle discrimination on the basis of sex. Not a feminist by any account, President Kennedy had inadvertently unleashed, through his initiation of the commission, untapped female talent and undirected female interest in women's opportunities and their status in American life, and he facilitated the beginnings of conversations among women and women's organizations from diverse backgrounds that ultimately led to the dramatic escalation of the women's movement.

Liberalism's Architects in the Age of Transformative Social Change

While the PCSW had been hard at work, two events unmistakably shifted the social and cultural ground on which many Americans had stood. In February 1963 Betty Friedan, who lived in the suburbs of New York City, published her historic book, *The Feminine Mystique*. Countless middle-class women, especially white suburban women, gained a powerful tool with which to deconstruct and analyze their hitherto unspoken discontent. In its wake, women across the nation began to seek out others who shared not only their malaise but also their increasing anger and determination to chart a new way forward. The second transformative event took place on a hot day in August 1963. Peaceful yet filled with determination, hundreds of thousands of people, mostly though not exclusively African Americans, gathered in Washington, D.C., to assert in songs, speeches, and through mass action that "we shall overcome." The decade-long mass movement for racial equality was given an unmistakable boost that day that neither President Kennedy nor the nation could ignore. Though more blood would be shed before a civil rights law was passed, the tide had clearly turned, and the day of national reckoning with history had arrived. African American women, including the handful who had spent formative years in New York City politics and community organizing and who also participated in the various dimensions of the PCSW work, helped usher these events along to their climaxes.

A third event which unfolded on the streets of Dallas, Texas, in November 1963, just weeks after the PCSW concluded its work, sealed the year as a dramatic and transformative one, a notable distinction particularly in a decade that would be marked by its national turmoil, triumphs, and tragedies. In the wake of President Kennedy's assassination, African Americans who had been fighting for decades for the most basic rights of citizenship marshaled support from across the nation to finally make civil rights legislation a reality. With Southern senators at the ready to filibuster any bill that advanced racial equality, they would need the armies of supporters they called to Washington. At the same time, with the unexpected change in leadership, African Americans found an important ally in Lyndon Johnson who was determined to make the civil rights bill his own by making it a tribute to the slain president.[43] Black women, too often unrecognized for the pivotal role they played in this chapter of history, were central to the lobbying efforts on Capitol Hill as well as orchestrating mass action outside it.

Part I: Sex and Racism in the Civil Rights Act of 1964

As the civil rights bill wound its way through the House of Representatives, the National Woman's Party (NWP), always attentive to opportunities to advocate for women's equal rights, strategized to get "sex" added to it as grounds to prohibit discrimination. They tapped a long-time supporter of the ERA, Democratic Representative Howard Smith from Virginia and the chair of the House Rules Committee, to introduce an amendment to Title VII of the legislation which addressed discrimination in employment. Like many of the NWP members, Smith opposed government regulations of business and protective labor legislation, and he had been a regular sponsor of the ERA legislation since the 1940s. Much has been written about Smith's motivations for inclusion of the "sex" amendment, given his hostility to the civil rights bill and his tongue-in-cheek repartee with Representative Emanuel Celler (Democrat from New York) after he introduced it.[44] If the addition of "sex" killed the bill, Smith would have been more than happy to see it die; but if the civil rights bill passed extending rights to African Americans, Smith was likely interested in guaranteeing that white women had those same benefits. Hardly a feminist, Smith's vote *against* the final House bill *with* the "sex" amendment attached demonstrated that his resistance to the advancement of African Americans was stronger than his commitment to women's equal rights. Nevertheless, once his legendary amendment was introduced, others in the House spoke out in support, especially the majority of women in Congress.

The congresswomen defended the amendment on a number of grounds. Martha Griffiths, a Democrat from Michigan, spoke at length and most forcefully. Although she commenced by pointing out that the derision and amusement with which her male colleagues considered it was proof enough of the need for the amendment, the substance of her argument was an explicit defense of white women who, she feared, "will be the last at the hiring gate."[45] She argued that without the "sex" amendment, black women seeking jobs would have a distinct advantage over white women because employers would worry about lawsuits on race discrimination grounds. While identifying a potential though unlikely consequence, if "sex" was excluded from the bill, Griffiths's line of argument was nonetheless marked by its racist tenor. She also asserted that "so-called protective legislation has really been to protect men's right to better paying jobs," but she quickly circled back to a position that resonated especially with her Southern male colleagues. Referencing the Fifteenth Amendment, Griffiths declared, "It would be incredible to me that white men would be willing to place white women at such a disadvantage except that white men have done this before . . . your great grand-fathers were willing prisoners of their own prejudice to permit ex-slaves to vote, but not their own white wives."[46] She concluded where she started, not with a defense of *all* women's rights of economic citizenship, but rather *white* women's rights, seemingly untroubled by the evident racism she used to justify the inclusion of the "sex" amendment in a civil rights bill that was crafted to eliminate racial discrimination.[47] Catherine May (Republican from Washington) further advanced Griffiths's point. She cited an NWP letter that expressed a similar concern for white women, quoting specifically that "government officials have interpreted 'race, color, religion, and national origin' in a way that has discriminated against the white, native-born American woman of

Christian religion."[48] Black women considering a feminist alliance with white women had ample grounds for skepticism and for keeping their distance, at least based on this debate.

Oregon Democratic Congresswoman Edith Green, former member of the PCSW and chair of its Committee on Civil and Political Rights, rose to speak against the amendment; she was the only woman to do so. A proven advocate for women's rights, Green nevertheless worried that the "sex" amendment would undermine the bill. "The main purpose of this legislation today is to try to help end the discrimination that has been practiced against Negroes," she implored. Like her PCSW colleague Esther Peterson, Green believed that racial discrimination was a more serious and pervasive problem than sexual discrimination and that it was a mistake to equate or address the two forms of inequality in one piece of legislation.[49] But in her effort to undermine Smith's amendment, she inadvertently showed why black women continued to face immense challenges in finding effective legal, political, or economic recognition or redress in much of white American society. Green argued sympathetically, "For every discrimination I have suffered, I firmly believe that the Negro woman has suffered 10 times that amount of discrimination. She has a double discrimination. She was born as a woman and she was born as a Negro."[50] Striking the "sex" amendment was her way to defend black women because it eliminated a likely threat to the civil rights bill. In taking this approach, she suggested that black women suffered from racial discrimination, not sexual discrimination. Green recognized the fact that black women were *women* insofar as she noted their "double discrimination," but she gave no indication that she understood that the racial discrimination they faced was different from that which black men faced in some important ways and that eliminating sexual discrimination could help black women as well. Like others in the House debate, Green assumed that black women and men were hindered by racial discrimination, and that white women were hindered by sexual discrimination, and that there was no social group positioned at the nexus of the two.[51] Despite her efforts, on February 10, 1964, the civil rights bill with the "sex" amendment attached cleared the House by an impressive majority (290–130), although few if any of the white Southerners who spoke in favor of the amendment, including Smith, voted for it.[52]

The House debate did not address the racialized sexual discrimination that black women faced in society, but it was strategically and effectively raised when the Senate discussion commenced in the spring of 1964. Pauli Murray was kept current on the civil rights bill's progress by women with whom she had forged a network during her work with the PCSW's Committee on Civil and Political

Rights. These included Catherine East of the Interdepartmental Committee, Mary Eastwood of the Justice Department, and Marguerite Rawalt, former member of the PCSW and an appointee to the Citizen's Advisory Council on the Status of Women. A co-author of the PCSW's statement to use the Fourteenth Amendment rather than an ERA to pursue women's rights, Murray was nonetheless "overjoyed" by the passage of the House bill with the "sex" amendment intact: "Particularly because as a Negro woman," she said, "it was difficult to determine whether I was being discriminated against because of race or sex and felt that the sex provision would close a gap in the employment rights of all Negro women."[53] Protective labor legislation had rarely benefited black women the way it had white women because of the ways racism undermined black men's and black women's economic opportunities, and so black women, including labor organizers, were much more ready to see it go.[54] Despite its odd origin, the amendment was part of the bill brought over from the House, and Murray and her others wanted to make sure it remained.

Those who favored the "sex" amendment were troubled to learn that Senate Republican leader Everett Dirksen of Illinois sought to eliminate it, ostensibly because he supported some protective labor legislation for women.[55] At the request of her former PCSW colleagues, Murray, a compelling proponent of the amendment, prepared a memo in support of it that was to be circulated around the Senate and sent to the White House. She crafted a thorough indictment of sexual discrimination and also painted a grim picture of the economic inequalities that specifically affected black women. In so doing, Murray effectively addressed the arguments raised in the House debate and rooted the basis for the amendment firmly in individual rights, not the specious racist grounds that Griffiths and others evoked. She responded to Edith Green's opposition to the amendment by arguing that even if racial discrimination had more vicious manifestations than sexism, it "in no way diminishes the force of the equally obvious fact that the rights of women and the rights of Negroes are only different phases of the fundamental and indivisible issue of human rights."[56] Moreover, Murray countered the argument that racism and sexism were so different that they could not be dealt with together. That argument was unnecessarily cautious, generally fallacious, and "cloaks both timidity and paternalism," she charged.[57] Taking a bold and comprehensive stance on economic rights for all women, Murray's memo challenged key positions that white activists had advocated, including during the recent PCSW.

And finally, under the heading "The Inclusion of the 'Sex' Amendment is Necessary to Protect Negro Women," Murray responded to the concerns Martha Griffiths had raised on behalf of white women and at the same time gave clear evidence why black women's particular problems were integral to discussions on women's economic inequality. Whereas Griffiths had made a case for the "sex" amendment on grounds that it would protect white women from black women's economic competition, Murray countered that this was an unlikely outcome because black women also faced sexual discrimination. She maintained that it was "exceedingly difficult for a Negro woman to determine whether or not she is being discriminated against because of race or sex." These forms of discrimination were deeply interconnected, a reality "that Negro women are uniquely qualified to affirm," she argued. She foresaw that without the "sex" amendment, Title VII would benefit black men but not black women.[58] Murray included detailed census data in her memo that illuminated the disproportionate barriers and responsibilities black women faced in education, jobs, health, marriage, and family life. More than any other social group, she argued, the black woman "is literally engaged in a battle for sheer survival."[59] The memo was, by Murray's own account, a powerful document that highlighted "the historical interrelatedness of the movements for civil rights and women's rights and the tragic consequences in United States history of ignoring the interrelatedness of all human rights."[60] Rather than fracture or compartmentalize her understanding of herself and the needs of black women more generally into discrete identities of black or female, she articulated the concept of intersectionality that black feminists twenty years hence would name. She embraced this complexity and advocated for a transformative politics of inclusion, human rights, and equality.

Copies of Murray's memo were sent to the attorney general, members of the Senate (including Dirksen), and to Lady Bird Johnson, a personal friend of Marguerite Rawalt's. In her letter to the First Lady, Murray asked specifically that Mrs. Johnson "discuss the matter with the President."[61] Bess Abell, Mrs. Johnson's secretary, wrote in response, "I am pleased to advise you that as far as the Administration is concerned, its position is that the Bill should be enacted in its present form [with the sex amendment]."[62] Both Johnson and the majority of the Senate proved favorably disposed to the amendment. When the bill was signed into law Rawalt wrote a congratulatory note to Murray asserting, "To you comes a real measure of credit for the ultimate successful passage of Title VII of the Civil Rights Bill with its protection for women in employment."[63] While Rawalt's accolade was understandable, it was also perhaps overenthusiastic. The history of Title VII's "sex" amendment was much more complex than the oft-repeated story of Howard Smith's mischievous effort to undermine the civil rights bill, and it survived in the Senate because of more than simply

Murray's memo. A diverse set of arguments rooted paradoxically in racism, racial equality, the rights of the individual, the rights of white women, and the rights of all women, converged at critical junctures in the legislative debates to keep the "sex" amendment alive. While not singlehandedly responsible, Pauli Murray is unquestionably among those deserving credit. She articulated a broad vision of human rights that refused to prioritize race over sex, or sex over race but rather saw these two elements as deeply interconnected and also only part of the more expansive human whole.

Part II: Women and the War on Poverty

Even before President Johnson signed the civil rights bill into law, he had initiated another part of his liberal agenda. He intended to use the full resources of the government, he said in his first State of the Union address, to eradicate poverty in America. Although President Kennedy had originally formulated an antipoverty agenda, it was Johnson who gave it shape and put it into practice.[64] Johnson called on Sargent Shriver, the head of the popular Peace Corps program, to design and launch the "unconditional war on poverty." The Job Corps, a key part of the antipoverty program in the Office of Economic Opportunity (OEO), was targeted at unemployed men in cities. It was designed as a residential training program that would restore the damaged male breadwinner ideal and simultaneously remove enrollees from their immediate, impoverished environments.[65] Edith Green, a member of the House Committee on Education and Labor, fought to have women included in the jobs program.[66] She pressed her point with administration witnesses during the congressional hearings, and "by the first week of hearings she had an ironbound commitment to open up the Job Corps to women," wrote Christopher Weeks, one of Shriver's assistants.[67]

Once women were added to the Job Corps, President Johnson evaluated possible candidates to launch the program. At Green's suggestion, he turned to Jeanne Noble. He had met her in 1963 during the Delta Sigma Theta's fiftieth anniversary celebrations. In an interview, Noble recalled the exchange: "President Johnson called me and asked me to come down and see him. He said, 'You thought I had forgotten about the Deltas, didn't you.' And I said to myself, 'Hmm, Lord, yes I did.' But he hadn't. He remembered all those ladies because he had probably never in his life been in a room with just thousands of highly educated black women."[68]

Prior to Johnson's call, Noble had been fighting against racism and sexism for years as an undergraduate at Howard University and a doctoral student at Columbia University, through the Deltas, as a government appointee, and as a professor at New York University. Explaining how she got involved with the Deltas during her graduate years in Harlem, Noble recalled, "Dorothy [Height] would call on the phone in the dormitory that I lived in and would ask me to do little projects for the Deltas. And that was a good thing, because at that particular time there were *so few blacks*. . . . There was no affirmative action, no scholarships, *nothing*."[69] Only thirty-two years old when she was elected to office, she served as the president of the Deltas from 1958 to 1963. During those critical years of the civil rights movement, the sorority moved in a new direction, and historian Paula Giddings credited Noble with the change.[70] Noble asserted that it was only when young college-aged sorors started getting thrown in jail for civil rights protests that the older women really became engaged.[71]

Not only that, she was a member of the Harlem Youth Opportunities Unlimited community action study (HARYOU-ACT) and was very familiar with the needs of the poor black community especially in Harlem. Noble's educational background, her sorority work, and her commitment to civil rights led her into national policy discussions about women's rights, racism, and poverty. From 1961 to 1963, she had served on the PCSW's Committee on Federal Employment.[72] The favorable impression Noble made on Edith Green and on the president opened yet more doors at the highest levels of government. After consultation with Green about Johnson's request, she agreed to head up the Women's Job Corps, much to Johnson's delight and Shriver's chagrin.[73]

Weighing the challenges she faced in launching a woman's branch of the jobs program, and echoing a bygone notion of gender norms, particularly in relation to women's employment, Noble told Shriver, "the real problem here is the respectability factor. No mother really wants her daughter to go into something called the job corps." As a way to break down anticipated resistance, she proposed that they give the contract for recruitment and training to a coalition of women's organizations. "And he told me it was the dumbest idea he had ever heard of. He did not want all of those women running around in tennis shoes in his job corps," she recalled.[74] But Noble ultimately had her way. When asked about women in the program, Shriver introduced Noble's suggestion as his own idea in front of a national audience. Noble recounted her reaction: "I looked at the television set, and there [Shriver] was on one of the Sunday morning shows. They put the question to him, 'Well, who's going to let anybody go to a job corps? Women in the job corps, that's ridiculous.' He opened up his big mouth and said, 'Oh, I'm going to give the contract to an organization called WICS. It consists of seven women's organizations.' He got into a corner and that's what he said."[75] WICS, Women in Community Service, was the successor to Women's Inter-

Organizational Committee (WIC), which was an interracial, interfaith coalition that Dorothy Height forged in Atlanta in March 1964 from the groups she had worked with on the PCSW and in the aftermath of the March on Washington. Member organizations included the National Councils of Catholic, Jewish, and Negro Women as well as the YWCA and Church Women United.[76]

Having won her first battle, Noble turned to the daunting task of setting up a federal program. She relied heavily on what she knew best: her huge network of women's organizations. From 1960 to 1963 Noble had served on the Defense Advisory Commission on Women in the Services (DACOWITS), which oversaw the recruitment and treatment of women in the military.[77] Impressed with what the military women were doing, Noble tapped them and her academic contacts to administer the program. Major June Henry, with whom Noble had worked on the DACOWITS, was brought in as a project manager for the OEO; Dr. Bennetta B. Washington, who was based in New York City and taught at NYU with Noble, was named director of the Women's Training Centers of the Job Corps.[78] Noble gave WICS the contract for recruitment and training.

The volunteer organizations immediately began enrolling young women from all across the country. Their reach was impressive—the WICS organizations counted 16,726 local units among them. As the *Norfolk Journal & Guide* noted, "27 million women volunteers joined in the war on poverty with the completion of agreements between the U.S. Office of Equal Opportunity and Women in Community Service."[79] A year into the program, WICS volunteers had referred more than twenty thousand applicants to the Job Corps, and more than nine thousand were enrolled in eighteen residential centers.[80]

Despite these advances, Congresswoman Edith Green vigilantly monitored women's status in the Job Corps compared with men's, and she found much to criticize. The program discriminated against women by design, she argued. Men outnumbered women by more than ten to one, even though there were relatively equal numbers eligible.[81] Shriver conceded that the program was unbalanced but argued that there was insufficient funding for the women's program.[82] At best, he promised to allocate one-third of the training slots for women. In this environment Green and Noble could not dismantle the entrenched belief that poor men needed jobs more than poor women did. Daniel Patrick Moynihan's study a year later, *The Negro Family: The Case for National Action*, would only bolster that assessment. In practice, young women ended up with approximately one-sixth of the training slots.

Policymakers such as Shriver and even Noble held particular views of women's economic needs and their desire for steady and well-paying jobs that had troubling implications for families headed by women, of whom nearly 50 percent were in poverty.[83] Although she was committed to designing a useful program for poor women in need of work, Noble had certain educational and class privileges that created a chasm between her and the women who sought jobs through the Job Corps. Her class-biased views about poor women's needs, in addition to those even deeper and more problematic ideas held by Shriver and much of the public about poor women of color, inclined Noble to take a pragmatic approach to the design of the program, one that would "develop basic educational skills, homemaking skills and marketable skills, such as those of nurses' aides or secretaries."[84] Even with these limited goals, she could not get more training slots opened for women. At the same time, as a number of historians have recently demonstrated, poor women—especially poor mothers—did not wait quietly for policy makers to focus attention on their desperate plights. They forged alliances and engaged in creative activism in cities like Harlem, Philadelphia, and Las Vegas that redefined the ways maternalist activism was understood at the same time that they demanded government attention, resources, and respect.[85]

Inside the OEO, Noble and Shriver were often at odds. Tasked to coordinate a controversial and under-resourced federal program, Noble turned to her networks—those rooted in women's voluntary organizations, not corporate boardrooms or political clubs. Shriver treated these women as interlopers and resented Noble's management approach, which included her asking the First Lady to host a luncheon to announce the Women's Job Corps. Noble's style differed from Shriver's, but what was more significant was her distant location from the decision making and resources. Shriver was already ensconced in arenas of power. Experience, access, and tradition all worked to men's benefit both as leaders and as participants in the War on Poverty programs. Noble's capacity to influence the Women's Job Corps was highly circumscribed from the start. Even if she had wanted to propose innovative ways to think about women's work, it would have been all but impossible to implement something drastically different, given the original conception of the Job Corps. After all, it had been necessary to convince the men who designed the program that it was important to include women in any way.

Noble left the Women's Job Corps as soon as she got the program off the ground. Uninterested in becoming a government bureaucrat she nevertheless served as a government consultant when asked.[86] After the Job Corps, she lent her talents to President Johnson's National Advisory Commission on Selective Service, established to study and make recommendations for the draft during the

Vietnam War, and New York Governor Rockefeller's panel on auto insurance, in addition to her ongoing commitments to HARYOU-ACT in Harlem.[87] Similar to Pauli Murray, Noble's experience on the PCSW led to further engagement in policymaking that had the potential to significantly affect the lives of black women. Although she had a very difficult time securing adequate resources and respect for the program from the men at the OEO, her selection indicated a significant step forward in the Democratic Party's appreciation for the importance of including black women in public leadership roles.

Part III: Constance Baker Motley and LBJ Make Legal History

President Johnson not only lent support to the post-PCSW agenda, the addition of the "sex" amendment to the Civil Rights Act of 1964, and the Women's Job Corps, he also made notable progress in appointing women to high-level federal jobs.[88] In January 1966 Constance Baker Motley received a call from the White House; President Johnson wanted to meet with her. She had won nine out of the ten civil rights cases she argued before the U.S. Supreme Court, and she had risked her life numerous times in the South, but particularly in 1962 when she defended James Meredith in his integration case against the University of Mississippi. Without question, Motley had stellar legal and civil rights credentials. Additionally, she was proving herself a popular and talented politician. Not only had she won a seat in the New York State Senate, but she was currently serving as the Manhattan borough president, the first woman in the city's history to be elected to that post.

As successful as she was at City Hall, Motley preferred a closer engagement with the law and wanted a federal judgeship. When she received the call from the president, she grew hopeful that he was considering her for an appointment, especially as a number of civil rights leaders and New York Senator Robert Kennedy had spoken on her behalf.[89] To her surprise and delight, her meeting with Johnson was not an interview but an announcement of her appointment to the federal court. Johnson was again following through on his commitment to appoint women to influential and visible federal posts. That he appointed Motley, an African American woman, indicated that the work that women like Height, Noble, and Murray had been doing was helping shift the views of the nation's highest leaders about the importance of having African American women in positions of power and leadership—women, not coincidentally, who had all spent formative years in the dynamic world of Harlem.

Letters of congratulations flooded in for Motley. Her old friend and Columbia law school classmate Bella Abzug wrote, "I have no doubts that you will bring great honor to the bench. . . . [Y]our appointment is a significant step for women and Negroes everywhere."[90] Pauli Murray's note was brimming with elation. "I cannot let this day go by without saying Bravo! Hooray for our side! My prayers and best wishes for a brilliant career on the bench," she wrote, and added optimistically, "You just might make it as the first on the nine."[91] There were scores of congratulatory letters from New Yorkers, especially Harlem residents, women's organizations, church groups, and civil rights leaders across the country. Motley's elevation to the bench was recognized as a moment of historical importance that reflected some of the hard-won struggles that had been waged.

The appointment also came at a pivotal time for the evolving women's movement, particularly with the founding of the National Organization for Women (NOW) in mid-1966. Whether or not they understood themselves as championing women's advancement, women in public life were both asked and increasingly inclined to reflect on their accomplishments through a gendered lens. Weighing the importance of her sex in Johnson's nomination, Motley determined, "I did not get to the federal bench because I was a woman. I understood my appointment as based on my accomplishments as a civil rights lawyer." She admitted, moreover, that although her career was a string of historic firsts for black women, she "had no particular attachment to the newest women's rights movement."[92] She was so disinclined to consider the importance of her place in history as a black *woman* that she turned down numerous invitations from professional organizations and women's groups to speak about women in public life.[93] At the same time, even though she did not evaluate her judgeship through a gendered lens, many people across the country did. While United Church Women in Kansas "rejoiced" over her appointment, a group of women in Florida wrote of their pride in Motley's achievement, emphasizing that they believed she had "done so much for all of US, especially women."[94]

Motley was attuned to the broad social currents and within a year of her appointment had shifted her thoughts about women's activism at least somewhat. During a speech in Connecticut in April 1967, she noted that the movement for equality that stemmed most forcefully from the struggles for racial equality was spreading to other areas. "Women, although not a minority in this country, have long labored under the handicap of a second-class citizenship," she maintained. "Discrepancies between the equality we preach and the discrimination we practice have lately become the targets of legal and judicial disapproval." As an example, Motley noted that "Title VII of the CR Act of 1964 . . . prohibits job discrimination on the basis of race, but on sex as well."[95] This was hardly a declaration of feminism, but for a woman who understood the struggle for social justice through a racial lens, even this subtle change indicated that the steady efforts that women's activists inside and outside of government had been making were beginning to gain attention and command comment.

Ten years later, Motley was much more comfortable speaking publicly about sexism, its effects on her, and the women's movement. In her commencement address to the Spelman College graduates in 1979 she declared, "The difference between the women of my generation and those of you who are graduating today is that the women of my generation had at least two excuses for failing to develop their God-given abilities. One was that they were women. The other was that they were black. Those two excuses are denied to the black women graduates of the class of 1979 as a result of the achievements of the civil rights movement and the achievements of the women's rights movement. The sum total of the effect of those two revolutions has been to level two of the greatest barriers to the advancement of mankind that this society has ever posed."[96] Although she was not an active participant in the evolving women's movement, Motley's own professional successes in the courts and in New York City politics helped open doors for other African American women. Additionally, she embodied yet another way that women in public life, particularly those who had understood their struggles for justice and equality through a prism of race, came to embrace and publically express a feminist perspective on women's historical challenges and their current opportunities.

Upping the Ante on the Liberal Establishment

In the early 1960s, political contestations within the administrative, legislative, and judicial dimensions of the state were beginning to yield some modest gains for African Americans' and women's rights. At the same time, many outside of government felt change was too slow in coming and too limited in scope. A number of black women who had been schooled in political activism in New York City now shifted their focus to the national stage even as they maintained their commitments to organizational and grassroots efforts. They knew that change happened most effectively when people in their communities were empowered, and that politicians had to be pushed, sometimes very hard, by the mobilization of the masses. While the violence in the South refused to abate and civil rights leaders like Medgar Evers were gunned down, and with Kennedy cautiously and unenthusiastically advancing civil rights legislation, African American women rallied not only their tried-and-true base, but also new organizations and new allies as well.

Dorothy Height, first engaged in struggles for economic, social, and racial justice in Harlem in the 1930s, now capitalized on her experience on the PCSW and began to build relationships with the leaders of the other national women's organizations, including Viola Hymes of the National Council of Jewish Women, Margaret Mealey of the National Council of Catholic Women, and Cynthia Wedel of the National Council of the Churches of Christ.[97] In the fall of 1963, after not only the momentous March on Washington but also the devastating bombing of the 16th Street Baptist Church in Birmingham that left four young girls dead and scores of others injured, she gathered a group of women together to evaluate civil rights priorities and to strategize about how women could advance them. She had found it difficult to get the male civil rights leaders "to accept the fact that the conditions affecting children, affecting youth, and affecting women," including child care and jobs for women, "were all a part of civil rights." She was encouraged by the different response she got from the women she had called together, noting that they understood "the relationship between decent housing, schooling, and child care, to employment, and employment to job opportunities."[98] A short time later, Height asked them for assistance after she received a call from James Forman, a SNCC organizer. African Americans in Selma, Alabama, were facing considerable resistance to their voter registration efforts, and Forman hoped the respectable women of the NCNW could lend a hand. After what she described as a stressful and dangerous trip to Selma, Height called her new interracial women's coalition together and asked them collectively to help address the situation in the South.[99] The group became known as Women's Inter-Organizational Committee or WIC, the organization that Jeanne Noble readily tapped for the Women's Job Corps.

Throughout her more than sixty years of activism and leadership, Height worked tirelessly to make the nation live up to its commitments to democracy, freedom, and equality. She did so with full awareness and thoughtful consideration of radical critiques of the United States, including Communism and Black Nationalism, but she always remained dedicated to working through the liberal establishment and in interracial coalitions.[100] In 1964 she led the NCNW into frontline, grassroots activism that frequently put members' lives at risk, in order to compel the government to live up to its promises to black people in the American South. "Wednesdays in Mississippi," the project she launched with a handful of white women, was an integral part of Freedom Summer in 1964. Interracial pairings of women went to Mississippi each week to deliver resources, build cross-race dialogue, and bear witness to the atrocities visited upon African Americans in Mississippi. Not only did the program continue for three summers, the NCNW grew increasingly active in addressing local housing, education, and economic needs. Their housing program quickly garnered the attention of national policymakers at the Office of Economic Opportunity and the Department of Housing and Urban Development.[101]

In thinking back over the contributions the NCNW made to the struggles for racial equality, Height recalled proudly that "[M]any groups came into Mississippi. NCNW never left. . . . Whether it was carrying books and art supplies to the freedom schools during Wednesdays in Mississippi, keeping Head Start on track, setting up pig banks, or building houses, we were helping people meet their own needs, on their own terms. Women knew that if they joined the National Council of Negro Women, they were going to help themselves by helping others."[102] The NCNW under Height's leadership fully embraced the struggle for racial equality, seemingly at the expense of a sustained focus on the needs and lives of black women.[103] While this was the case in some important respects (especially the lack of challenge to the racist misogyny, including from African American men, that rained down on black women in the wake of the Moynihan report), looked at from another perspective, Height tried to empower poor women in substantive ways that would enable them not only to survive in an economically and socially hostile world, but to also live in dignity.

Height was hardly the only black female activist to emerge from New York City's fertile political ground to put her decades of experience to use in the heated national debates about racial equality and social justice in the 1960s. Notable among others who did were Ella Baker and Anna Arnold Hedgeman. Baker had spent some of her earliest activist years during the Great Depression helping Harlem residents navigate the treacherous economic climate through a grassroots consumer cooperative movement. She spearheaded the effort to increase NAACP membership nationally in the 1940s. Her contributions to the civil rights struggle were legion and legendary. They have been thoughtfully documented by biographer Joanne Grant and historian Barbara Ransby. She remained deeply wedded to the ideals of participatory democracy and pursued no positions in the government or politics after her campaign of the 1950s, but her activism unmistakably shaped the national civil rights movement in the 1960s in profound ways. Like too many others, Baker had to risk her life on a regular basis to help bring the basic rights of citizenship and the light of human dignity to the disenfranchised and the disempowered. In the wake of the Montgomery bus boycott, Baker shifted her focus more completely from New York, where she had been at the forefront of the fight against racial segregation in the New York City schools and against police brutality, to the Southern struggle. A lone woman among the male leadership, she served for two years as the executive director of the Southern Christian Leadership Conference, but, discouraged by the elitism and sexism that ran through the organization, Baker decamped in 1960. When courageous young people acted on their frustrations with not only racial injustice but also strategy choices made by civil rights veterans, Baker was there to facilitate a new path forward. Through her orchestration, the Student Non-Violent Coordinating Committee (SNCC) was born in the wake of a meeting she organized at Shaw University in April 1960. Never comfortable with the spotlight but rather determined to help people find their own capacity for growth, change, and leadership, Baker served as sage and strategist, but not the public face of the movement. She maintained a different approach to activism than Height did. Whereas Height, a nationally prominent leader, traded on her status to gain access to the leadership of the Democratic Party and the civil rights movement, Baker's firm belief in participatory democracy shaped her activism for decades and was manifest in all she did. It also informed the distance she maintained from formal political structures and leaders. Given this, it was not surprising that other than her 1930s work in New York City's New Deal administration and her single pursuit of elected office in Harlem in the early 1950s, Baker kept her distance from the various arms of the state.

Anna Arnold Hedgeman, another seasoned civil rights veteran, was at a personal crossroads in 1960. Disheartened by its intransigence, she had left Mayor Wagner's administration in 1958. In the succeeding few years, she agonized over strategies and institutional vehicles for bringing about a more just world. An early ally of—as well as a candidate for office on—the Democratic reform ticket in New York City, Hedgeman became disillusioned, sensing that it had little capacity and worse, no real will to transform city politics.[104] As she groped her way forward, she moved toward the church. Inspired by a young white minister, Dr. Robert Spike of the National Council of Churches (NCC), Hedgeman took a position with the organization's Commission on Religion and Race.

Hedgeman served as the NCC's coordinator of church participation in the March on Washington and shortly afterward spearheaded its lobbying effort for the civil rights bill, wanting to capitalize on the new interest local churches had in civil rights in the wake of the march.[105] Having honed her political skills over four decades, she went full tilt into the battle to get the legislation passed. Her political strategy encompassed a variety of actions. She traveled the country relentlessly, going from a demonstration in "violence scarred" Cambridge, Maryland, to Kalamazoo, Michigan, to speak with Michigan's United Church women. There, she gave a talk titled "The Civil Rights Struggle—Challenge to Religion" and made a plea for individual action. She asked her audience directly, "What are your churches like—may I come with my husband and four children or would I have to come alone and sneak into the back pew? . . . What are your restaurants, clubs, elected officials, homes and jobs like?"[106] Additionally, she coordinated with SNCC and SCLC activists to get firsthand information from the field. When Representative Howard Smith of Virginia held up the bill in the House Rules Committee, she organized letter-writing campaigns asking members of Congress to sign a discharge petition. She also prepared delegations who would travel to Washington to lobby senators after the bill was released from the House.[107] Years of experience had taught her that the only hope of moving the president or Congress on race issues was through direct engagement and dramatic pressure.

The House Rules Committee finally discharged the bill with the famous "sex" amendment attached, but civil rights activists around the nation knew that the battle had barely begun. The Senate had the capacity to filibuster the bill, and with the powerful Southern contingent, that fear became a reality. Days of resistance begot weeks and then months of despair, but stalwarts like Hedgeman refused to give up. The Commission on Religion and Race summoned delegates from every state in the nation to Washington. More than a thousand people came to meet with legislators and demand that the bill be made law. The interfaith effort, Hedgeman noted, was "extraordinary."[108] Despite months of resistance from Southern segregationists, the pressure worked. The Senate finally discharged the bill after "a record-shattering Southern filibuster" that lasted 82 days.[109] The Civil Rights Act became law in July 1964.

Like Height, Hedgeman was committed to working for racial equality through the liberal establishment, although she was "grateful for the thunder of rebels" like James Baldwin and Malcolm X.[110] Despite her early contemplation of Black Nationalism in the 1920s, she embraced the promise of democracy and the potential for white America to seek racial justice. Deeply rooted in her faith and the belief in humanity's capacity for good, Hedgeman endeavored to build coalitions across race lines and national borders, between secular and religious institutions, and between men and women. She also continued to believe that meaningful change in race relations, in rights of citizenship, and in economic justice could happen through the vehicles of the state. But she never stopped appreciating the need for outside pressure groups to raise issues and force them into national discussions. This was the case for a problem that shadowed her during her years of civil rights activism and political work—namely, sexism.

Feminist Stirrings in the Civil Rights Movement

In 1962, when A. Philip Randolph, architect of the 1941 March on Washington movement and leader in the fight for a permanent Fair Employment Practices Commission, called on Anna Hedgeman again to help initiate a march on Washington for job opportunities, she readily responded, eager to take on a project with broad reach and national significance.[111] She worked closely with Randolph laying the groundwork for the march. He had originally planned the event for October 1963. But by the early summer, Randolph had merged his idea for a march with Martin Luther King's, and an August date was set. The collaboration and the event itself bore Hedgeman's imprint, which the *Baltimore Afro-American* recognized when it referred to her as "a major architect" of the march.[112]

In her 1964 autobiography Hedgeman wrote about the march and the organizing effort. In addition to detailing the machinations that went on behind the scenes, she leveled a noteworthy and pointed criticism at the march's founders and leaders. Her strongest objection stemmed from her feeling that African American female activists were treated like second-class citizens by the male leadership who neither sought their input nor recognized their contributions. For example, Hedgeman was the only woman on the march's nine-member organizing committee.[113] Moreover, with all that black women had done in pursuit of racial equality, she felt they deserved a voice at the event. She and Dorothy Height, who at that time was not only engaged in the PCSW but in her capacity as president of the NCNW had also been meeting with male leaders of the civil rights organizations for more than a year, insisted that women be recognized for their tremendous contributions to the movement. But the men rejected their demands. Hedgeman was angry that she had to fight just to get Rosa Parks publically acknowledged for her role in the movement.[114] Similarly, despite her joyful recollections of the day, Height remarked that Bayard Rustin, the march's masterful coordinator, resisted even the last-minute appeals made the morning of the march to include a woman speaker. "That moment was vital to awakening the women's movement," she declared.[115]

Airing her complaints publicly, Hedgeman was willing to express frustrations rooted in sexual discrimination, even if it risked exposing tensions within the civil rights movement. In an interview with the *New York World-Telegram and Sun*, she argued: "I'm no feminist. But I'm for women. . . . Right along with Negroes, women are discriminated against just for being what they are. I honestly think women are the most discriminated against of all the minorities. . . . I'm

anxious to see women join the human race."[116] There
reasons for her to have disavowed the feminist mantle in
a product of the liberal establishment to which Hedge
ted, did not adopt it even as it chronicled women's une
society. Additionally, the book most often associated wi
Feminine Mystique, which was published the same year
tive of white, middle-class suburban women. And finall
enthusiastically embracing the feminist label was the often racist NWP. It was
not at all surprising that Hedgeman emphatically rejected the term even as she
articulated ideals that would be recognizable and embraced by most feminists.

Pauli Murray also had much to say about the exclusion of women from the
march's speaker list. Shortly before she engaged in lobbying efforts to secure
both racial and gender equality in the civil rights bill, Murray took a bold step
and penned a critical response to the exclusion of women among the speakers or
recognized leaders at the 1963 March on Washington. Like Hedgeman, she was
one of the few voices willing to critique the landmark event. Her essay entitled
"The Negro Woman in the Quest for Equality" was delivered as an address
to an NCNW leadership conference in November 1963 and published in *The
ACORN*, the newsletter for Lambda Kappa Mu sorority, a national organization for African American business and professional women; thus it reached a
large audience of black women. In the piece, she argued that women in the civil
rights movement had not been treated as partners but that they were relegated
to "secondary, ornamental or 'honoree' role[s]." She was forceful and blunt in
describing how she and other African American women felt. It was "bitterly
humiliating," she remarked poignantly, "for Negro women on August 28 to see
themselves accorded little more than token recognition in the historic March
on Washington." She highlighted women's exclusion from the speakers' list and
the delegation that went to the White House to meet with President Kennedy.
Murray reminded her audiences that the men had been told of the women's
desire to participate and the importance of recognizing their contributions, but
the women were ignored. "This omission was deliberate," she contended.[117]
Black women's voices and their contributions to the movement were largely
and intentionally disregarded.

In the same piece, Murray used her analogy of Jim Crow and Jane Crow as a
framework to analyze the hurdles women, especially African American women,
faced in a predominantly white, patriarchal society. She criticized the media for
its complicity in obscuring positive representations of black women's lives, their
aspirations, and their significant contributions to the civil rights movement.[118]

rray wrote and spoke out further, distressed by the unevenness with
n civil rights measures—designed to ameliorate racial inequality—were
ad through a male-gendered lens throughout much of society, including
among black men. She co-authored a groundbreaking legal article with Mary
Eastwood of the Justice Department in which they analyzed ways the U.S.
Constitution should guarantee women equal rights. They stated that there
were "striking parallel[s]" between discriminatory attitudes toward women and
African Americans.[119] Arguing that sex was not "a reasonable basis for legislative classification," they determined that the Fourteenth Amendment's equal
protection clause should protect women from sexual discrimination, especially
in employment.[120]

And a few years later in testimony before Congress, she spoke from her
own social positioning as a self-supporting, single, African American woman
who had graduated with a doctorate in law from Yale University and had subsequently "pursued so many job leads which failed to materialize" that she finally
stopped looking for law school teaching jobs.[121] Murray insisted that she could
not afford to privilege one aspect of her identity over another: "I have observed
the interrelationships between what is often referred to as racism and sexism
and have been unable to avoid the conclusion that discrimination because of
one's sex is just as degrading, dehumanizing, immoral, unjust, indefensible,
infuriating and capable of producing societal turmoil as discrimination because
of one's race."[122] In language much more explicit than Hedgeman's and with
more frequency in policy debates, Murray staked a claim for sexism to be taken
seriously as a problem all women faced in work, in their communities, schools,
health clinics, and in their homes.

She found allies who were determined to fight for women's rights beyond government action. The PCSW stimulated the creation of state-level
commissions on the status of women. These met annually to address issues
related to women and to assess the progress made on advancing the goals of
the original PCSW. During the third annual meeting, a number of women,
including Murray, turned their dissatisfaction with the weaknesses of the state
commissions into action and formed the National Organization for Women
(NOW). This new feminist organization was dedicated to organizing and directly challenging women's inequality. Anna Arnold Hedgeman and New York
State Assemblywoman Shirley Chisholm (who will be discussed extensively in
chapter 5) were also some of NOW's earliest members, and all three women
assumed leadership positions.[123]

Murray was active in the organization its first year, including serving on NOW's board of directors. But she came to find herself at odds with the majority of the membership over the same divisive issue that had plagued women's activists for nearly fifty years. At the annual meeting in November 1967 more than one hundred members gathered in Washington, D.C., to discuss, among other issues, the ERA. Betty Friedan, NOW's president, proposed that the membership support a resolution calling on Congress to pass the ERA. Murray spoke up immediately, arguing that NOW should instead form a study group to determine if women's rights were effectively covered under the Fifth and Fourteenth Amendments. She was already engaged in a number of legal efforts to test the issue.[124] Additionally, she worried that if NOW took an assertive position on the ERA, it risked losing support from a variety of women's organizations, including the UAW, which supplied the nascent organization with much needed supplies. Murray's proposal was overwhelmingly defeated. When someone else then proposed that the word "equal" in the ERA be replaced by "human" so as to read Human Rights Amendment, Murray supported the change. Pat Trainer, the chair of NOW's Task Force on Image of Women in Mass Media, responded vehemently, stating, "I must resign from NOW if *human* rights is a substitute for *equal* rights."[125] When the vast majority of the meeting members voted in favor of Friedan's initial resolution to push Congress on the ERA, Murray likely felt herself in increasingly unfriendly company. She resigned from the board by the year's end, aware that the needs of poor women, especially black women, were not given the same attention as the needs of middle-class white women, and she remained at odds with most members over the ERA.[126]

As a clear indication of how far her frustration with sexism had carried her and at the same time how quickly the critiques that feminists were leveling became part of the mainstream, Hedgeman not only joined NOW shortly after it was founded, but she was appointed to its Board of Directors.[127] Hedgeman stayed with NOW for nearly two years, but like Murray she came to question its priorities, strategies, and vision. Critical of liberal feminism's driving concern to attain for women full, individual rights equal to men's, Hedgeman remarked that women "have accepted that pattern which men have developed, and tried to get into it." Even as she was committed to working through it, Hedgeman maintained a healthy skepticism about the political system in the United States, and did not feel that the changes NOW pursued were enough to bring about a more just world. She preferred a broader human rights agenda, "a liberation program which should be thought of in terms of both men and women," and envisioned a system free of the gendered and racialized power dynamics that shaped the current economic and political systems. But with NOW, she worried aloud that "we've set up a whole new competition."[128]

Over the course of her public life Hedgeman had worked in single-sex, mixed-sex, majority-black, and interracial organizations. In her opinion, NOW's exclusive focus on women precluded the possibility of building meaningful and necessary coalitions, and so in 1968 she resigned from the board.[129] From her years of experience with the NCNW, the YWCA, and from working on the inside of city government as a lobbyist, and running three times as a candidate, Hedgeman had developed a strong feminist consciousness, but she actively— even insistently—denied the label. Her criticism was sharp, but she spoke from her deepest convictions that NOW's approach failed to address the very real needs of poor women, women of color, and other marginalized people. From her perspective, feminism as praxis was left wanting, and so she not only left NOW but also did not join any other feminist organizations. Declaring early on and throughout the 1960s, "I'm not a feminist, but I'm for women," Hedgeman offered a competing way to articulate her genuine resentment of patriarchy at the same time that she indicated her distrust of a movement and a label that she found too narrowly focused.

Conclusion

The advent of the 1960s ushered in not just an energetic young president but also new opportunities for African American women to weigh in on the most important domestic debates of the decade for the first time from *within* the halls of government, which was led by increasingly sympathetic Democrats, as well as from their more familiar position outside it. These openings emerged primarily because of the efforts black women put into organizations like the NCNW, the Deltas, and the NAACP over decades, as well as their activism in Democratic Party politics and civil rights activism, especially in New York City, where many of them had learned their political and leadership skills. Struggles for racial justice remained paramount, but the same women who fought for racial equality became increasingly aware of the lack of women's equality. As members of society positioned at the nexus of race and sex, a handful of African American women, many of whom had spent years in New York City contributing to its social, political, and economic transformations, especially with regard to race relations, began to speak out about the need to address not just each of these forms of injustice but also the heavy burden of living at their intersection.

The first occasion to address women's rights or, more cautiously, "women's status," was the President's Commission on the Status of Women. Created at a time when consensus liberalism dominated the political dialogue, the commission was nevertheless perched on the horizon of change. A small number of influential African American women participated in various dimensions of the commission's work, yet for black women the PCSW was less useful for what it ultimately told the nation about the distinct challenges they faced in society, which was very little, than for the networks it facilitated. The coalitions that Dorothy Height formed from her PCSW connections—WIC, and Wednesdays in Mississippi—provided critical support to civil rights activists as well as countless poor black women in the South. Jeanne Noble, another PCSW participant, chose WICS, the successor organization to WIC, as the Women's Job Corps' mechanism with which to respond to the economic crisis facing poor women. The women whom Pauli Murray had worked with on the PCSW's Committee on Civil and Political Rights became friends and comrades-in-arms in the debate over the "sex" amendment in the civil rights bill, in the founding of NOW, and in legal efforts to secure women's rights. Well positioned from their years of experience, especially in New York City, they contributed substantively to national-level policy decisions and social movement activism in the 1960s that affected the lives of millions of African Americans, women, and the poor. They also assumed leadership roles, but they still had to contend with deep levels of racialized gender discrimination.

The often blatant disregard for African American women's contributions to the struggle for racial equality led Hedgeman and Murray to publically express their anger, and it is significant that they did so by availing themselves of the feminist rhetoric and ideas that were gaining currency in the wake of the PCSW and the publication of *The Feminine Mystique*. A mere five years later, it was difficult for women in public life to avoid taking a position on feminism. Disinclined to assess her achievements through a gendered or a feminist lens, for example, Constance Baker Motley nevertheless absorbed enough of the feminist ethos that was circulating through mainstream America to appreciate that the women's movement had the power to transform society. Still, feminism's close association with white female activists was too uncomfortable for some of these women to claim it even as their various articulations of a more just society assumed women's equal and equally valued position, which were very much feminist ideals.

Regardless of their relationship to the feminist label, Murray and Hedgeman believed in women's equality and they worked for it directly. They both served on NOW's board of directors its first year, indicating their commitment to working across racial divides on behalf of all women. NOW, however, began to tilt its energies toward the ERA and women's reproductive rights. The specific and immediate challenges that poor women and women of color had to contend with went largely ignored. As a result, both women left the board. Scholars have written extensively about the ways middle-class white feminists minimized or ignored many of the concerns black women had.[130] While many of NOW's members were personally concerned about racism and class-based inequality, there is no denying that the organization committed tremendous energy to the fight for the ERA and for abortion rights. Neither of these issues had been priorities for black women, and so it became increasingly difficult for Murray or Hedgeman to see themselves or their needs represented in NOW as well as some of the prominent feminist organizations. As the decade wore on, however, one African American woman in particular emerged not only to claim the mantle of feminism, but also to use her new, historic position in Congress to fight for the ERA, abortion rights, and a number of issues that were important to women across the class spectrum and the racial divide, such as childcare and minimum wages for domestic workers. Shirley Chisholm, the first black woman elected to Congress in 1968, would spend the remainder of her political career trying to transform not only feminism to be inclusive of all women's needs, but also party politics, especially Democratic Party politics, to be the platform to fight for women, African Americans, the aged, young people, veterans, draft resisters, and the poor. Hers is the story to which we now turn.

CHAPTER FIVE

On the Shirley Chisholm Trail
in the 1960s and 1970s

When the Ninety-first Congress convened in January 1969, the Democratic caucus gathered to approve the committee assignments for the new session. Shirley Chisholm of Brooklyn, the first black woman elected to the House of Representatives, found her committee assignment unacceptable, and she stood up to protest.

> Every time I rose, two or three men jumped up. . . . Men were smiling and nudging each other as I stood there trying to get the floor. After six or seven attempts, I walked down an aisle to the "well," the open space between the front row of seats and the Speaker's dais, and stood there. I was half afraid and half enjoying the situation.
>
> "For what purpose is the gentlewoman from New York standing in the well?" Wilbur Mills, chair of the Ways and Means Committee asked.
>
> "I'd been trying to get recognized for half an hour, Mr. Chairman, but evidently you were unable to see me, so I came down to the well. I would just like to tell the caucus why I vehemently reject my committee assignment."[1]

Chisholm had clear grounds for complaint. She represented the Bedford-Stuyvesant section of Brooklyn, one of the poorest urban communities in the nation. Her assignment on the Rural Development and Forestry subcommittee of the Agricultural Committee seemed thoroughly inappropriate. She remarked, "I think it would be hard to imagine an assignment that is less relevant to my background or to the needs of the predominantly Black and Puerto Rican people who elected me, many of whom are unemployed, hungry and badly housed."[2] After her protest, Chisholm was reassigned to the Veterans Affairs Committee.[3]

Chisholm later wrote that several members in the chamber spoke to her sympathetically afterward, but they implied that she had made a huge mistake. One went so far as to say that she had committed political suicide. Her constituents, however, did not think so. Word of her action on the Hill made it back to New York in no time, and the local audience loved it. A headline in the *Amsterdam News* read, "Shirley Is a 5-Alarm." The article portrayed Chisholm as a political renegade and an independent fighter. Conveying her sense of urgency and loyalty to her constituents, the new legislator asserted, "I am a woman of action, in action. . . . I know the independence I exhibit is not acceptable to the professional politicians, but is perfectly acceptable to the people of the community who elected me."[4] She simultaneously explained why she would likely be an ineffective legislator, and won the hearts of the people for it.

Introduction

Shirley Chisholm's political career, from her grassroots activism in Brooklyn to her election to the House of Representatives and her 1972 campaign for the United States presidency, is part of a longer history of African American women in New York City politics. Before the turn of the century Victoria Earle Matthews, Irene Moorman, and Lyda Newman commenced the struggle for women's suffrage, contending with racism from white suffragists and gendered hostilities from society more generally. With the vote in hand, women like Layle Lane, Sara Speaks, Ada B. Jackson, and Anna Hedgeman reached higher and strived to represent people who hitherto had little or no voice in Congress. Their goal was finally achieved when Chisholm was elected to the House of Representatives in 1968. Her victory was also a crucial step in the process of breaking down barriers that kept black women from powerful positions within the federal government. Starting in 1961 with the President's Commission on the Status of Women, Dorothy Height, Jeanne Noble, and Pauli Murray were brought into national policy discussions about women, race, rights, work, and poverty. Then in 1966, President Johnson appointed Constance Baker Motley to the federal bench. By the mid-1960s the Democratic Party had come to consider African American women at least symbolically important participants in the administrative and judicial dimensions of the state. With Chisholm's election, a black woman finally held a seat in the national legislature as well.

Shirley Chisholm carefully navigated the inhospitable political terrain to victory, contending at each step in the process with racial and gender discrimination deeply embedded in the culture. How did she win when others before her had lost? Her political career and professional ambitions clearly benefited from the changes that the civil rights movement, the women's movements, and the eight years of Democratic Party dominance had yielded. Yet her success at the polls was the result of far more than a timely campaign. She won because of a combination of factors, including her ideas about equality and justice; her political skills and strong personality; the consistent support she received from black women in her district; the tireless activism of two generations of politically inclined women who came before her; and the support of the Democratic Party.

As much as Chisholm's election was the conclusion of black women's long struggle to attain a voice through the electoral process, it was also the beginning of a new chapter in political history. When Congress convened, for the first time there was a black woman sitting among its 435 members. Chisholm held strong opinions about the ongoing struggles for racial justice, causes of poverty, and women's rights, and she wanted not only to weigh in on them in national debates, but she wanted also to craft policies to address them. Theoretically, she was in a position to do so now, but could she succeed as a lone black woman in this unfamiliar chamber of power? Additionally, 1968, the year Chisholm was first elected to Congress, saw the largest number of America's young men sent off to war in Southeast Asia. Chisholm had strong feelings about that as well, and she was not inclined to keep her thoughts to herself. But could she help bring an end to the war in Vietnam that was devastating growing numbers of American families and siphoning desperately needed funds from the War on Poverty? Her political career in Congress helps shed light on some of these important questions.

As with a number of other nationally prominent black women, Chisholm learned her political skills and sharpened her ideas about the state in New York City's formal and informal political arenas. She became a vocal advocate for an activist government to redress economic, social, and political injustices and frequently used her national prominence to bring attention to racial, sexual, and class-based inequality. Like Height, Murray, Noble, and Hedgeman, she maintained a commitment to the promise of the political system, even though an increasing number of African American female activists all but abandoned hope in the liberal establishment and pursued increasingly radical means to bring about a different world.[5] But Chisholm was hardly naïve and understood why so many young people were drawn to the Black Power movement and its critique of the United States. And she was unafraid to say so.

Once Chisholm gained access to the nation's most influential chambers, she struggled to navigate around entrenched power dynamics that made it hard to effect change. The preexisting structures of government, especially the committee system with its privileging of seniority and the informal networks that had been cultivated over the years in elite environments like private schools, country clubs, and corporate boardrooms, made it difficult for most newcomers to make headway. It was even more complicated for Chisholm, who as a black woman had to contend with racism and sexism and the force of their intersectional dynamics. Not only that, Chisholm won her seat in Congress the same year the Democratic Party lost its grip on the presidency. The New Deal coalition was dealt a powerful blow in 1968 with Richard Nixon's election, but it was only in the ensuing years that the full implications of the national political realignment became clear. Chisholm was unapologetically liberal, but she arrived in Congress at the moment when an increasing number of white working-class and middle-class Americans abandoned the Democratic Party and rebuked her progressive vision of government. With few powerful allies to help usher her bills through committee or a vote, she remained a historic symbol and inspiration, but could she be an effective legislator?

Chisholm was far more willing to call herself a feminist and to align with the predominantly white feminist movement than other African American women. Her ideas and values, her political ambition, and the spirit of the times worked together to enhance her openness to claiming the feminist mantle. In arguing for women's rights, Chisholm forced the New York State Assembly and then Congress to contend with sexual discrimination in ways that they had not done before. At the same time, she pushed members of the predominantly white, middle-class feminist establishment to address their weaknesses in thinking about the needs of women of color. Although she is rarely integrated into histories of the "second wave," she deserves to be.

Finally, Chisholm's political life offers a valuable perspective on the changes that had transpired within the Democratic Party by the late 1960s. Her election marked the culmination of a process that began in the late 1910s, when African Americans in New York City migrated to the Democratic Party well ahead of the 1936 national realignment. That shift yielded some patronage jobs and eventually campaign support for black men, but black women had to work much harder to get the male-dominated world of party politics to take them seriously as political operatives and candidates. As late as 1964, Chisholm was only the third African American woman elected to the New York state legislature; in 1968 she was the first elected to the U.S. Congress. The Democratic Party clearly felt no urgency to support African American women as candidates. Black women, however, did not wait to be invited. Once they realized that the Republican Party had reneged on its promises to African Americans, they began their long struggle to gain positions in the Democratic Party. Often one of the hardest steps was getting male party leaders to take them seriously. But as a handful of other black women before her had done, Chisholm defied the odds and proved her mettle as a candidate. As she advanced from state office to a national forum, she endeavored to expand the Democrats' agenda to secure rights and benefits for women, workers, the poor, the elderly, children, and African Americans. Her vision of government pushed beyond the edges of liberalism, but could her contributions represent a meaningful shift in the party's priorities, or would they mark its boundaries in a rapidly changing political environment? Time would soon tell.

Early Influences

Shirley Anita St. Hill was born in Brooklyn, New York, in November 1924. She was the first of four daughters born to Ruby Seale and Charles St. Hill, who immigrated from the Caribbean in the early 1920s. Early in her life, economic challenges compelled Chisholm's parents to send the girls to live with their maternal grandmother in Barbados. Six years later, in March 1934, Shirley and her sisters returned to the now unfamiliar streets of Brooklyn. It was the middle of the Depression, and Chisholm's mother, a seamstress by trade, accepted domestic work to keep the family afloat. Charles St. Hill, a member of the Confectionery and Bakers International Union, struggled to maintain steady work. He moved from a bakery to a factory and then became a janitor. His employment struggles did not dampen his political passion, however. He and friends spent many a night in the family's kitchen discussing their inspiration, Marcus Garvey, while the young St. Hill girls laid in bed listening. Chisholm asserted years later that her father had "instilled a pride in ourselves and our race."[6]

Chisholm's parents imposed strict rules on studying and religious practice. A strong student, Chisholm graduated from the prestigious Girls High School in Brooklyn in 1942 and was offered scholarships to two highly selective colleges, Oberlin and Vassar. Prohibitive boarding expenses kept the future politician much closer to home, however; she enrolled in Brooklyn College in the fall of 1942. On campus, Chisholm joined a number of organizations. As a member of the Harriet Tubman Society, she and the others fought for a course on "Negro history" and circulated petitions demanding an end to poll taxes for voting. In response to the exclusion of black students from a number of social clubs, Chisholm started Ipothia (In Pursuit of the Highest in All) as a black women's student organization.[7] She also honed her public-speaking skills in the Debate Society. These organizations and the generally progressive atmosphere of Brooklyn College all contributed to her growing racial and political consciousness. Reflecting back years later, Chisholm acknowledged that with a deepening understanding of the nature of racial discrimination, "in college I became angry."[8]

Despite graduating *cum laude* from Brooklyn College in 1946, Chisholm knew that she, like most college-educated African American women, had few professional options. Gender discrimination and racism as independent forces were difficult enough to overcome in the 1940s and 1950s, but to be the target of their combined dynamic meant even more difficulties for black women. After initial difficulties finding work in part because of her slight size and young appearance, Chisholm began her career in early childhood education.[9] Over the next two decades, she advanced from a teacher's aide at Mt. Calvary Child Care Center in Harlem to a consultant for the New York City Division of Day Care, overseeing ten daycare centers.[10]

Her personal life progressed during these years as well. While pursuing a graduate degree at Columbia University, the young teacher met Conrad Chisholm, a Jamaican immigrant. Conrad did not share his future wife's political passion, but by Shirley's own account, he did all he could to support her. Conrad worked as a private investigator and later for the city government. He also accepted the reality that the couple would not have children. Neither spoke publicly about the issue. It is unclear whether health issues or Shirley Chisholm's political aspirations ultimately kept the couple childless.[11]

In 1953, a friend introduced Chisholm to Wesley "Mac" Holder who at the time was organizing local activists to fight for the election of a black judge in Brooklyn. Chisholm joined Holder's group and campaigned for Louis Flagg Jr.'s election (see chapter 3 for details). Despite fierce resistance from the regular Democratic political club, the group scored a considerable victory. For the first time in history, an African American would serve as a judge in Brooklyn.[12] In the aftermath of the campaign, Chisholm worked with Holder to convert the election committee into the Bedford-Stuyvesant Political League (BSPL) and proudly asserted, "We were rebels."[13] Like the grassroots organizations led by

Ada Jackson and Maude Richardson a decade earlier, the BSPL brought together local residents who were fed up with political neglect. They fought for better housing, jobs, and community improvement.

Yet Chisholm's rhetorical bravado about being a rebel was not fully matched by her actions. Even as she helped orchestrate the Flagg victory with the insurgents, she attended meetings of the Seventeenth Assembly District club, the traditional Democratic organization. Although Bedford-Stuyvesant was a predominantly African American district, the leadership of the club remained all white and all male.[14] The machine "bosses" had not only resisted addressing systemic racism, they had actively contributed to it. Chisholm remarked on the segregation in the club—black people sat on one side of the room, white people on the other, all waiting to be called on by the club's leadership who sat on the dais up front. African Americans did not feel empowered by the club, she insisted, "They went because they needed help."[15] Despite these oppressive circumstances Chisholm, a political pragmatist, tried to work for change through the club leaders.

Initially, she was assigned to do fundraising, a task typically relegated to women.[16] But she spoke out at weekly meetings, questioning Vincent Carney, the district leader, and others about trash on the streets and unfulfilled promises. She pressed them for more resources for the district. Rather than responding to her demands, she contended that the leadership tried to keep her quiet by making her part of the "in group." They elected her to the board of directors—a position she had not pursued. "The trouble was," Chisholm asserted, "I didn't behave."[17] She continued to harass speakers about community problems. Shortly afterward she got a letter thanking her for her service, which let her know that she was no longer on the board. As Chisholm described it, "I had my own early education in politics, in the toughest and most instructive school possible, New York City's old-time clubhouses."[18] The hybrid political education served her well. She was a strategic politician-in-the-making, and she seized the resources available to advance her professional goals even as she fought for community betterment.

In 1958, Chisholm and Holder had a falling out over the leadership of the BSLP, and Chisholm left the organization, but her absence from grassroots politics did not last long. In 1960, Thomas R. Jones, a veteran progressive activist and a former member of the "Elect Flagg" committee, decided to take on the entrenched political machine. His first step was to create a new community-based organization, the Unity Democratic Club (UDC), which Chisholm promptly joined. After two years of concerted community organizing and political educating, the Bedford-Stuyvesant insurgents took over the district and drove the old-guard Democrats out. Not only did Jones win the state assembly seat in the fall of 1962, but he won the coveted district leadership position as well. The old white male leadership sustained a critical blow from which it would not recover. For only the second time, African Americans in Brooklyn had a black man representing their interests in Albany. But what about a black woman? Twenty years earlier Bedford-Stuyvesant had come within a hundred votes of electing Maude Richardson to the state assembly, but still no African American woman had ever won. In 1964 Chisholm was ready to write a new chapter in Brooklyn history.

Breaking Through the Walls of Resistance— Chisholm's First Campaign for Office

"From the time I was two my mother said I was born to lead," Chisholm boldly asserted in an interview.[19] When Tom Jones gave up his assembly seat for a judicial appointment, she was ready to embrace her destiny. As with politically ambitious African American women in the past, Chisholm encountered gendered resistance. The UDC threw up her first hurdle; the club was reluctant to run a woman. She held her ground, believing herself the rightful heir to Jones's seat. Constituents hostile to a female candidate were similarly frustrating for Chisholm. One man sarcastically inquired whether she had fixed her husband's breakfast before campaigning. She ignored the reproach and replied by highlighting her long history of community activism.[20] She felt she had earned the right to govern and said as much to hecklers.

Although some people inside and outside of the political clubhouse questioned her ability to serve in public office because she was a woman, many others in Bedford-Stuyvesant were comfortable with women's public leadership. Black women had a history of spearheading struggles for human rights in Brooklyn. In the immediate postwar period, for example, Ada B. Jackson, Maude Richardson and Pauli Murray had sought political office as part of their efforts to remedy the inequalities in their community. Chisholm followed in their path.[21]

In time, Chisholm realized that being a woman and sensitive to gendered concerns could have its advantages. There were nearly five thousand more women registered to vote in the Seventeenth Assembly District than men.[22] When Bessie Buchanan won her seat in 1954, her district in Harlem had similar demographics, and she had made the most of it. Chisholm targeted her appeals to this underestimated majority by asking them to "elect me to dramatize the problems as black women."[23] Despite her claims that she did not like doing so, Chisholm used her race and sex strategically, turning her two biggest potential liabilities into useful assets.

And women responded, especially a local group called the Key Women of America, of which Chisholm was the Brooklyn branch president. Founded in 1954 by Bertha Nelms Harris, Key Women was a black women's civic organization committed to children, family services, and community needs.[24] It provided poor women in Bedford-Stuyvesant with sewing and speech classes. In addition, during Chisholm's presidency, the Brooklyn branch hosted a garden party for the Home of the Aged for Colored People and volunteered at the Kings County Pediatric Hospital.[25] Reminiscent of black women's clubs of the past that focused on respect and uplift, Key Women nevertheless appreciated the window of opportunity that presented itself for black women to advance in the state, and they helped launch Chisholm's formal political career in 1964.[26] As Constance Rose, one of the organization's officers, explained during an interview, "We all got out and pitched for her. We went with petitions and everything. We were actually her backbone."[27] Local, politically liberal African American women were essential foot soldiers in Chisholm's campaign.

Equally important, the Unity Democratic Club came around to supporting Chisholm in her bid for the state assembly seat, despite its initial hesitation. With the backing of black women and the now-dominant political club, she won the June 1964 Democratic primary, beating her opponent, Harold Brady, by a significant margin.[28] With the same grassroots activists working feverishly for her in the general election, Chisholm took a giant step forward in her political career on Election Day in 1964. Garnering more than eighteen thousand votes, she won a decisive victory against her opponents, Charles Lewis, the Republican Party candidate who had fewer than nineteen hundred votes, and Simon Golar, the Liberal Party candidate who finished a distant third with under one thousand votes.[29] Chisholm's noteworthy victory was part of the larger forces of change that were registered across New York in 1964. Chisholm joined seven other African American legislators in Albany, the largest number of black leaders to head to the state capital ever.

Her victory had roots in the long struggles that Bedford-Stuyvesant activists like Jackson, Richardson, and Murray had waged. It also benefited from the nationally changing climate on civil rights and Democratic liberalism, and from local supporters who knew her commitment to racial equality and economic justice. Not only that, Chisholm's explicit appeal to black women, a strategy Buchanan had used with success ten years earlier in Harlem, worked now in

Brooklyn. And finally, Chisholm secured the Democratic Party's backing. The party still dominated city politics, which meant that this endorsement was key. The UDC's takeover of the district two years earlier had been critical as had Chisholm's work with the organization. She was a maturing politician who had sharpened her skills during a fifteen-year period in political clubhouses as well as in community groups. She knew how to relate to her constituents and she was not afraid to be in the limelight. Chisholm was ready to take on Albany.

Trying to Legislate for Change— Assemblywoman Shirley Chisholm

During her four years in the New York State Assembly (1965–68), Chisholm made good on her campaign promises to fight for the poor and against racial inequality. She proposed legislation to eliminate racial discrimination in banking, investment, and insurance practices, and to require city police to complete a course on civil rights. She advocated for unemployment insurance for agricultural workers and hospital employees, and she fought for an improved minimum wage law. For the poor, especially constituents like hers in Bedford-Stuyvesant, she advocated more affordable public housing and an education bill for a program called Search for Education, Elevation, and Knowledge (SEEK), which would enable men and women from disadvantaged backgrounds to go to college.[30]

As the national women's rights movement gained momentum and prominence, Chisholm's legislative efforts demonstrated her emerging feminist consciousness. More so than many of the white female leaders, she was particularly attentive to the ways class and race compounded problems for poor women and women of color. She proposed legislation for daycare centers for working women and women on public assistance, unemployment insurance for domestic workers, and seniority protection for teachers who took maternity leave. Chisholm often faced resistance on many of these progressive bills, but the changing national debates on gender issues, race relations, and poverty, including President Johnson's announcement of a War on Poverty, enabled her and others to make slow but identifiable headway in New York. SEEK, her bill to extend support for talented, underserved students, became law. So did the unemployment insurance bill for domestic workers, most of whom were poor women of color. And she prevailed in a third significant piece of legislation that assured that female faculty who took maternity leave would not lose accrued time toward tenure.[31] Although not the only progressive voice in Albany,

Chisholm was integral to the fight to make the state more responsive to the poor, to women generally, and to women of color.

As a lawmaker, Chisholm tried to accomplish two goals that were frequently in tension with each other. She wanted her constituents to see her as an independent people's advocate, but she also wanted to be an effective politician. In order to navigate legislation through the state assembly, Chisholm had to make alliances and likely compromises as well. In her four years as a state assemblywoman, she proved herself an able legislator, much more successful than Bessie Buchanan had been. Buchanan, the first African American woman elected to the New York State Assembly ten years earlier, failed to see any of her progressive legislative goals achieved. Chisholm had clearly learned some valuable lessons about political deal making. But she also worked hard to cultivate a reputation as a political maverick. This was especially evident in her election victories, which, because of a series of reapportionments, happened three times in four years.[32] Whatever compromises she may have made, her constituents enthusiastically supported her. To an *Amsterdam News* reporter Chisholm said, "I really feel that so long as I fight for the people I have nothing to worry about."[33] She remained dedicated to improving Bedford-Stuyvesant through the legislative process. At the same time, she was equally committed to and successful in advancing her own career, although she was careful not to speak about her ambitions in personal terms. There were very few women—and even fewer black women—in politics during the 1960s and they avoided appearing personally motivated for fear of being stereotyped, undermined, or dismissed.[34] Nevertheless, there was no mistaking the fact that Shirley Chisholm was a politician on the rise.

Fighting Shirley Chisholm—Unbought and Unbossed

In 1966 former UDC member Andrew Cooper spearheaded a legal challenge to have Brooklyn's congressional boundaries redrawn. "The black community was broken up into five districts. There was no single black district that could send a Congressman to Washington," Cooper observed.[35] The plaintiffs in the case charged that the way the state had drawn up the congressional districts violated the Constitution and "[imposed] an invidiously discriminatory impairment of the electoral rights of the Negro and Puerto Rican inhabitants of the Bedford-Stuyvesant community."[36] The judge referred the case to a federal panel, and ultimately the court found in favor of the Bedford-Stuyvesant activists.[37]

With a new congressional district mandated by the court, the Committee for a Negro Congressman from Brooklyn (CNCB) convened in December

1967 to begin the process of choosing a candidate.[38] In a clear rebuke to the Democratic Party county establishment, the CNCB stated that they were "resolved to see to it that the white machine bosses no longer called the tune for black people." After interviewing many potential candidates, the organization decided in favor of Shirley Chisholm. Recognizing her work in Albany and her political viability, the CNBC declared, "Mrs. Shirley Chisholm has already established a reputation for political independence," and she had "successfully challenged the machine at the polls."[39] Soon afterward, Mac Holder of the former BSPL contacted Chisholm, and the two patched up their decade-long disagreement. The "Dean" of Brooklyn politics was going to run her campaign. Chisholm's campaign platform, which demonstrated her progressive ideals and represented many familiar and long-held concerns for Bedford-Stuyvesant residents, included federal support for affordable housing and the expansion of childcare services, improved public education, better hospital and nursing home facilities, and the enforcement of antidiscrimination laws. The CNCB leadership enthusiastically endorsed it.[40]

Chisholm, however, did not have universal support from the black community. She had to fend off challenges in the Democratic Party primary from State Senator William Thompson and former secretary of the New York Department of Labor, Dollie Robinson, both of whom were African American. Thompson had the backing of the King's County Democratic Party machine, and Robinson, who had worked with Esther Peterson in the Women's Bureau and participated in the PCSW Consultation on Negro Women's Problems, had strong support from Assemblyman Bertram Baker and from labor organizations.[41] In assessing her opponents, Chisholm was more concerned about Thompson, a standing legislator with party support, than she was about Robinson, a former labor organizer and then bureaucrat. She noted, "Willie Thompson was so sure he would win with the organization behind him that he was up at Cape Cod vacationing" while she was campaigning.[42] The outcome of the June primary proved Thompson's confidence unjustified and Robinson's lack of name recognition a fatal liability. Chisholm maintained her winning streak and, despite the party's support of a rival, became the Democratic contender in the November election.[43]

Chisholm now turned her full attention to James Farmer, the nationally prominent civil rights leader and her sole opponent in the race. Farmer entered the campaign in March on the Liberal Party ticket, which had fielded a number of politically progressive African American candidates in the past, including Pauli Murray, Ella Baker, and James Robinson. Although they lost, a number of other candidates had won on the party's ballot since its origins in New York City in the 1940s. Two months after Farmer launched his campaign, the Republican Party drafted him to run on their slate as well.[44] Despite the party's lack of popularity in the city, Farmer agreed and set about gaining support. As the founder of the Congress of Racial Equality (CORE) and its president from 1961–66, Farmer easily garnered the organization's endorsement yet Chisholm secured a number of key endorsements as well. The *Amsterdam News* had backed black female candidates as early as 1934, when the paper endorsed Edith Hunton Carter, and now it supported Chisholm over Farmer, whom many Brooklynites considered an outsider. Chisholm was also formally backed by a number of labor unions, including the AFL-CIO of New York.[45]

During the fall 1968 campaign, the candidates weighed in on the explosive situation over public school decentralization in the Ocean Hill–Brownsville section of Brooklyn. The battle was over the board of education's creation of an experimental community school board formed in response to African Americans' demand for more and better jobs in the New York City public school system, the largest in the nation, and about greater control over the way schools in their communities were run. From the 1930s and into the 1960s, the teachers union—the United Federation of Teachers—and the school system's teaching staff and administration were disproportionately white and included a significant percentage of Jews. When black parents demanded that black teachers and administrators get hired to teach in predominantly black neighborhoods like in Ocean Hill–Brownsville, white teachers and administrators were fired. The union saw the local board's control over hiring and firing as a threat to its authority, and it fought back with a series of strikes that were ultimately successful in undermining the experiment's goals. In the midst of the conflict and a month before the November election, Chisholm joined the newly formed Emergency Citizens Committee to Save School Decentralization and Community Control.[46] Both she and Farmer not only favored local community control, they came out against the teacher's union president, Albert Shanker.[47]

At the same time, Farmer's campaign strategy centered less on issues and his extensive and impressive civil rights record than on a highly gendered appeal to voters. In the wake of the controversial Moynihan Report, which argued that black families' matriarchal patterns accounted for their high rates of poverty, and the Black Power movement with its extremely masculinist rhetoric, Farmer emphasized the need for a "good strong voice that could be heard across the country."[48] The *Amsterdam News* reported that to bolster his tough male image,

Farmer traveled throughout the campaign with an "eight-man Afro group with bongo drums."[49] His attempt to woo voters by highlighting his masculinity was unmistakable.

But Holder, Chisholm's campaign manager, was unconcerned. He saw her local position as an assemblywoman, her party affiliation, and *her* gender as significant strengths that could readily counter Farmer's emphasis on masculinity. Chisholm was also upbeat about her chances in the general election. She had the backing of the UDC and the Citizens' Committee, and she was the Democratic candidate in a city dominated by her party. Her state assembly district was right in the center of the new congressional district, and she had the strong support of black women. Annie Bowen of Bedford-Stuyvesant chaired the Shirley Chisholm for Congress Committee, which worked tirelessly for her victory.[50] When Chisholm reflected on Farmer's campaign, she observed, "It was not my original strategy to organize womanpower to elect me.... But when someone tries to use my sex against me I delight in being able to turn the tables on him."[51] In an interview with the *New York Times* she argued, "We have to help black men, but not at the expense of our own personalities as women. The black man has to step forward but that doesn't mean the black woman has to step back."[52] Chisholm's feminist sensibilities were clearly growing, and she counted on women's groups and female voters to assist her.

The local press focused on the gendered stereotypes that both candidates were exploiting. In their reports on a series of debates between Chisholm and Farmer, journalists never failed to mention Chisholm's size. The *Amsterdam News* called her a "tiny yet torrid lawmaker" and the *New York Times* mentioned that she "looked slight at 96 pounds."[53] But because her political persona dramatically contradicted her physical stature, they felt the need to highlight both; it was clear that they considered her strong personality the oddity. That she was a woman who weighed less than one hundred pounds was often contrasted to her hard-hitting, "fiery" style. Chisholm cultivated the image of an independent, tough, streetwise fighter, committed only to her community. Her famous slogan, "Fighting Shirley Chisholm—Unbought and Unbossed," captured the spirit she wanted to project. She insisted that she had no political ambition. But even before she stepped foot in the House of Representatives, Chisholm had gained a substantial amount of political experience and indeed had become a savvy politician.

Farmer was unable to overcome the considerable forces working against him. He ran on the Republican-Liberal ticket against a popular, Democratic native of Brooklyn with four years in the state assembly and twenty years of community-based experience. Chisholm beat Farmer by a margin of more than two to one.[54] Local loyalty, gender, race, and her Democratic Party affiliation all worked together to yield a momentous outcome. Shirley Chisholm made history thirty-five years after Layle Lane had first run for Congress, and she was on her way to Washington.

Life in Congress

Chisholm's victory was unprecedented, but what would it mean for the poor people in her district, for black women, and for African Americans and women generally? Would it be an opportunity for lasting change, or would it prove as frustrating and limiting for Chisholm as Jeanne Noble found her work on the Women's Job Corps? Was it to be a victory of substance or primarily of symbolism?

Chisholm fought for fourteen years for it to be a victory of substance, but she also understood the power of symbols, and there was no denying that her election represented a historic milestone for African American women in politics. Even as she began her struggle over resources on the floor of Congress, the bold New Yorker seized the momentum of her election to capitalize on and define its meaning. Unlike any of her African American female predecessors in politics, Chisholm was a master at using the press to make bold statements and to strengthen her image. She recognized that new members of Congress were expected to wait their turns and hold their tongues in deference to their senior colleagues. "But," she told the *New York Times*, "I have no intention of being quiet."[55] The press responded enthusiastically. As Susan Brownmiller noted in her feature article on Chisholm, "She is good copy for political reports across the United States, for European journalists, members of the Negro press, the women's pages, the college press, and Washington's regular Capitol Hill corps, and TV and radio."[56] Chisholm encouraged journalists' lenses to settle upon her. With an unprecedented audience, she set the mood for her national political career and intentionally crafted a way for her constituents and the rest of the nation to think about her.

The Brooklyn lawmaker was more than capable of garnering favorable attention, but her greater challenge was to convert that public support into political power in the U.S. Congress. While Chisholm had run a successful race, she faced an uphill struggle in securing the progressive legislation she advocated, particularly given the changing national political climate following Richard Nixon's election to the presidency in 1968. Without well-placed senior legislators who would support her legislative agenda, and with only very small cohorts of white women and African American men in Congress, Chisholm anticipated that the congressional arena would be a very difficult one in which to effect change.[57] But that did not keep her from trying.

In her first few months in Congress, the contours of Chisholm's political agenda emerged. Her legislative program exhibited a political vision that went beyond most of her liberal colleagues. An articulate and passionate speaker, Chisholm was unafraid to advocate the primacy of federal authority over state governments in policy making and spending. Putting the needs of African Americans, women, and the poor at the center of her legislative program, she accused the middle-class liberals who designed the War on Poverty of not understanding the realities of poverty and discrimination.[58] Not only that, she challenged what she considered to be the intransigence in the political structure and argued that the two-party system was outdated. Coalitions of the disempowered, she argued, should replace the current structure.[59]

Further, she co-sponsored bills on domestic policy that proposed increased federal support for workers' rights to unionize, the elimination of all forms of discrimination, government-guaranteed full-employment programs, educational opportunities for those who needed it, health insurance for domestic workers, increased federal funds for housing, reformed welfare laws that substantively supported poor women without punishment or judgment, the passage of the Equal Rights Amendment, and the repeal of laws that made abortion illegal. And she was equally clear about her foreign policy agenda, which called for the immediate cessation of the war in Vietnam, the abolition of the draft, amnesty for draft resisters, and a dramatic curtailment of federal spending on the military.[60] Her vision was bold and activist. Her capacity to shepherd it through Congress was proving to be another matter altogether. A few key examples demonstrate her political vision, her legislative strategy, and ultimately the limits she faced.

In March 1969, the Brooklyn congresswoman questioned her colleagues about their spending priorities. In a markedly gendered appeal, Chisholm addressed her colleagues in the House as "a teacher and a woman." She attacked the Nixon administration and Congress for spending huge amounts of money on "unnecessary and impractical weapons" when children in the nation's capital "get nothing." She challenged both the ideological basis and unbalanced outcomes of America's domestic and foreign policies. "Unless we . . . defeat the enemies of poverty and racism in our own country and make our talk of equality and opportunity ring true, we are exposed as hypocrites in the eyes of the world when we talk about making other people free," Chisholm charged. Arguing against the continuation of the Vietnam War, she promised to vote "No" on every bill that funded the Department of Defense until "the monstrous waste and shocking profits in the defense budget have been eliminated."[61] Chisholm courageously but unsuccessfully fought to get Congress to redirect money away from the war in Southeast Asia and back to the war on poverty.

Chisholm also used her unique position as the only black woman in Congress to address two issues of particular importance to the intensifying women's movement. In a speech to the House of Representatives in May 1969, she spoke of the need for an Equal Rights Amendment (ERA). At the time few black women publicly supported the possibility of improving women's lives through an organized women's movement. Early on, Anna Hedgeman, Pauli Murray, and Flo Kennedy worked with the National Organization of Women (NOW) but left it in frustration over its narrow agenda. Chisholm briefly served as vice president of NOW's New York City chapter, but it was Aileen Clarke Hernandez, a union organizer and civil rights activist, who was most identified with the predominantly white-led women's organization by 1970. She served as NOW's second president.[62] When NOW picked up the forty-year fight for the ERA that the National Woman's Party had been waging, Chisholm brought the issue of women's equality right to the floor of Congress.[63] She addressed the members of the House on the system of prejudice that kept women in subordinated positions: "As a black person, I am no stranger to race prejudice. But the truth is that in the political world I have been far oftener discriminated against because I am a woman than because I am black . . . Prejudice against women is still acceptable. There is very little understanding yet of the immorality involved in double pay scales and the classification of most of the better jobs 'for men only.'"[64]

As debate about the ERA ensued in the early 1970s, Chisholm argued that laws designed to protect women's health actually intended to deny them good pay, promotions, and positions of power. She raised a compelling point that had also been offered by women during the 1964 debate over the "sex" amendment in the Title VII debate. "Women have been protected from working as waitresses at night when the tips are large," she argued, "but they have never been protected from working as charwomen, scrubbing floors all night long."[65] Conducting her battle as a congressional insider, she exposed one of the weaknesses of protective labor laws. Contrary to nationally prominent liberal African American women like Dorothy Height, Jeanne Noble, and Pauli Murray, and radical African American women like Angela Davis, Kathleen Cleaver, and Frances Beal, Chisholm had clearly cast her lot with the mainstream feminist organization on this issue, trusting or perhaps hoping that her bold support of the ERA would not cost her much local support.

At the same time, Chisholm took on an even more controversial issue, abortion rights. Many men in the Black Power movement were adamantly against birth control and abortion, seeing it as a tool of white America to control or eliminate the African American population.[66] Alternatively, the Brooklyn congresswoman became the honorary president of the National Association for the Repeal of Abortion Laws (NARAL) in 1969.[67] She saw the organization's creation as "a turning point in the struggle against this country's cruel, inhuman and archaic abortion laws." She argued a feminist position that "every woman must be guaranteed—as her inalienable right—the freedom to choose whether or not she will bear children."[68] Because of her distinctive status as the lone black woman in Congress, Chisholm's outspoken stance, particularly on such a contentious issue, drew a great deal of attention. Major print and television media covered a press conference she gave in September 1969. At the event Chisholm explained, "NARAL's moral responsibility is to get women the finest medical consultation on abortion by licensed physicians at a moderate price. We consider it a national disgrace that these referral services have been forced to operate in a twilight zone."[69] She acknowledged that her public support of abortion touched off a heavy flow of mail to her Washington office. To her surprise, the responses were overwhelmingly favorable. Also in favor of it were radical black women like Frances Beal, Patricia Robinson, and Nina Harding who, although they shared concerns that birth control could be a tool for the state to control the black population, appreciated even more that it was a means for women to control their own lives.[70]

In addition to heading NARAL, in December 1969 Chisholm proposed abortion legislation in Congress. "Compulsory pregnancy costs money," she argued. Chisholm substantiated her point by providing her colleagues with the number of so-called illegitimate children on Aid to Families with Dependent Children (AFDC) rolls.[71] A tactical politician, Chisholm knew her audience and played to its interests. An economic justification at the expense of an unpopular program, albeit one she supported, was the approach she chose with her overwhelmingly white male audience. She also urged the New York legislature to repeal its abortion laws, asserting, "There is no reason at all for the State to enter into this medical decision-making process."[72] There were limits to the government's authority, in her opinion, and women's bodies were outside of them. Abortion legislation made little headway in Congress despite her impassioned speech, but in 1973 the issue was decided by the U.S. Supreme Court in *Roe v. Wade*.

Chisholm did not just advocate for women's issues that were most associated with the liberal feminist movement, namely, the ERA and abortion rights. She fought for issues that poor women, including those in the National Welfare Rights Organization (NWRO), had recently raised through a series of protests and dramatic actions in cities across the nation from Las Vegas to Philadelphia to New York. These included increased welfare support, access for poor children to better schools, housing, universal daycare, and a minimum wage for domestic workers.[73] For example, in 1970 when President Nixon attempted to turn the management of the Manpower Training program over to the states, Chisholm responded aggressively, noting, "Manpower programs came into existence [because] state employment agencies were not doing their jobs." Not only did the liberal Democrats' efforts save the program, but Chisholm even tried to expand it by proposing daycare centers so that mothers could work more easily.[74] Additionally, in April 1971 Chisholm was one of twenty members of the House to co-sponsor the Adequate Income Act. The plan, which the NWRO supported, was designed to benefit low-income families until their income reached $11,000 per year.[75] Chisholm testified at the committee hearings, but she also urged her colleagues to hear from poor women themselves, arguing that it was vitally important to "secure testimony from many of those whose lives will be affected." She went further, addressing the ways racialized gender discrimination limited black women's access to good jobs and living wages, noting pointedly, "Black families and black women especially are being crushed by this economic vice."[76]

Chisholm's commitment to working mothers went beyond the Manpower Act and the needs of poor and working-class women. In 1971, she and fellow New York Representative Bella Abzug collaborated on a comprehensive child development program. They fought for twenty-four-hour childcare centers, a proposal that incorporated the night shifts that many women had to work. While her proposed legislation was vital for working-class mothers, she also argued that all women, regardless of class distinctions, deserved to make their employment decisions without concerns about childcare.[77] Although their version was defeated, another version was passed in Congress. It was killed, however, by a Nixon veto.[78]

Domestic workers had specifically benefited from Chisholm's legislative efforts when she was in the New York State Assembly, and she took up their cause again in the House. Joined by D.C. delegate Walter Fauntroy and Assistant Secretary of Labor Esther Peterson, Chisholm addressed a crowd of six hundred women at the First National Conference of Household Workers. Fauntroy proposed an amendment to the Fair Labor Standards Act to benefit domestic workers.[79] Chisholm led the fight in Congress to extend minimum-wage benefits to nearly six million new workers, including domestic workers.[80] It took two years, but victory came in 1974, when the minimum-wage increase was approved.

As she engaged these struggles that often emerged from the intersection of gender, race, and class politics, Chisholm wrote about her political philosophy in her 1970 autobiography, *Unbought and Unbossed*, and in so doing she addressed the ideas and tactics of radical black activists. The Student Non-Violent Coordinating Committee (SNCC), which between 1960 and 1964 had worked assiduously to engage in the liberal political establishment through voter education efforts and the Mississippi Freedom Democratic Party, expelled its white members in 1966 and came to critique the system and the strategy of collaboration most associated with Martin Luther King Jr. Stokely Carmichael, SNCC's new leader, went on to make Black Power the clarion call of a new generation. Huey Newton and Bobby Seale, students at a community college in Oakland, California, formed the Black Panther Party for Self-Defense (BPP) in October of the same year. Focused especially on ending police brutality in black communities, the organization also articulated a radical critique of American society, including its prison system, military practices, politics, and its capitalist economic structure.[81] Declaring herself "a militant" in sympathy with racial militants' critiques of the United States, Chisholm nonetheless defended her decision to engage "the system" in the particular ways she did. She argued that hers was a difference of tactics, not of ideology, when she referenced and cautiously committed to the "ballot" side of Malcolm X's "Ballot or the Bullet" speech.[82] She elaborated on the treacherous position she felt African Americans were in:

> I'm not a fool, brothers and sisters. I'm a pragmatist. What is the sense of shooting, burning, killing? . . . All they have to do is press a button in Washington and every black neighborhood will be surrounded with troops and bayonets. What are you going to do against the massive forces of government? . . . You are 14 or 15 percent of the population, with no real economic or political power. When you get through burning, won't you still have to go to the Man and ask for an apartment? . . . I know I'm here in Congress, part of the Establishment, but . . . I haven't sold out. I'm fighting within the system. There is no other place to fight, if you only understood it. There's no other way for us to survive, because we really don't have anything.[83]

Here was Chisholm's most explicit and comprehensive assessment of the society she was not just living in but the government in which she served. That she could so effectively position herself as an "insider/outsider" speaks not only to Chisholm's skills as a politician but also to the complexity of her political vision, which was at once highly critical of the system but also appreciative of its potential for change.

In expressing her understanding as to why so many young African Americans were turning toward more radical outlets Chisholm was similar to Dorothy Height and Anna Arnold Hedgeman. Height spent decades striving to make the nation live up to its commitments to democracy, freedom, and equality through interracial coalitions. Yet she did so with full awareness and thoughtful consideration of radical critiques of the United States issued by Communists and Black Nationalists. In the 1930s she had been active in the Harlem Youth Council and met frequently with Communists, Socialists, and others who made up the Popular Front. Because of the lessons she learned, Height explained in her autobiography, "I cannot necessarily say that the actions of people who are 'radical' or 'militant' are wrong," even as she acknowledged that she could not be a Communist.[84] She demonstrated that same open-mindedness numerous times, including in 1964 when she met with Malcolm X at a small gathering at Sidney Poitier's home in Westchester, New York, and as she weighed the charges Black Power leaders leveled at the liberal establishment, including white civil rights activists and black integrations.[85] Reflecting back on her decades of activism, years later Height poignantly noted, "We had been treating symptoms rather than causes . . . and a more direct approach was urgently needed."[86] As difficult as this admission may have been, she retained her commitment to integrationist rather than separatist methods such as those pursued by SNCC, CORE, and the Black Panthers.

Hedgeman had also reflected on her political philosophy in her 1964 autobiography, *The Trumpet Sounds*. Fully aware of the economic, social, and political ravages of racism, Hedgeman acknowledged that aspects of Black Nationalism appealed to her. Like Chisholm and Height, she understood black radicals' arguments and their pull. She was "grateful for the thunder of rebels" like James Baldwin and Malcolm X but felt that separatism and armed self-defense would not, in the end, yield the goal African Americans so clearly wanted and deserved—to be full and respected citizens of the nation.[87] She believed in the promise of democracy and the potential for white America to seek racial justice, despite frequent setbacks and disappointments. But Hedgeman also never let go of her understanding of the need for outside pressure groups to raise issues and force them into national discussions.

Not only was she a passionate social critic and outspoken legislator, Chisholm also collaborated with black male leaders and with feminists to form special-interest pressure groups. In 1970, she and the twelve other African Americans in the House of Representatives formed a working group. A year later, it was officially recognized as the Congressional Black Caucus. The group requested that President Nixon meet with them so that they could discuss the needs of "the poor and minorities of the country" and gain commitments for action.[88] After being sidelined for more than a year, the caucus boycotted the president's State of the Union address; only then did they win Nixon's attention.[89] At their meeting, they demanded, among other things, a jobs creation program, an end to the war in Vietnam, an increase in domestic spending, and a boycott of products from South Africa.[90] The thirteen black representatives in Congress, all Democrats, endeavored to bolster their political power by building a national network. Despite their best efforts, however, Nixon rejected many of the recommendations.[91] Nevertheless, the Caucus persisted, continuing to raise concerns about poverty and racial discrimination in Congress.

Chisholm also collaborated with nationally prominent feminists, including Bella Abzug, Betty Friedan, and Gloria Steinem, to found the National Women's Political Caucus (NWPC) in July 1971.[92] The women crafted a platform that had much in common with the Congressional Black Caucus's agenda. Among other elements, the NWPC called for "the immediate end to the war in Vietnam and stressed the elimination of racism, violence and poverty." The *Amsterdam News'* editor, Clarence Jones, "hailed the move" and pledged that his paper would "play a leading role in their movement." "We agree," he said, "with their objectives and are responsive to them." In explaining its purpose, Chisholm stated that the NWPC was not out to compete with men. "However," she noted, "we are no longer going to be the silent majority and watch quietly what is happening to the United States."[93] Chisholm deserves more recognition for her role in the feminist movement than she has received to this point because of the positions she advocated for and because of her prominence in this organization, along with a number of other feminist organizations, including predominantly white women's organizations but also predominantly black women's organizations like the Coalition of 100 Black Women and the National Black Feminist Organization.[94] Her foundational and influential role helps complicate arguments about the movement that reduced it to a narrowly focused group of middle-class white women. Chisholm may have been one of a handful of black women to take such a public role, but she was indisputably one of its leaders.

Because of enduring gendered norms that helped sustain the political sphere as a male domain, women in public life were vulnerable to derision and hostility, and the prominent leaders of the NWPC were no exception. President Nixon and some of his leading department heads belittled the NWPC, and through their actions they gave permission to the nation to continue ignoring women in politics. According to the *New York Times*, Secretary of State William Rogers told Nixon of a newspaper photograph of the four "militant" NWPC leaders, Steinem, Friedan, Abzug, and Chisholm. As documented in the article, when Nixon asked what the picture looked like, Rogers said, "Like a burlesque." And the President responded, "What's wrong with that?"[95] Their tone was hostile, demeaning, and sexist. The women's caucus had its work cut out in such an antagonistic environment. The paper's description of the women as "militant" subtly gave credence to the administration's reaction. Despite the hostilities the new organization faced, Chisholm remained committed to it, appreciating that black women and their concerns needed to be part of this movement.

Moreover, knowing that the impact would be far greater if many others joined the effort, Chisholm encouraged other African American women to embrace the feminist struggle and emphasized the importance of their participation. She gave civil rights activist Fannie Lou Hamer special recognition for her work with the NWPC. "For the first time in a movement such as this we had many Blacks participating. . . . It was a wonderful cross-section of Black, White, and Indian women. . . . And they came from all classes, all colors, and all political persuasions," she explained.[96] Black women's participation was a vital step, but Chisholm pushed further. She was mindful of their double oppression and aired her concerns about racial prejudice that prevailed in the NWPC. Prioritizing the needs of poor women and women of color, Chisholm advised the mostly white, middle-class audience, "Black women want to be part of the women's movement, but we are also part of another movement—the liberation of our own people."[97] She urged them to address poor women's *and men's* wages, childcare, housing, and health issues. She tried to build a coalition between the white women in the mainstream movement and women of color who were tentatively exploring its potential for change. The alliance, she insisted, could be very powerful politically, but she was working against deeply rooted discriminatory forces. Historian Paula Giddings argues that "history had offered little comfort to Black women," when it came to joining forces with white women, and African Americans had grounds to distrust the women's movement.[98] Not only had black suffragists experienced racism fifty years earlier, but as recently as 1964 Congresswoman Margaret Griffiths fought to include "sex" in Title VII of the Civil Rights Act in part because she feared white women would be disadvantaged in comparison to black women. As did Pauli Murray in the prior debate, Chisholm now fought to change that. The challenges she faced in trying to bridge gaps between women created by distinct racialized and also class experiences was difficult in the NWPC. It proved impossible a year later.

On the Chisholm Trail—
The Presidential Campaign of 1972

At the founding meeting of the NWPC in 1971, Betty Friedan suggested, "It is not so impossible that a woman may run for president in 1976—and win!" The *Amsterdam News* decided to poll its readers on the idea of a female president the following week. Reactions were mixed, but a number of respondents supported the idea and proposed that Shirley Chisholm would make a good president. Their comments included: "Congresswoman Shirley Chisholm would make a very capable first woman president" and "I would like to see Shirley Chisholm become president of the United States" and "Shirley Chisholm has proven herself. She would be my choice for lady president."[99] Two weeks later, the congresswoman from Brooklyn floated the idea herself during a press conference. By September, she promised she would "shake up the system" and declare her candidacy if she could raise enough money.[100]

On January 25, 1972, Chisholm turned the prospect into a reality. Standing in front of an enthusiastic crowd of seven hundred at the Concord Baptist Church in Brooklyn, she announced her candidacy for president of the United States. Speaking for the historically disempowered, African Americans, women, Native Americans, and the poor, Chisholm reaffirmed her dedication to those who had been "boxed out of the opportunities to participate equally and enthusiastically in building a strong and just society."[101] She sought to build an even broader base, adding college students, among whom she was popular, and veterans for whom she was a strong advocate. Her campaign platform was consistent with what she had been fighting for in Congress: she advocated for an activist federal government and called for the elimination of poverty, justice for those who suffered discrimination, a greater commitment to the environment, a new housing program, and much more.[102] These issues were evidence of her vision of justice and equality.

In a fashion similar to her Brooklyn campaigns, women across the country responded to Chisholm's entry into the race. Among the numerous local responses, State Representative Gwen Cherry urged Chisholm to come to her hometown in Florida. Members of the Berkeley, California, chapter of NOW exuded enthusiasm and hope as they pounded the pavement fund-raising and campaigning for Chisholm. A woman in New Mexico borrowed $500 to enter

Chisholm's name in her district. Brooklyn women once again organized to raise funds for her campaign.[103] She also inspired black women in the South on her campaign swing through the region. The *Amsterdam News* reported, "In the early dawn as they waited for the buses, . . . or at a poultry plant, the women reached out with pride and wonderment to touch the hand of the fashionably dressed, 95-pound dynamo who symbolized their liberation."[104] Chisholm represented more than the poor urban community she hailed from in New York City. She was now a national symbol of black women's defiance of social, economic, and political norms that had historically sought to relegate them to the bottom tier of society.

There was of course excitement for Chisholm's candidacy beyond that of women. She represented the hope and social justice that many politically disempowered people and radicals had been seeking. The Black Panther Party endorsed her candidacy and called on "every black, poor, and progressive person in the country to help elect her."[105] Although the organization's most radical leaders had been undermined or killed by the FBI's Counter Intelligence Program (COINTELPRO) by this time, the Panthers' endorsement worried a number of moderate supporters who wanted Chisholm to disavow them. But Chisholm stood her ground and accepted their backing, noting, "the Black Panthers are citizens of the United States and they have a right to endorse whomever they decide to endorse."[106] Similarly, two self-described Marxist-Humanist revolutionaries wrote an open letter to Chisholm suggesting that in her decision to run for the presidency she was "throwing off thousands of years of oppression" and was eagerly anticipated.[107]

The *Amsterdam News* also gave its support to the hometown candidate, stating that she had the intelligence, courage, integrity, leadership, and interest necessary to run.[108] The newspaper was willing to defy the sentiment of many of its male leaders who intentionally remained quiet or even hostile to Chisholm's candidacy. Regular contributors to the paper, including Bayard Rustin, Roy Wilkins, and Floyd McKissick, wrote next to nothing about her efforts in Congress or her presidential campaign.[109] The same held true for black male leaders across the rest of the country. With the exception of Congressman Ronald Dellums of California and Manhattan Borough President Percy Sutton, their silence was almost audible.[110] At the same time, others were overtly hostile to the Brooklynite's campaign. The acting chief of SCLC's Operation Breadbasket, Rev. William Jones, attacked Chisholm and described her career in Congress as "purely symbolic rather than substantive." Going further, he argued that if she were "confronted by a strong and dynamic candidate, her political career in the nation's capitol will be brought to an immediate halt."[111] Many black male leaders were clearly uncomfortable with Chisholm's lack of deference to them, and they refused to work with her to build a coalition.

This was most evident at the National Black Convention held in Gary, Indiana, in March 1972, where thousands of delegates from across the country came together to develop a National Black Agenda. Political scientist Hanes Walton Jr. explained that leaders focused on the potential influence of the black electorate in the 1972 presidential campaign and debated how to compel the greatest commitments from the parties regarding its goals and priorities. They floated the notion of fielding an African American candidate for president, but they refused to back Chisholm.[112] Not waiting for anyone to give her the green light, she had already tossed her name into the ring, believing that she should run for the presidency. An outsider among the national black leadership in part because of her independence, but also because of gender discrimination, Chisholm wrote about the Gary meeting, "I was not asked to participate and I did not intrude."[113] Rather than making overtures to the Gary delegates in order to craft a united front, she remained distant. It is hard to imagine, given the conflicting views that emerged at the Gary convention, that any overtures by Chisholm would have yielded much. Her effort to court support from her fellow CBC members had yielded coolness, eye rolling, and frustrated sighs.[114] Still, especially during her presidential campaign, Chisholm was reminded of the steep price she paid for often going it alone. Her constituents in Bedford-Stuyvesant may have loved her independence, but it was not the way to build effective alliances, particularly among already wary black men.

Chisholm was frustrated by more than just the lack of support from black leaders. She was also disappointed by the tepid response she received from the national heads of the women's organizations, including those she had helped create. Bella Abzug, fellow New York congresswoman and co-chair of the NWPC, was cautious about Chisholm's candidacy. She "encouraged" her but did not explicitly endorse her or campaign for her.[115] Black female leaders—Dorothy Height, Pauli Murray, Ella Baker, Anna Arnold Hedgeman, and Coretta Scott King—who had been active in national policy debates within the Democratic administrations and in civil rights struggles of the 1960s, were similarly silent.[116] Whatever their personal thoughts about Chisholm as a person or a politician, those who were desperate to see an end to the Vietnam War were likely unwilling to gamble on her candidacy. The majority of Democrats who wanted to see Nixon out therefore backed the Democratic front-runner, the prominent liberal and strong antiwar candidate, George McGovern. Radical black feminists also failed to take a public stand for Chisholm, even though groups like the Black Panthers supported her. While she had enthusiastic support from women in pockets around the country, including from local and regional NOW groups and women in the National Welfare Rights Organization, feminist activists overall failed to take what would have been a politically bold step and back Chisholm wholeheartedly.[117] Whether it was gender discrimination, racism, political pragmatism, or some combination of the three, black male leaders as well as nationally prominent black female leaders and white feminists kept her campaign at arm's length.

At the same time, despite its lofty promises, Chisholm's campaign suffered from internal disagreements and a lack of experienced management. There was no coordinated strategy, and so the disparate efforts were not marshaled into one strong surge of support. The professional she hired to run her campaign, Gerald Robinson, quit after just one month, disillusioned with "the confused mess of squabbling groups he had to work with."[118] Instead, the individual state primary campaigns were organized by disparate but enthusiastic grass-roots supporters such as James Pitts in Massachusetts, Tashia Young in New Mexico, Roxanne Conlon in Iowa, and Jacqui Hoop in Michigan.[119] Eschewing any romantic interpretation of these local efforts, Hanes Walton has bluntly stated that Chisholm's "amateurish and impoverished campaign needed more than optimism to sustain it."[120] At one point securing 151 delegates, in the final tally Chisholm finished with 101.45, placing fourth in the cacophonous field of Democratic Party challengers.[121]

In her autobiography, *The Good Fight*, Chisholm talked about the difficulty of bringing together white female activists and community organizers from the black community. Because she had no national campaign manager, volunteers ended up in power struggles with each other. Tensions over race and gender plagued her campaign in just about every state in which she ran.[122] Assessing the problems, Chisholm wrote, "The conflict between blacks and white women appeared to be a competition over which group was going to own me and my candidacy."[123] They also demonstrated the challenges of coalition building. Although she identified areas of common cause, Chisholm was unable to move the predominantly white women's organizations to address the pressing economic issues black women worried about most. Other potential supporters, including young people and anti-war activists, turned to McGovern instead. The kind of coalition Chisholm described and had hoped to build did not materialize. The groups to whom she appealed had histories that prevented them from easily uniting with others for whom they maintained a level of mistrust.[124] Such a coalition would have taken years to build, if it were even possible. What was clear in 1972 was that Chisholm did not have the resources to build it through her hastily constructed presidential campaign.

The trailblazing presidential hopeful tried to minimize her disappointment about the failure of different constituencies to back her, but the conflicts brought to the surface by Chisholm's presidential campaign clearly took a toll. Although she did not often speak of it directly, she was disheartened by the lack of support she received from African American and women's groups alike. Black men, she felt, were not really ready to champion black women in politics. The price for the divisiveness between African American men and women was "a tremendous hindrance to the progress of the race," Chisholm maintained. Sounding resentful and even personally hurt, she told a visitor to her Brooklyn office in 1973, "I want Black politicians to leave me alone. . . . I have been in this business for 18 years and I'm now reverting to being a loner. . . . My responsibility will always be to the people."[125]

The lack of support hurt, but it was not her only impediment in the campaign, which in reality was disorganized and had limited resources. Moreover, Chisholm's maverick style hurt her. The zest that led her to disregard the House of Representative's protocol and demand a new committee assignment when she arrived in Congress was a mainstay of her political approach. While it inspired her constituents, it did not go over as well among those more willing to accommodate the status quo in exchange for gradual but tangible victories for African Americans and all women. Full endorsement of Chisholm's presidential campaign would have been a risky political move for mainstream civil rights organizations and feminist groups. But had they provided her some support, Chisholm could have had more than her 151 delegates to trade in exchange for input in the party's platform at the Democratic National Convention. Perhaps the delegates to the DNC were just too cautious, but Chisholm's style did not help.

Back to Congress

Even though she was disappointed by the presidential campaign, Chisholm returned to the House of Representatives in 1972, winning her seat back with more than 80 percent of the vote.[126] The political and economic landscapes that Chisholm and other liberal Democrats had to negotiate grew increasingly treacherous as the 1970s wore on, however. Nixon may have resigned in disgrace, but President Ford was hardly more sympathetic to liberal Democratic policies. The economy heaved simultaneously under the burdens of war costs, an oil embargo, and the residuals of the Great Society spending. In the face of an escalating crisis, one article in the *New York Times* argued that the city's congressional delegation was "big, but politically toothless." Seemingly overwhelmed by the events unfolding around her, Chisholm sounded like a different person in 1975 than she did in 1969. Referring to Washington's lack of support, she said defensively, "They don't understand our fantastic cost of living. They don't understand how our tax base has been eroded by the flight to the suburbs."[127] Chisholm, the *Amsterdam News* reported a year later, was "sick and tired of being blamed for everything that happens in her constituency."[128]

At times feeling beaten down, she battled on. She continued to fight for welfare reform, an extension of minimum-wage coverage, job development and public service employment, and adequate childcare programs.[129] In February 1975, for example, Chisholm participated in the House floor debate on food stamps. In response to escalating costs and swelling recipient rolls, the Ford administration proposed a reduction in federal expenditures by increasing the share of food-stamp costs paid by recipients. Charging that the president's proposal "strikes hardest the elderly poor, women, minorities, and blue-collar workers who have the least resources to fall back on in this period of economic unrest," Chisholm called for a reversal.[130] She pointed out that a recent tax cut had not helped the elderly, the poor, and the majority of food-stamp recipients, who paid little or no income tax. With Chisholm as a leading voice, the president's program came under sharp attack in Congress. She and other liberal Democrats pushed again for a daycare bill as well. Knowing the level of hostility welfare recipients faced among her colleagues in Congress (as well as society at large), Chisholm made a strategic appeal based on economic concerns rather than human need. Making an argument similar to one she had made for abortion legislation seven years earlier, Chisholm explained, "Forcing day care centers to close down only would increase welfare costs because many mothers would be unable to work without day care services."[131] She wanted to expand the use of the state to support women and children, but she was cautious about the ways she made her case to the predominantly white male audience in the House. Initially she and the other progressive forces scored a significant victory as the bill passed both chambers of Congress. But when President Ford vetoed the legislation, the Senate sustained it, thus eliminating the chance to make a meaningful difference in the lives of poor women.

While her efforts in Congress fell on increasingly inhospitable soil, Chisholm's influence in the women's movement yielded considerable and positive outcomes. At the 1973 NWPC convention she addressed the crowd, unafraid to speak about divisive issues. She asked the women gathered there to "extend the movement beyond the white middle class to the black and Mexican-American women who suffer double discriminations." She pointed out, "The use of the word 'Ms.' is not a burning issue to them. They are more concerned about extension of the minimum wage . . . about welfare reform. They are not only women, but women of color and they are subject to more discrimination than whites."[132] As historian Elsa Barkley Brown has argued, white middle-class women needed to acknowledge the ways in which racial privilege shaped their lives.[133] Chisholm used her position to pressure white feminists to do just that. Although at times too limited, the changes she and other women of color helped bring about were apparent especially at the National Women's Conference in Houston in 1977. The conference had a much broader representation of women of color and poor women than earlier movement gatherings. Not only that, the majority of the more than twenty thousand women who attended passed the "National Plan for Action" to address the diverse needs of women.[134]

Over the course of the 1970s, however, conservative and reactionary forces gained momentum in the social debates in the same way that they were compelling changes in Congress. Under the masterful leadership of conservatives like Phyllis Schlafly, they managed first to slow and then to stop many feminist efforts. In 1976, conservatives secured the passage of the Hyde Amendment, which banned the use of federal funding for abortions, thus denying poor women a critical resource. Simultaneously, the ERA, which had been effectively making its way through the state ratification process, stalled out in the late 1970s. Despite Congress's granting a three-year extension for ratification, the amendment died in June 1982, three states short of passage. Working against this swelling tide of conservatism, Chisholm fought for her liberal agenda until 1982. After serving one term under the Reagan administration, she concluded that her vision of the state was under severe attack and could make no further headway. And so Shirley Chisholm, the "unbought and unbossed" woman of action from New York City, retired from office.

Conclusion

Shirley Chisholm's 1968 election to Congress was at once the conclusion of a half-century-long effort for black women from New York City to gain a voice in electoral politics and the beginning of a new chapter in women's history. Justifiably recognized as a political "first," Chisholm was much more than that. She was the product of two generations of grassroots struggles in Brooklyn for social justice, economic rights, racial equality, and control over local political processes. She was a female activist who, over time, developed a keen, complex feminist consciousness. She was a civil rights advocate and a founding member of the Congressional Black Caucus. She was a liberal Democrat—one who may have placed too much hope in the state but who believed there was really nowhere else to turn. The beneficiary of historical good timing, she seized the openings created by the social movements of the 1960s, especially the civil rights movement. She was a courageous fighter who contended with men who questioned her abilities because she was a woman. And finally, she was an extraordinary woman who believed she could be president of the United States and ran to prove it.

The trajectory of black women's political activism in New York City—from women fighting for entry into political clubs in the 1920s to Chisholm's campaign for the presidency of the United States in 1972 and her arrival at the Democratic National Convention with over one hundred delegates to bargain with—suggested that African American women's political stature in the city and in the Democratic Party had altered significantly. In the course of fifty years, they successfully confronted white women's racism to join the suffrage movement, they proved their loyalty and worth to male political party bosses so that they could have a chance at the polls, and then they won over voters, first for city and state seats, and then for national office. As this history proved, it was essential for a black woman from New York City to gain acceptance among Democratic Party stalwarts if she hoped to advance her political career. Bessie Buchanan succeeded in getting party support in 1954, and she trail-blazed into the New York State Assembly. Constance Baker Motley was the party favorite ten years later and went first into the New York State Senate. And Chisholm, under the auspices of an insurgent Democratic club, compelled party support in 1968, and she scored a historic victory by winning a seat in Congress. Those who ran on other party ballots in the 1920s, 1930s, 1940s, and 1950s helped accustom voters to seeing women as candidates, but they lost every election they ran in.

As with black women who had worked in various branches of government earlier, Chisholm helped challenge racist and gendered assumptions about who could legitimately serve as a public leader. However, she did so not by working through women's organizations like the NCNW, the Deltas, or the YWCA or through traditional civil rights organizations like the NAACP or SNCC, but rather by working her way through one of the toughest political schools of all, New York City's Democratic Party clubhouses. As she and the others attained new levels of access to the state, they became "outsiders-within" in the manner

that Patricia Hill Collins has written about. Their relative marginality "provided
a distinctive angle of vision" on the political world in which they worked.[135]
For Chisholm in particular as the lone black woman in Congress, it informed
not just her political philosophy but also her strategies.

Chisholm understood her career as part of something larger than herself.
It was an effort to make the path easier for those women who would come
after her and to make black women's lives visible. Her autobiographies and her
work as an educator, a community activist, and most important as a politician,
all contributed to an intellectual and social movement tradition that aimed to
foster more black women's activism. Chisholm's social thought and political
action focused on opposing oppression, even as she advanced her own career.
Throughout her tenure in politics, she spoke out on and supported legislation
to benefit African Americans, women, the working-class, the poor, students,
Vietnam veterans, the elderly, and children. It was less Chisholm's achievements
than her efforts on behalf of the disempowered, that inspired African American
women in New York City and around the nation to become politically active.[136]
Melody Murphy from Kentucky, for example, wrote Chisholm, "What a marvel-
ous trailblazer and inspiration you are to thousands of women from all over the
country. Many of us hold you as an ideal and a role model."[137] Moreover, in her
historic congressional victory, Chisholm was a symbol of resistance to forces
of racialized gender oppression that had until 1968 kept black women from
the inner chambers of political power. And finally, her victory was an essential
piece of trailblazing. Within four years of her first House election Chisholm was
joined in Congress by three more African American women: Barbara Jordan of
Texas, Yvonne Braithwaite Burke of California, and Cardiss Collins of Illinois.

At the same time, she appreciated that it would take much more than nominal
insider status to get her legislation enacted. With few political allies or networks
to tap into, Chisholm proved a relatively ineffective legislator. Her success in
the state assembly was the result of good timing, party strength (her first victory
coincided with President Johnson's landslide victory), and her ability to build
alliances within the comparatively smaller chamber. It was much more difficult
to secure necessary majorities in a chamber with national authority, and at a time
when the Democratic Party, with its fragile and fractious New Deal coalition,
was falling apart. Further, more liberal than most of her colleagues, Chisholm
found that in the face of rising conservatism, her vision of the state, based on
aggressive federal activism on behalf of the socially, politically, and economically marginalized, was in retreat in the 1970s and under outright attack by the
early 1980s. If Chisholm had been able to secure the legislation she fought for

over the course of her fourteen years in Congress, she could have helped lead the Democratic Party and the nation on a path of renewed yet bolder political progressivism, because she put the concerns of people of color, women, and the poor at its center. Instead, much of the legislation she proposed fell outside the boundaries of political feasibility even in 1969, and so her career served not as the start of a new path toward equality and justice but instead as a marker of the price of party dissension and the rise of the New Right.

Conclusion

In her autobiography, *The Good Fight*, which documents her run for the nation's highest office, Shirley Chisholm poignantly recounted the speech she gave at the Democratic National Convention in July 1972. "What I said that night was that most people had thought I would never stand there, in that place, but there I was. All the odds had been against it, right up to the end," she wrote. "I never blamed anyone for doubting. The Presidency is for white males. No one was ready to take a black woman seriously as a candidate. It was not time yet for a black to run, let alone a woman, and certainly not for someone who was both. Someday . . . but not yet. Someday the country will be ready," Chisholm maintained somewhat wistfully.[1] I have argued through the telling of this new narrative of black women's politics, that Chisholm's election to Congress and her presidential campaign concluded an important dimension of black women's political history. Yet her achievements also marked the beginning of a fresh chapter which is very much still being written. In their campaigns for the U.S. presidency in 2008, Barack Obama and Hillary Rodham Clinton made important strides forward in breaking down racialized and gendered barriers to political power which Chisholm as a black woman confronted nearly forty years earlier and tried to overcome simultaneously. She would likely have celebrated their achievements, but she would not have been content. The "someday" Chisholm hoped for when a black woman is elected to the U.S. presidency has not yet arrived, and so the story and the struggle continue.

African American Women's Political Accomplishments

At the same time, politically active African American women accomplished a great deal between the 1910s and the 1970s. To begin with, they helped secure women's right to vote in New York and nationally. Aware that living in the North gave them a tool their Southern sisters could not safely exercise until 1965, African American women in New York City used their votes to help the black communities of Harlem and Bedford-Stuyvesant and, though less acknowledged, also helped themselves gain political clout—slowly, but surely. Specifically, as new voters they deliberated carefully over their political choices and joined with African American men in New York City in migrating from the Republican Party to the Democratic Party starting in the late 1910s. In response to their votes, Tammany Hall began to direct patronage to African Americans. Not only that, through their dogged persistence and increasing political savvy, they began to undermine the Democratic Party's resistance to running black women as candidates, which was critical because of the party's near-complete dominance in the city. Although it took until 1954 for Tammany Hall to put its full weight behind a black female candidate, as soon as it did, the candidate, Bessie Buchanan, won. As they forged forward into the deeply masculine domain of party politics, African American women also contributed to the long and as yet incomplete process of wearing down the tightly-linked association of politics with white masculinity.

In addition, from the 1930s forward, black women seized the opportunities generated during times of economic, social, and political upheaval to secure positions inside the apparatus of the state that gave them unprecedented access to power brokers and, at times, to the levers of power themselves. As appointees of New York City mayors and New York State governors, for example, they fought for jobs, better housing and schools, safe and clean streets, and for the elimination of racist business practices. While many efforts were unsuccessful, sometimes they secured new laws and policies, and they raised issues on behalf of communities that were too often neglected; not only that, they helped shift and expand the Democratic Party's focus on racial equality.

At the national level starting in the early 1960s, African American women cleared new ground in the liberal establishment while serving on the President's Commission on the Status of Women, during debates about the Civil Rights Act of 1964, by developing the Women's Job Corps, and on the federal bench. In most of these arenas, they spotlighted the severe economic and social challenges African American women faced because of the intersections of racial and gendered discrimination. While the PCSW offered few specific recommendations to benefit African American women, it provided an unprecedented opportunity for a handful of black women to participate in a national discussion on women in American society. Dorothy Height, Pauli Murray, and Jeanne Noble parlayed their experiences on the PCSW into influential engagement with Democratic Party leaders. Murray made a significant contribution to Title VII of the Civil Rights Act, Noble organized the Women's Job Corps at President Johnson's request, and Height mobilized various interracial coalitions from her PCSW network that provided invaluable support to the grassroots civil rights movement in the South. As a federal judge, Constance Baker Motley attended to her duties with a commitment to making the law truly fair, aware of the historic ways it had so inadequately served people of color and the poor.

Finally, as elected officials, African American women introduced legislation in the New York State Assembly, the New York State Senate, and in the U.S. Congress to address concerns of the poor and working class, the unemployed, and those who had to contend with racism and gender discrimination. For example, Bessie Buchanan proposed bills to address sex-based pay inequities and race-based discrimination in banking, education, and insurance. Constance Baker Motley introduced legislation to eliminate the category of race on marriage licenses, to prohibit discrimination in volunteer fire departments and labor union apprenticeships, and to eradicate school segregation. She also fought against the abuse of police authority and for public housing. Shirley Chisholm had a similarly progressive legislative record in Albany. She battled to eliminate racial discrimination in business practices and to require city police to complete a course on civil rights. She advocated for unemployment insurance for agricultural workers and hospital employees, an improved minimum-wage law, more affordable public housing, and an education bill to support economically disadvantaged students. Not only that, she was sensitive to the ways that class, gender, and race compounded problems for poor women and women of color. She proposed legislation for daycare centers for working women and women on public assistance, unemployment insurance for domestic workers, and tenure protection for female faculty who took maternity leave. The force of her personality and her ability to forge alliances with other legislators in the state assembly, in addition to the emergence of national dialogues on race relations, poverty, and women's rights during the 1960s, led to a number of beneficial legislative victories, including those for poor students, domestic workers, and new mothers.

It was harder for Chisholm to succeed in Congress because she lacked the kinds of networks or seniority necessary to navigate the process. Still, she and other progressive legislators tried to secure more federal support for public housing and schools, a jobs program, the Equal Rights Amendment, twenty-four-hour daycare centers, abortion rights, an end to the Vietnam War, benefits for domestic workers, and a number of other programs that required robust government action. Despite the Democrats' loss of the presidency in 1968, liberals won some significant battles in the early 1970s. Among others, a law was passed to insure that domestic workers received minimum wages; Title IX of the Education Act significantly benefited women's access to higher education; and Congress voted favorably for the ERA and a daycare bill. These last two measures met subsequent resistance in the states and in the White House, bellwethers of the national political swing to the right that began the year Chisholm entered Congress and which was fully manifest by 1980 when Ronald Reagan won the U.S. presidency.

Not only did they help transform politics, but through their activism African American women made substantial contributions to the civil rights movement, especially in the North, and the women's movement as well. From the moment they unpacked their bags in Harlem in the 1910s through the conclusion of this story in the late 1970s, African American women remained committed to mitigating and eliminating the scourge of racism. They took to the streets, they organized, and they lobbied government officials for anti-lynching laws and an end to Jim Crow policies in the South, and called for practices in the North that included decent and affordable housing, jobs, municipal services for their neighborhoods, unbiased media coverage, and more responsive political representation. Many of these were the same issues that black women fought for once they were inside the state. Because of the persistence of racism, grassroots activists found that even when they succeeded in their immediate goals of getting rents lowered or a new school built, obtaining jobs, or garnering resources for their neighborhoods, for example, many of these struggles had to be waged more than once. Regardless of their political affiliations, the women in this story understood that the most enduring changes were those that were codified in law. It was often the combined efforts of those working from the inside and others pressuring from the outside that yielded more lasting changes. In these ways black women in New York City were part of the struggle for racial equality, especially in the North.

African American women's efforts to advance women's social, political, and economic rights throughout the twentieth century have been underappreciated by scholars of women's history and by the popular culture. Although few of them would have called themselves feminists, the women in this book left an indelible mark on women's movements for greater rights starting in the 1910s and continuing through the apex of the "second wave" women's movement. In addition to their integral role in gaining women's right to vote in New York, black women worked to break down gendered resistance to women in politics more generally by working as canvassers, lobbyists, candidates, and finally as elected officials.

They also used their positions of authority to address women's concerns in other ways. In the 1930s they exposed the horrific labor situation for black women and demanded that the city government address it. As they trail-blazed into government positions, they brought other women along with them. Whether it was as employees of New Deal agencies, in the New York State Assembly, on the President's Commission on the Status of Women, with the Women's Job Corps, or in Congress, they addressed the injustices women faced in all aspects of the work force, from unequal access and decent jobs to discrimination in wages and benefits, and unfair treatment of pregnant women. In addition to using their leadership in long-established women's organizations like the NCNW, the YWCA, and the Delta Sigma Theta sorority to advance women's rights, they also served as founders or leaders of some of the most influential women's organizations in the late 1960s and early 1970s: the National Organization for Women, the National Association for the Repeal of Abortion Laws,[2] the Coalition of 100 Black Women, the National Women's Political Caucus, and the National Black Feminist Organization. Attentive to the ways a number of these organizations were inclined to focus on priorities set by upper-middle-class white women, they endeavored to broaden the feminist agenda to more fully address issues of concern to women of color, including economic inequalities, and racial and ethnic discrimination. In addition to their organizational work, the black women in this story also wrote critical essays, poems, autobiographies, and books that informed public conversations about diverse women's concerns and aspirations. For all of these reasons, African American women should be more fully included in the history of women's activism in the twentieth century.

African American Women's Vision of Politics

In the course of documenting their political activism, I have illuminated the broad vision of politics African American women developed. Aware of its historic limitations, the state was not an automatic ally for African American women to turn to, especially for those who had migrated from the South in the wake of the Jim Crow takeover. At the same time, mindful of the ways political patronage worked in a city as rapidly changing as New York between 1900 and 1920, they decided to work with it strategically, to neutralize it as an obstacle, and,where possible, to make it a productive tool in the fight for social, political, and economic rights. Their deliberate engagement with various arms of the state found increasing numbers of black women gravitating toward the Democratic Party as early as the 1910s, but they were hardly monolithic in their political perspectives. The first black woman to run for office in New York City, Grace Campbell, did so on the Socialist Party ticket. She was followed by others who maintained a commitment to leftist politics, but there was also a minority who remained loyal to the party of Lincoln through the 1940s because of the Dixiecrats' role in the national Democratic Party.

With the emergence of the Cold War in the late 1940s, politically left-leaning black women found themselves targeted by vitriolic silencing campaigns, as was the case for the majority of progressive activists. Yet for the growing numbers of black women who ensconced themselves in the Democratic Party, the goals were to expand its agenda and to secure positions of leadership. Mary McLeod Bethune did trail-blazing work in the Democratic Party during the New Deal. Building on that effort, Anna Hedgeman served as an appointee in the Truman administration during the late 1940s, and continuing through the 1970s, African American women generally came to represent the most liberal wing of the Democratic Party. Long after the McCarthy era did its damage, they remained committed to and fought for a progressive vision of social, political, and economic justice that scholars have previously not recognized.

African American Women's Influences on Politics and Social Movements

African American women's efforts to influence the Democratic Party and public policy met with varying degrees of success. The Democratic Party did not come readily to support black women as candidates. Only when they outnumbered black men on voter registration rolls in a number of Manhattan and Brooklyn districts and made themselves an important constituency did local Democratic leaders finally respond. Bessie Buchanan's election to the state assembly in 1954, Constance Baker Motley's election to the state senate in 1963, Shirley Chisholm's election to the U.S. House of Representatives in 1968, and (although she is not a subject of this study) Carol Mosley Braun's election to the U.S. Senate in 1992—all historic firsts for African American women in politics—demonstrate black women's persistent efforts to expand the Democratic Party's inclusiveness and, once they were in office, its agenda. These women succeeded in widening the path for other black women to follow on, which was evidenced by the increasing numbers of African American women on ballots at the city, state, and national levels. In the decade after Chisholm's historic victory, for example, a number of black women were elected to the House of Representatives (including Barbara Jordan of Texas, Yvonne Braithwaite Burke of California, and Cardiss Collins of Illinois), to the New York State Assembly, and to legislative office in other cities and states.[3]

At the same time that African American women achieved legislative, policy, and symbolic victories through their work in politics and government, they also crashed up against the seeming limits of what they could accomplish by working through the state. The vast majority of the progressive legislation they introduced never made it out of committees. For one thing, their expansive ideas about the role government should play in redistributing resources through social and economic policies frequently outpaced much of the electorate's ideas and those of most political leaders. For another, the traditions of the state were gendered in ways that precluded women from organizing effective coalitions inside formal political structures that could have at least enabled them to strike some productive compromises. For black women, these boundaries were even more substantial and qualitatively different because of the insidious workings of racial discrimination combined with gender discrimination. Class privilege, advanced degrees, and national prominence were enough by the 1960s for women like Height, Noble, Motley, or Chisholm to gain recognition and a place at the table, but such assets were rarely sufficient to give them sustained power or access to resources that they could distribute to others. The limitations on their ability to more fully influence the Democratic Party agenda and to redirect resources—including government money, jobs, and political positions—had consequences for the people in need on whose behalf they most frequently fought.

African American women, who had honed their political skills in New York City, had perhaps a greater influence on the long struggle for racial equality, including but hardly limited to the days of mass mobilization in the 1950s and 1960s, and on the movements for women's rights. Their participation and leadership in the civil rights movement was vital to securing the passage of laws at the municipal, state, and national levels, most obviously in the Civil Rights

Act of 1964. Many of these women also shaped the women's movements of the 1960s and 1970s. They frequently married a politics of race—one that was ever mindful of the historic oppression African Americans had experienced throughout U.S. history—with a consummate belief in women's human rights. As a result of their efforts and those of other women of color, new organizations emerged: NOW in 1966, the Coalition of 100 Black Women in 1970, the NWPC in 1971, and the National Black Feminist Organization in 1973. They also foregrounded issues that were of paramount concern to poor women and women of color, including labor rights, forced sterilization, and racial and ethnic discrimination. Their efforts helped create lasting institutional changes such as the establishment of women's studies and African American studies programs at colleges and universities. And finally their influences were felt at the National Women's Conference in Houston in 1977. The conference had a much greater representation of women of color and poor women than earlier movement gatherings had. Not only that, the majority of the more than twenty thousand women who attended passed the "National Plan for Action," which addressed the needs and concerns of diverse women.

"Someday"—Challenges for the Future

The history of black women's political activism between the 1910s and the 1970s offers some complicated lessons for activists in more current times. The effects of their efforts as well as the impacts of the civil rights and women's movements of which they were integral contributors continue to unfold in measured, uneven ways. On the one hand, the political events of 2008, including Barak Obama's historic victory and the notable achievements of Hillary Rodham Clinton and Sarah Palin suggest that changes may be underway regarding the gendered and race-related lenses through which the electorate evaluates presidential candidates. On the other hand, there has been only gradual progress for women at the congressional level. In the One hundred twelfth Congress, which began in January 2011, ninety women took the oath of office (seventy-three in the House of Representatives and seventeen in the U.S. Senate), which represents 16.8 percent of the total membership. Among those ninety women were twenty-four women of color, including thirteen African American women.[4] This is an obvious improvement over the late 1960s, when there were eleven women in Congress, and Chisholm made her first successful foray into that office, but it still represents a very slow pace of change, especially compared to other democracies around the world. The United States ranks seventy-first out of 188 nations in the number of women in its national legislature.[5]

Specifically for African American women in politics, there are barriers that have been particularly hard to dislodge. Not only was there a twenty-four-year gap between Shirley Chisholm's breakthrough and Carol Mosley Braun's, but Braun's election to the U.S. Senate remains, at the time of this writing, a singular event for African American women. Moreover, Braun's 2004 bid for the U.S. presidency received no serious attention in the press or from the Democratic Party. Ellen Goodman, a journalist for the *Boston Globe*, noted that when Braun announced her candidacy, "CBS used her announcement to lead-in a story on bottom-tier candidates, asking 'Why are they running?' and an interviewer on *Good Morning America* asked, 'Why don't you work for another candidate who has a real shot at victory?'" At that time, Braun was in range of a number of Democratic male candidates, including John Edwards and Bob Graham, but as Goodman commented, Braun and her campaign were labeled "symbolic," "not a strong contender," a "no-shot" and a "distraction."[6] The *New York Times* argued that she was running for her own ego, calling her campaign "a vanity affair."[7] The lack of financial support, the withering press attacks, and the cool reception from the Democratic Party—issues African American women who had run for office in the past had faced—compelled Braun to pull out of the race before the first primary.[8] Clearly at the federal level, the tight association of politics with white masculinity is much harder to undermine than it is at other levels of government.

The picture looks somewhat better at the state level. Of the 1,745 women serving in state legislatures nationwide in 2011, 348 (19.9 percent) were women of color, of which 242 (69 percent) were African American women. Women of color made the Democratic Party their political home by overwhelming numbers, as is evidenced by the fact that of the 348 women of color in state legislatures, 330 are Democrats, 16 are Republicans, and two are nonpartisan.[9] This level of loyalty is rooted in the party's somewhat more sympathetic policies regarding race, gender, the working class, and poor people's issues—issues that demand a more activist government regarding expenditures and programs.

While African American women have attained some important positions of political leadership, more has to be done to secure laws to address unemployment and underemployment, housing needs, poorly funded schools, racial profiling by the police, and poverty more generally. Because of the increased feminization of poverty in the 1980s, many of these issues fell with disproportionate heaviness on women's shoulders, especially women of color. During the 1980s and 1990s African American women, with few allies among white women or black men, were unable to defend against the hostile policies of the Reagan, Bush Sr., and Clinton administrations. Over the course of twenty years, these three presidents curtailed or eliminated government programs that served the constituencies for whom African American women in this study had most often fought. Many of the attacks were delivered by using thinly veiled misogynistic and racist stereotypes, the most mean-spirited and destructive of which was the "welfare queen." In the 1930s, while working as an assistant to Mayor LaGuardia, Anna Hedgeman had to fight against the pervasive belief that African American women took ready "handouts" from the government. She would likely have been deeply saddened—though perhaps less surprised, given her sixty years of activism for racial and gender justice—that this issue reared its head yet again.

Taken together, the political lives of the women in this historical narrative serve as an inspiration about the possibilities and promises of the state, and a caution regarding the extraordinary struggle that must be waged to force the deeply entrenched systems of power to give even a little, never mind to bring about the world of justice, equality, and dignity to which the women in this story dedicated their lives. The persistence today of some of the largest and most intractable problems African American women fought to eradicate indicates that there is still further to go before the political system is made fully responsive and truly representative. Yet the path to leadership is wider now, and more women of color are able to walk on it in large part because of the efforts of three generations of black women from New York City. Perhaps the next chapter in this history will find that Shirley Chisholm's hoped for "someday" has arrived.

Appendix

African American Women's Campaigns for Elected Office, 1919–1972

Year	Name	Political Party	Office	Borough
1919	Grace Campbell*	Socialist	21st State Assembly District (A.D.)	Manhattan
1920	Grace Campbell	Socialist	19th A.D.	Manhattan
1934	Layle Lane	Socialist	U.S. Congress	Manhattan
	Jane P. Morgan	Socialist	19th State Senate	Manhattan
	Alma Crosswaith	Socialist	19th A.D.	Manhattan
	Eunice Hunton Carter	Republican	19th A.D.	Manhattan
1936	Layle Lane	Socialist	U.S. Congress	Manhattan
	Jane Bolin	Republican	19th A.D.	Manhattan
1937	Jane Morgan	Socialist	19th A.D.	Manhattan
	Ruth Whitehead Whaley	Democrat	19th A.D (Primary election only)	Manhattan
	Layle Lane	Socialist	20th A.D.	Manhattan
	*Sara Pelham Speaks**	Republican	21st A.D. (Won primary, lost general election to incumbent)	Manhattan
1938	Alma Crosswaith	Socialist	17th A.D.	Manhattan
	Layle Lane	Socialist	21st A.D.	Manhattan
1942	Layle Lane	Socialist	U.S. Congress Representative-at-Large	Manhattan
	Maida Springer	American Labor Party (ALP)	21st A.D.	Manhattan
1943	Layle Lane	Socialist	City Council	Manhattan
1944	Sara Pelham Speaks	Republican	U.S. Congress	Manhattan
	Adam Clayton Powell, Jr. **	Democrat/ALP	U.S. Congress (Defeated Speaks)	Manhattan
	Ruth Price Brown	Democrat	12th A.D. (Primary election only)	Manhattan
	Ada B, Jackson	Republican/ALP	17th A.D.	Brooklyn
1945	Layle Lane	Socialist	City Controller	Manhattan
	Ruth Whitehead Whaley	Democrat	City Council	Manhattan
	Maude Richardson	Republican	City Council	Brooklyn

Year	Name	Political Party	Office	Borough
1946	Layle Lane	Socialist	State Controller	Manhattan
	Maude Richardson*	Republican	17th A.D. (Defeated Jackson in primary, lost general election to incumbent)	Brooklyn
	Ada B. Jackson	Republican	17th A.D. (Lost primary against Richardson)	Brooklyn
1947	Ada B. Jackson	ALP	17th A.D. (General election)	Brooklyn
	Layle Lane	Socialist	23rd State Senate	Manhattan
	Ada B. Jackson	ALP	City Council	Brooklyn
1948	Ada B. Jackson	ALP	U.S. Congress	Brooklyn
	Maude Richardson	Republican	17th A.D. (Lost general election against Baker)	Brooklyn
	Bertram Baker **	Democrat/ALP	17th A.D. (Defeated Richardson in general election)	Brooklyn
1949	Ada B. Jackson	ALP	Borough President	Brooklyn
	Pauli Murray	Liberal Party	City Council	Brooklyn
1950	Hattie Brisbane	ALP	5th A.D.	Brooklyn
1952	Wilhelmina Rowe Carter	Republican	11th A.D.	Manhattan
	Lucille Pickett	Republican	12th A.D.	Manhattan
	Hattie Brisbane	ALP	5th A.D.	Brooklyn
	Catherine Brown	ALP	23rd A.D.	Brooklyn
	Gwendolyn Mahon	ALP	5th A.D.	Queens
1953	Ella Baker	Liberal Party	City Council	Manhattan
	Hattie Brisbane	ALP	5th A.D.	Brooklyn
1954	Lucille Pickett	Republican	12th A.D. (Lost general election against Buchanan)	Manhattan
	Bessie Buchanan* (served 1955–1962)	Democrat	12th A.D. (Defeated incumbent in primary election, Pickett in general election)	Manhattan
1960	Anna Arnold Hedgeman	Democrat	U.S. Congress (Primary election only)	Bronx

Year	Name	Political Party	Office	Borough
1964	**Constance Baker Motley*** (served 1964–1965)	Democrat	21st State Senate	Manhattan
	Shirley Chisholm (served 1965–1968)	Democrat	17th A.D.	Brooklyn
1965	Anna Arnold Hedgeman	Democrat	City Council President	Manhattan
	Constance Baker Motley* (served 1965–1966)	Democrat/ Republican/ Liberal Party	Borough President	Manhattan
1968	Anna Arnold Hedgeman	Democrat	72nd A.D. (Lost primary election to incumbent Charles Rangel)	Manhattan
	Dollie Robinson	Democrat	U.S. Congress (Lost primary against Chisholm [and William Thompson])	Brooklyn
	Shirley Chisholm* (served 1969–1982)	Democrat	U.S. Congress (Won primary, won general election against James Farmer)	Brooklyn
1972	Shirley Chisholm*	Democrat	U.S. President (Primary election only)	National
1992	**Carol Mosley Braun*** (served 1993–1998)	Democrat	U.S. Senate	Illinois

All elections are general elections unless specified as primary elections only.

Women's electoral victories in primary elections only are *italicized*.
Women's electoral victories in general elections are in **bold**.

* Marks historic firsts for African American women.
** Marks significant historic firsts for African American men referenced herein.

Note: There are a number of elections in the early 1950s included here that are not mentioned in the book. They are representative of the ALP's and the Republican Party's continued support of African American female candidates. They also show the persistence of a minority of African Americans in New York City to support political parties other than the Democratic Party.

Notes

INTRODUCTION

1. "Statement of Candidacy for the Office of President of the United States by the Honorable Shirley Chisholm, New York, N.Y.," January 25, 1972, Shirley Chisholm Papers, Rutgers Special Collections.

2. See Evelyn Brooks Higginbotham, *Righteous Discontent: The Women's Movement in the Black Baptist Church, 1880–1920* (Cambridge, Mass.: Harvard University Press, 1993); Glenda Elizabeth Gilmore, *Gender and Jim Crow: Women and the Politics of White Supremacy in North Carolina, 1896–1920* (Chapel Hill: University of North Carolina Press, 1996); Floris Barnett Cash, *African American Women and Social Action: The Clubwomen and Volunteerism from Jim Crow to the New Deal, 1896–1936* (Westport, Conn.: Greenwood, 2001); Deborah Gray White, *Too Heavy a Load: Black Women in Defense of Themselves, 1894–1994* (New York: Norton, 1999); Stephanie Shaw, *What a Woman Ought to Be and to Do: Black Professional Women Workers during the Jim Crow Era* (Chicago: University of Chicago Press, 1996).

3. Jane Dabel, *A Respectable Woman: The Public Roles of African American Women in 19th Century New York* (New York: New York University Press, 2008); Rosalyn Terborg-Penn, *African American Women in the Struggle for the Vote, 1850–1920* (Bloomington: Indiana University Press, 1998); Lisa Masterson's recent book on African American women's early political activism in Illinois stands to be an important contribution to this emerging dimension of African American and political history. See *For the Freedom of Her Race: Black Women and Electoral Politics in Illinois, 1877–1932* (Chapel Hill: University of North Carolina Press, 2009).

4. Kimberlé Williams Crenshaw, "Demarginalizing the Intersection of Race and Sex: A Black Feminist Critique of Antidiscrimination Doctrine, Feminist Theory, and Antiracist Politics," *1989 University of Chicago Legal Forum* (University of Chicago Law School), 139–67; Patricia Hill Collins, *Black Feminist Thought: Knowledge, Consciousness, and the Politics of Empowerment*, 2nd ed. (New York: Routledge, 2000 [1990]); Elsa Barkley Brown, "'What Has Happened Here': The Politics of Difference in Women's History and Feminist Politics," in *"We Specialize in the Wholly Impossible": A Reader in Black Women's History*, ed. Darlene Clark Hine, Wilma King, and Linda Reed, 39–54 (Brooklyn, N.Y.: Carlson, 1995).

5. Stephen Skowronek, *Building a New American State: The Expansion of National Administrative Capacities, 1877–1920* (New York: Cambridge University Press, 1982), ix, 285; Elisabeth S. Clemens, "Organizational Repertoires and Institutional Change: Women's Groups and the Transformation of American Politics, 1890–1920," in *Civic Engagement in American Democracy*, ed. Theda Skocpol and Morris P. Fiorina, 91 (Washington, D.C.: Brookings Institution Press, 1999).

6. Gilbert Osofsky, *Harlem: The Making of a Ghetto, Negro New York, 1890–1930* (Chi-

cago: Elephant, 1996 [1963]), 160; Nancy Weiss, *Farewell to the Party of Lincoln: Black Politics in the Age of FDR* (Princeton, N.J.: Princeton University Press, 1983), 3–12; Richard Valelly, *The Two Reconstructions: The Struggle for Black Enfranchisement* (Chicago: University of Chicago Press, 2004), 60–62, 121–48; Michael McGerr, *The Decline of Popular Politics: The American North 1865–1928* (New York: Oxford University Press, 1986), 186.

7. Matthew Countryman, *Up South: Civil Rights and Black Power in Philadelphia* (Philadelphia: University of Pennsylvania Press, 2005); Martha Biondi, *To Stand and Fight: The Struggle for Civil Rights in Postwar New York City* (Cambridge, Mass.: Harvard University Press, 2003); Alan Brinkley, *The End of Reform: New Deal Liberalism in Recession and War* (New York: Knopf, 1995); Steven Fraser, "Sidney Hillman: Labor's Machiavelli," in *Labor Leaders in America*, ed. Melvyn Dubofsky and Warren Van Tine, 207–33 (Urbana: University of Illinois Press, 1987); Steve Fraser and Gary Gerstle, eds., *The Rise and Fall of the New Deal Order, 1930–1980* (Princeton, N.J.: Princeton University Press, 1989).

8. Vicki L. Crawford et al., eds., *Women in the Civil Rights Movement* (Bloomington: Indiana University Press, 1990); Belinda Robnett, *How Long? How Long? African American Women in the Struggle for Civil Rights* (New York: Oxford University Press, 1997); Barbara Ransby, *Ella Baker and the Black Freedom Movement* (Chapel Hill: University of North Carolina Press, 2003); Kimberly Springer, ed., with preface by Beverly Guy-Sheftall, *Still Lifting, Still Climbing: African American Women's Contemporary Activism* (New York: New York University Press, 1999); Bettye Collier-Thomas and V. P. Franklin, eds., *Sisters in the Struggle: African American Women in the Civil Rights–Black Power Movement* (New York: New York University Press, 2001). Of the emerging literature on the Northern struggle for racial equality, only Jane Dabel's recent book, *A Respectable Woman*, and Thomas Sugrue's *Sweet Land of Liberty: The Forgotten Struggle for Civil Rights in the North* (New York: Random House, 2008) give black women's activism sustained attention. See also Countryman; Biondi; Craig Steven Wilder, *A Covenant with Color: Race and Social Power in Brooklyn* (New York: Columbia University Press, 2000); Wendell Pritchett, *Brownsville, Brooklyn: Blacks, Jews, and the Changing Face of the Ghetto* (Chicago: University of Chicago Press, 2002). For recent scholarship on the welfare rights movement, see Premilla Nadasen, *Welfare Warriors: The Welfare Rights Movement in the United States* (New York: Routledge, 2005); Annelise Orleck, *Storming Caesar's Palace: How Black Mothers Fought their Own War on Poverty* (Boston: Beacon, 2005); Felicia Kornbluh, *The Battle for Welfare Rights: Politics and Poverty in Modern America* (Philadelphia: University of Pennsylvania Press, 2007); Lisa Levenstein, *A Movement without Marches: African American Women and the Politics of Poverty in Postwar Philadelphia* (Chapel Hill: University of North Carolina Press, 2009).

9. Leila Rupp and Verta Taylor, *Survival in the Doldrums: The American Women's Rights Movement, 1945 to the 1960s* (New York: Oxford University Press, 1987); Cynthia Harrison, *On Account of Sex: The Politics of Women's Issues, 1945–1968* (Berkeley: University of California Press, 1988); Melanie S. Gustafson, Kristie Miller, and Elisabeth I. Perry, eds., *We Have Come to Stay: American Women and Political Parties, 1880–1960* (Albuquerque: University of New Mexico Press, 1999); Jo Freeman, *A Room at a Time: How Women Entered Party Politics* (New York: Rowman & Littlefield, 2000); Ruth Rosen, *The World*

Split Open (New York: Penguin, 2000); Jo Freeman, *We Will Be Heard: Women's Struggles for Political Power in the United States,* (Lanham, Md.: Rowan & Littlefield, 2008). Although they are not specifically women's political histories, Alice Kessler-Harris's *In Pursuit of Equity* (New York: Oxford University Press, 2001) and Nancy MacLean's *Freedom Is Not Enough: The Opening of the American Workplace* (Cambridge, Mass.: Harvard University Press, 2008) have given Murray's contributions to the Civil Rights Act of 1964 far greater attention than past studies. In addition, Duchess Harris, in her book *Black Feminist Politics from Kennedy to Clinton* (New York: Palgrave, 2009), discusses Height's contributions to the PCSW as part of her extended discussion on the PCSW's Consultation on the Problems of Negro Women. Kessler-Harris also briefly discusses Height's contributions to the PCSW. None looks at the collective contributions of these African American women to the feminist movement, however.

10. Elizabeth Lindsay Davis, *Lifting as They Climb* (New York: Hall, 1996 [1933]); Higginbotham; White; Kevin Gaines, *Uplifting the Race: Black Leadership, Politics, and Culture in the Twentieth Century* (Chapel Hill: University of North Carolina Press, 1996); Shaw; Victoria Wolcott, *Remaking Respectability* (Chapel Hill: University of North Carolina Press, 2001); Robert Gregg, *Sparks from the Anvil of Oppression: Philadelphia's African Methodists and Southern Migrants, 1890–1940* (Philadelphia: Temple University Press, 1993).

CHAPTER I. FIGHTING FOR RIGHTS IN THE 1910S AND 1920S

1. Anna Arnold Hedgeman, *The Trumpet Sounds: A Memoir of Negro Leadership* (New York: Holt, Rinehart, and Winston, 1964), 44.

2. See Davis; Higginbotham, 14; White; Gaines, 2–4; Shaw; Wolcott; Gregg, 3–5.

3. See Dorothy Salem, *To Better Our World: Black Women in Organized Reform, 1890–1920* (New York: Carlson, 1990); White; V. P. Franklin and Bettye Collier-Thomas, "For the Race in General and Black Women in Particular: The Civil Rights Activities of African American Women's Organizations, 1915–1950," in Collier-Thomas and Franklin, *Sisters,* 21–41.

4. Joe William Trotter, Jr., ed., *The Great Migration in Historical Perspective: New Dimensions of Race, Class, and Gender* (Bloomington: Indiana University Press, 1991); Darlene Clark Hine, "Black Migration to the Urban Midwest: The Gender Dimension, 1915–1945," in Trotter, *Great Migration*; Elizabeth Clark-Lewis, *Living In, Living Out: African American Domestics and the Great Migration* (New York: Kodansha, 1996 [1994]); James N. Gregory, *The Southern Diaspora: How the Great Migrations of Black and White Southerners Transformed America* (Chapel Hill: University of North Carolina Press, 2005); Davarian L. Baldwin, *Chicago's New Negroes: Modernity, the Great Migration, and Black Urban Life* (Chapel Hill: University of North Carolina Press, 2007).

5. See Dabel; Carla Peterson, "And We Claim Our Rights": The Rights Rhetoric of Black and White Women Activists Before the Civil War," in *Sister Circle: Black Women and Work,* ed. Sharon Harley et al., 128–45 (New Brunswick: Rutgers University Press, 2002); Leslie Harris, *In the Shadow of Slavery: African Americans in New York City, 1626–1863* (Chicago: University of Chicago Press, 2003); Wilder; Harold Connolly, *A Ghetto Grows in Brooklyn* (New York: New York University Press, 1977); Edwin Lewinson, *Black Politics*

in New York City (New York: Twayne, 1974); Roi Ottley, *New World A-Coming* (New York: Arno, 1968); Philip Kasinitz, *Caribbean New York: Black Immigrants and the Politics of Race* (Ithaca, N.Y.: Cornell University Press, 1992), 41–44.

6. During the shirtwaist strike of 1909, strike leaders met with African Americans in Brooklyn, urging them to resist working as strikebreakers. African Americans expressed frustration with racism within organized labor, which labor leaders acknowledged. See David Von Drehle, *Triangle: The Fire That Changed America* (New York: Grove, 2003), 75.

7. *Thirteenth Census of the United States: 1910*, vol. 4, "Population," table 8, 574 (85.9 percent, or 22,654, worked in "domestic and personal service" in New York City, and 1.33 percent, or 603, worked in professional services).

8. *Fourteenth Census of the United States: 1920*, vol. 4, "Population," chap. 7, table 2, 1161–62 (71 percent, or 28,937, of African American women worked in "domestic and personal service" in New York City, and 2.27 percent, or 921, worked in professional services).

9. *Thirteenth Census*, vol. 4, table 8, 571–74; *Fourteenth Census*, vol. 4, table 2, 1157–61.

10. Jacqueline Jones, *Labor of Love, Labor of Sorrow: Black Women, Work, and the Family from Slavery to the Present* (New York: Vintage, 1995), 154, 208–9; Alice Kessler-Harris, *Out to Work* (New York: Oxford University Press, 1982), 219, 237; Connolly, 34; Wilder, 139.

11. James Weldon Johnson, *Black Manhattan* (New York: Da Capo, 1930), 127. See also Richard Rubenstein and Robert Fogelson, eds., *Story of the Riot* [Mass Violence in America Series] (New York: Arno, 1969).

12. Khalil Gibran Muhammad, *The Condemnation of Blackness: Race, Crime, and the Making of Modern Urban America* (Cambridge: Harvard University Press, 2010); Biondi; Ransby; Kevin Boyle, *Arc of Justice: A Saga of Race, Civil Rights, and Murder in the Jazz Age* (New York: Holt, 2004); Andrea McArdle and Tanya Erzen, eds., *Zero Tolerance: Quality of Life and the New Police Brutality in New York City* (New York: New York University Press, 2001).

13. Johnson, 58–59; Connolly, 8, 33, 89; Dabel; Higginbotham; Gilmore; Elizabeth Lasch-Quinn, *Black Neighbors: Race and the Limits of Reform in the American Settlement House Movement, 1890–1945* (Chapel Hill: University of North Carolina Press, 1993); Terborg-Penn, *African American Women*; Giddings, *When and Where I Enter: The Impact of Black Women on Race and Sex in America* (New York: Bantam, 1984); Elsa Barkley Brown, "Womanist Consciousness: Maggie Lena Walker and the Independent Order of Saint Luke," *Signs* 14 (Spring 1989): 610–33; Gerda Lerner, ed., *Black Women in White America: A Documentary History* (New York: Pantheon, 1972); Linda O. McMurray, *To Keep the Waters Troubled: The Life of Ida B. Wells* (New York: Oxford University Press, 1998).

14. Johnson, 143.

15. Cash; Darlene Clark Hine, *Hine Sight: Black Women and the Re-Construction of American History* (Brooklyn: Carlson, 1994); White; Shaw.

16. Boyle; Trotter, *Great Migration*; Gregory; James Grossman, *Land of Hope: Chicago, Black Southerners, and the Great Migration* (University of Chicago Press, 1989); Timuel

D. Black, Jr., *Bridges of Memory: Chicago's First Wave of Black Migration* (Evanston, Ill.: Northwestern University Press, 2003); Baldwin; Joe William Trotter, Jr., *Black Milwaukee: The Making of an Industrial Proletariat, 1915–1945*, 2nd ed. (Urbana: University of Illinois Press, 2007); Lillian Serece Williams, *Strangers in the Land of Paradise: The Creation of an African American Community, Buffalo, New York 1900–1940* (Bloomington: Indiana University Press, 1999).

17. *Survey Graphic, Harlem Mecca of the New Negro* (New York: Survey Associates, 1925.)

18. See Nathan Kantrowitz, "Negro and Puerto Rican Populations of New York City in the Twentieth Century," *American Geographical Society*, 1969, table I; Connolly, 7; Osofsky, 18; Lewinson; Ottley; John B. Manbeck, ed., *The Neighborhoods of Brooklyn* (New Haven, Conn.: Yale University Press, 1998); Clarence Taylor, *The Black Churches of Brooklyn* (New York: Columbia University Press, 1994). Between 1910 and 1920, the city's black population increased from 91,709 to 152,567, a 66 percent increase. From 1920 to 1930 it expanded to 327,706, a 115 percent increase (U.S. Census data cited in George W. Groh, *The Black Migration: The Journey to Urban America* [New York: Weybright and Talley, 1972], 50).

19. Groh, 59; Kantrowitz, "Negro and Puerto Rican"; Manbeck, xxiv. The population grew from 1.2 million in 1890 to 2.7 million in 1940. Brooklyn's black population grew from 10,287 in 1890 to 107,263 in 1940 (*U.S. Census, 1910, Fifteenth U.S. Census*, "Population," vol. 3, pt. 2, 1940; *Sixteenth Census of U.S.*, vol. 2, "Characteristics of the Population," pt. 5, New York; Taylor, 103.

20. Lewinson, 21, 27, 34; Wilder, chapters 2 and 3; Connolly, 5–9; Harris.

21. Claude McKay, *Harlem: Negro Metropolis* (New York: Harcourt Brace Jovanovich, 1968 [1940]), 16–17; Johnson, 59; Connolly, 52–55.

22. Terborg-Penn, *African American Women*, 118–32; Ann Gordon, et al., *African American Women and the Vote 1837–1965* (Amherst: University of Massachusetts Press, 1997).

23. The symbolic representation of Tammany Hall as a Bengal tiger started during William "Boss" Tweed's era in the 1860s. The tiger had been the chosen symbol of Tweed's beloved volunteer fire company, No. 6, and when he became the Tammany boss, the tiger symbol came with him. In the early 1870s, *Harper's Weekly* political cartoonist Thomas Nast popularized the image of the Tammany Tiger as a voracious, corrupt political machine. See Oliver Allen, *The Tiger: The Rise and Fall of Tammany Hall* (New York: Addison-Wesley, 1993), 83; Kenneth Ackerman, *Boss Tweed: The Rise and Fall of the Corrupt Pol Who Conceived the Soul of Modern New York* (New York: Carol & Graf, 2005), 36, 253–54.

24. Allen; Gustavus Myers, *The History of Tammany Hall* (New York: Dover, 1971); Roy Peel, *Political Clubs in New York City* (New York: Putnam's, 1935), 138, 153–59, 191–200; Lewinson, chapter 3.

25. The city had absorbed a small area of Westchester County in 1874 and a second area in 1895. Today that land is part of Bronx County. Allan Nevins and John Krout, eds., *The Greater City New York, 1898–1948* (New York: Columbia University Press), 45, 52.

26. In 1910, Manhattan's population was 2,762,522 and Brooklyn's was 1,634,351. In 1920, Manhattan's population was 2,284,103 and Brooklyn's was 2,018,356. By 1930,

Brooklyn's population, 2,560,401, had surpassed Manhattan's, 1,867,312. All figures taken from http://www.census.gov/population/cencounts/ny190090.txt (accessed August 31, 2011).

27. Nevins, 48–49; Allen, 190–91.

28. Tammany District Attorney Asa Bird Gardiner was quoted in Myers, 289n9; "Meeting of the Special Committee of the Democratic General Committee of Kings County, on harmonious and concerted action of Democrats," series 1, box 1, Brooklyn Democratic Party Papers (BDPP), Brooklyn College Special Collection (BC), 30, 48,67.

29. Osofsky, 160; Weiss, 3–12; Valelly, 60–62, 121–48; McGerr, 186.

30. "Tammany Hall vs. Fusion—or—Organized Democracy Against Disorganized Aristocracy and Bastard Reform," campaign literature by Tammany Hall United Colored Democracy of the County of New York, Kent State University microfilm, n.d. [1913?], 10.

31. "Tammany Hall vs. Fusion," 5; Richard Sherman, *The Republican Party and Black America from McKinley to Hoover, 1896–1933* (Charlottesville: University of Virginia Press, 1973), 110–11; Valelly, 121–48; Gustafson, *Women and the Republican Party* (Urbana: University of Illinois Press, 2001),125–29.

32. "Tammany Hall vs. Fusion," 5; Sherman, 110–11; Valelly, 121–48; Gustafson, *Women*, 125–29.

33. "Tammany Hall vs. Fusion," 3.

34. "Tammany Hall vs. Fusion," 12.

35. Lewinson, 45–46, 61–62; Hulan Jack, *Fifty Years a Democrat: The Autobiography of Hulan E. Jack*, (New York: Franklin House, 1982), 65; John C. Walter, *The Harlem Fox: J. Raymond Jones and Tammany, 1920–1970* (New York: State University of New York Press, 1989); George M. Furniss, "The Political Assimilation of Negroes in New York City," PhD diss., Columbia University, 1969, 62.

36. Lewinson, 59; Osofsky, 169.

37. *The Crisis*, January 1922, 106.

38. Lewinson, 60; Kasinitz, 213.

39. Connolly, 90; *New York Age*, July 25, 1925; March 29, 1930; *Negro World*, August 8, 1931, 1.

40. "Tammany Hall vs. Fusion," 5–7.

41. Terborg-Penn, *African American Women*, chapter 3.

42. Terborg-Penn, *African American Women*, 40.

43. Nell Irvine Painter, "Voices of Suffrage: Sojourner Truth, Frances Watkins Harper, and the Struggle for Woman Suffrage," in *Votes for Women: The Struggle for Suffrage Revisited*, ed. Jean Baker, 42–55 (New York: Oxford University Press, 2002).

44. Ellen Carol DuBois, *Harriet Stanton Blatch and the Winning of Woman Suffrage* (New Haven, Conn.: Yale University Press, 1997), 186–87.

45. Terborg-Penn, *African American Women*; Marjorie Julian Spruill, "Race, Reform, and Reaction at the Turn of the Century," in *Votes for Women*, ed. Marjorie Spruill Wheeler, 102–17 (Knoxville: University of Tennessee Press, 1995); Rebecca Edwards, *Angels in the Machinery: Gender in American Party Politics from the Civil War to the Progressive Era* (New York: Oxford University Press, 1997), 142–44.

46. See Materson; Tera Hunter, *To 'Joy My Freedom: Southern Black Women's Lives and Labors After the Civil War* (Cambridge, Mass.: Harvard University Press, 1997), 32–33; Elsa Barkley Brown, "To Catch the Vision of Freedom: Reconstructing Southern Black Women's Political History, 1865–1880," in *African American Women and the Vote, 1837–1965*, ed. Ann Gordon et al., 66–99 (Amherst: University of Massachusetts Press, 1997); White, 40–41, 49–50; Anne Meis Knupfer, *Toward a Tenderer Humanity* (New York: New York University Press, 1996), chapter 3.

47. Hallie Q. Brown, *Homespun Heroines and Other Women of Distinction* (New York: Oxford University Press, 1988, [1926]), 115; Charles Harris Wesley, *The History of the National Association of Colored Women's Clubs, A Legacy of Service* (Washington, D.C.: NACW, 1984), 77; Karen Garner, "Equal Suffrage League," in *Organizing Black America*, ed. Nina Mjagkij, 224–25 (New York: Garland, 2001); Gerda Lerner, *The Majority Finds Its Past* (New York: Oxford University Press, 1979), 86; Terborg-Penn, *African American Women*, 87, 94–95; Gordon et al., *African American Women*.

48. *New York Times*, February 7, 1910; Terborg-Penn, *African American Women*, 100–102.

49. *New York Times*, February 25, 1911. See also Osofsky, chapter 8.

50. Terborg-Penn, *African American Women*, 101.

51. *New York Times*, August 29, 1915; September 2, 1915.

52. *New York Age*, September 20, 1917; September 27, 1917; October 4, 1917; November 1, 1917; Robert Hill, ed., *Marcus Garvey and UNIA Papers* (Berkeley: University of California Press, 1986), vol. 1, 224–25; vol. 3, 698, 700; vol. 4, 941; vol. 5, 785, 834; Terborg-Penn, *African American Women*, 87, 92, 100–101. Anne Watkins was daughter of Luke Edward Wright of Tennessee, former Confederate general, U.S. Ambassador to Japan from 1906 to 1907, and Secretary of War from 1908 to 1909. She was married to John Humphrey Watkins, former railroad president and Wall Street bond dealer. Available at http://www.tngenweb.org/giles/history/bios/wright.htm (accessed August 31, 2011); *New York Times*, September 21, 1909.

53. *New York Age*, September 27, 1917.

54. *New York Age*, September 20, 1917; *Negro World*, February 24, 1923; Barbara Bair, "'Ethiopia Shall Stretch Forth Her Hands unto God': Laura Kofey and the Gendered Vision of Redemption in the Garvey Movement," in *A Mighty Baptism: Race, Gender, and the Creation of American Protestantism*, ed. Susan Lester and Lisa MacFarlane, 59 (Ithaca, New York: Cornell University Press, 1996).

55. Elisabeth Israels Perry, *Belle Moskowitz: Feminine Politics and the Exercise of Power in the Age of Alfred E. Smith* (Boston: Northeastern University Press, 2000 [1992]), 114.

56. Aileen Kraditor, *The Ideas of the Woman Suffrage Movement, 1890–1920* (New York: Norton, 1981 [1965]), chapter 7; Terborg-Penn, *African American Women*, chapter 6; Evelyn Brooks Higginbotham, "In Politics to Stay: Black Women Leaders and Party Politics in the 1920s," in *Women, Politics and Change*, ed. Louise A. Tilly and Patricia Gurin, 200–201 (New York: Sage, 1990).

57. *New York Age*, September 27, 1917; November 1, 1917; November 22, 1917.

58. *New York Times*, February 7, 1910; September 2, 1915; April 29, 1917; October 28, 1917; November 5, 1917; Ida Hustead Harper, ed., *History of Woman Suffrage, 1900–1920*,

212 / NOTES TO CHAPTER ONE

vol. 5 (New York: Arno, 1969), DuBois, *Harriet Stanton*, chapters 5–7; Freeman, *A Room at a Time*, 60–61; Kristi Andersen, *After Suffrage: Women in Partisan and Electoral Politics before the New Deal* (Chicago: University of Chicago Press, 1996), 77.

59. *New York Times*, November 7, 1917; November 8, 1917. The Socialists won ten seats in the state assembly, an increase of eight from the prior election. Moreover, although Morris Hillquit, the Socialist Party candidate for mayor, came in third behind the victorious Democrat John Hylan and Fusion candidate and incumbent John Purroy Mitchell, he beat the Republican Party candidate Bennett. Election totals were: Hylan, 293,386; Mitchell, 148,060; Hillquit, 138,793; and Bennett, 52,828.

60. *New York Times*, November 8, 1917; November 27, 1917. New York City gave the suffrage amendment a majority of 92,696. The amendment was defeated by 3,856 votes in the rest of the state. Eleanor Flexner, *Century of Struggle: The Woman's Rights Movement in the United States* (New York: Atheneum, 1972 [1959]), 290.

61. *New York Times*, January 6, 1918; January 7, 1918; January 8, 1918.

62. *New York Age*, November 22, 1917; September 18, 1920.

63. *The Crisis*, March 1920, 234. See also Judith Weisenfeld, *African American Women and Christian Activism: New York's Black YWCA, 1905–1945* (Cambridge, Mass.: Harvard University Press, 1997), 178; Higginbotham, "In Politics to Stay"; Terborg-Penn, *African American Women*, chapter 7.

64. Freeman, *A Room at a Time*, 108; Gustafson, *Women*, 3; Higginbotham, "In Politics to Stay," 206–7; Terborg-Penn, *African American Women*, 103–4.

65. *New York Times*, January 18, 1918; February 22, 1918; March 1, 1918; May 19, 1918; August 7, 1919; October 26, 1920. The minutes of the Brooklyn Democratic Party reveal that they began to include women in the Executive County Committee in September 1922 and continued to have women at both the county committee level and executive committee level thereafter. Brooklyn Democratic Party Papers, series I, box 3, Brooklyn College Special Collections. Andersen, 80–81; Freeman, *A Room at a Time*, chapter 6.

66. *The Crisis*, November 1918, 45. See also Sherman, 133, for mention of Democrats' success in local elections in New York City.

67. Lewinson, 59; Osofosky, 169–74.

68. Matthew Josephson and Hannah Josephson, *Al Smith: Hero of the Cities* (Boston: Houghton Mifflin, 1969), 194; Perry, *Belle Moskowitz*, 117.

69. Perry, *Belle Moskowitz*, 117–18.

70. "A Dozen Reasons Why Women Should Vote for Alfred E. Smith," campaign literature, Brooklyn Democratic Party Campaign Materials, 1898–27, available at Metropolitan New York Library Council Digital Collections, available at http://cdm128401.cdmhost .com/cdm/search/collection/bc; Allen, 228; Perry, *Belle Moskowitz*, 168–83; Josephson and Josephson, 197, 287–88; Lewinson, 59.

71. *New York Times*, November 7, 1918. Lilly won 7,572 to Ellenbogen's 7,388 and Vogel's 432 votes.

72. *The Crisis*, September 1918, 240; Lewinson, 63; Sherman, 138; Terborg-Penn, *African American Women*, 142; Elisabeth Israels Perry, "Defying the Party Whip: Mary

Garrett Hay and the Republican Party, 1917–1920," in Gustafson, Miller, and Perry, 97–107.

73. *New York Times*, November 8, 1917; November 7, 1918; Lewinson, 59. Healy won 6,977 votes to Johnson's 5,557 and Randolph's 1,078. Healy's plurality over the two men together was just 342 votes.

74. *New York Age*, August 30, 1919; September 6, 1919; *New York Times*, September 2, 1919; September 3, 1919.

75. Marcus Garvey Papers, vol. 1, 222; *New York Times*, November 7, 1918; October 26, 1920; October 1, 1922.

76. *New York Times*, November 8, 1917; November 6, 1918; November 7, 1918; August 7, 1919; July 5, 1920; November 3, 1920; July 11, 1921; October 1, 1922.

77. *New York Age*, August 19, 1919; July 10, 1920; September 18, 1920; reviewed *New York Age*, 1919–1920 for references to Grace Campbell.

78. *New York Times*, January 8, 1920; April 2, 1920.

79. *New York Times*, April 21, 1920; May 20, 1929.

80. Among others, A. Philip Randolph, Chandler Owens, Fannie Jacobs, and Mary McVicker ran for the state assembly; Fanny Witherspoon and Pauline Newman ran for Congress. *New York Times*, November 7, 1918; October 26, 1920; November 10, 1921; October 1, 1922; DuBois, *Harriet Stanton Blatch*, 229; *Marcus Garvey Papers*, vol. 1, 222.

81. Andersen, 80–102; Freeman, *A Room at a Time*, 23–24. For a discussion of the "gendered imagination," see Kessler-Harris, *In Pursuit of Equity*.

82. Helene Weinstein, *Lawmakers: Biographical Sketches of the Women of the NYS Legislature (1918–1988)* (Albany, N.Y.: Legislative Women's Caucus, 1989).

83. *New York Times*, October 5, 1919; *The Crisis*, October 1919, 293–98.

84. Hedgeman, 39–40.

85. *The Crisis*, May 1919, 23; September 1919, 241–44; December 1919, 56–61; *New York Age*, May 10, 1919; June 28, 1919; July 19, 1919; July 26, 1919; August 2, 1919.

86. W. E. B. DuBois, "Returning Soldiers," *The Crisis*, May 1919, 13.

87. Claude McKay, "If We Must Die," *The Liberator*, July 1919, 21.

88. Brown, 114–16; Roslyn Terborg-Penn, "Discontented Black Feminists," in *Decades of Discontent: The Women's Movement, 1920–1940*, ed. Lois Jensen and Joan M. Scharf, 269 (Westport, Conn.: 1983); Terborg-Penn, *African American Women*, 270, 271; White, 124, 174. See also Marcus Garvey, *Philosophy and Opinions of Marcus Garvey* (Arno Press, 1968), 55.

89. White, 134–39; Brown, 116; Terborg-Penn, "Discontented Black Feminists," 267–69; Ula Yvette Taylor, *The Veiled Garvey: The Life and Times of Amy Jacque Garvey* (Chapel Hill: University of North Carolina Press, 2002), chapter 4.

90. *Negro World*, February 24, 1923; April 19, 1930.

91. *Negro World*, September 8, 1923.

92. W. E. B. DuBois, *The Souls of Black Folk*, ed. David Blight and Robert Gooding-Williams (Boston: Bedford/St. Martin's, 1997), 38–39.

93. Hedgeman, 51.

94. *New York Age*, June 18, 1921; March 5, 1927; October 6, 1928.

95. *New York Age*, November 10, 1928.

96. *New York Age*, November 6, 1920.

97. *New York Age*, October 9, 1920; October 23, 1920; October 21, 1921; *The Crisis*, September 1920, 235.

98. Quote in Higginbotham, "In Politics to Stay," 212. See also Sherman, chapters 8 and 9.

99. *New York Age*, July 25, 1925; October 24, 1925; July 24, 1926; September 11, 1926; September 21, 1929; December 28, 1929; *The Crisis*, January 1928, 19; May 1928, 168; December 1928, 416, 418.

100. *The Crisis*, December 1922, 73; *New York Times*, June 13, 1924; August 29, 1924; *New York Age*, June 14, 1924.

101. *New York Age*, June 14, 1924; October 30, 1926; April 2, 1927; March 5, 1927.

102. *New York Age*, November 18, 1922; April 12, 1924; April 2, 1927.

103. *New York Age*, February 16, 1924.

104. *The Crisis*, October 1928, 346.

105. Perry, *Belle Moskowitz*, 204.

106. *The Crisis*, July 1924, 104; *New York Age*, October 13, 1928; October 20, 1928.

107. On the Dyer anti-lynching bill, see *The Crisis*, April 1922, 248; November 1922, 8; January 1923, 103–6; July 1923, 124; July 1924, 104. On African Americans' frustration with the Republican party, see *The Crisis*, October 1924, 262; *New York Times*, June 6, 1924; June 9, 1924.

108. *New York Age*, October 13, 1928; October 20, 1928; Higginbotham, 208–12; Freeman, *A Room at a Time*, 137, 184, 188; Terborg-Penn, *African American Women*, 145, 157; White, 134–35.

109. Andersen suggests that Democrats were slightly more welcoming to women than Republicans following the passage of the 19th Amendment (80–102). Freeman claims that Republicans were (*A Room at a Time*, 23–24). There was a tremendous amount of variability across the nation, so no simple statement can be made. What both scholars do show is that once the parties adjusted to women's inclusion at some minimal level in the political machinery, they made very few further changes until the late 1960s.

110. Andersen, 87–88.

111. Andersen, 105, 109; Higginbotham, "In Politics to Stay"; *New York Age*, June 18, 1921; September 15, 1928; November 3, 1928; *Crisis*, March 1921; *Crisis*, July 1926, 129.

112. *New York Age*, October 5, 1916; October 12, 1916; May 2, 1925.

113. *New York Age*, November 23, 1916; January 17, 1925.

114. *New York Age*, August 22, 1925; March 19, 1927; *New York Times*, April 3, 1920; September 26, 1920; April 19, 1921; April 23, 1922.

115. *New York Age*, August 11, 1923; February 16, 1924; March 1, 1924; May 17, 1924; January 25, 1925; February 21, 1925; October 10, 1925; *The Crisis*, October 1928, 333–35; Osofsky, 106–10. See also Biondi for an extensive discussion of the effort to change the city's housing laws in the late 1940s (chapter 6).

116. *New York Age*, November 1, 1919; May 28, 1921; August 15, 1925. The Civil Rights Law of the State of New York was first passed as the Malby Civil Rights Law in June, 1895. It was "introduced at Albany through the influence of Charles W. Anderson,

who is secretary to State Treasurer Colvin" (*New York Times*, June 19, 1895). See also Lewinson, 37–40; Osofsky, 162–68. The Civil Rights Law was amended a number of times throughout subsequent decades, including in 1907 and 1913 (*New York Times*, May 25, 1907; April 13, 1913). See also *Laws of the State of New York*, vol. 2, Civil Rights Law amended, chap. 196, 812–14; and Penal Law amended to protect civil rights, chap. 380, 1201; and Table of Laws and Codes amended, Civil Rights Law, 12 (Albany: Lyon/State Printers, 1918). For a discussion about the struggle to increase the number of black nurses at Harlem Hospital, which was allied with Bellevue Hospital, see Darlene Clark Hine, *Black Women in White: Racial Conflict and Cooperation in the Nursing Profession, 1890–1950* (Bloomington: Indiana University Press, 1989), 41–46.

117. *New York Age*, April 30, 1927.

118. Hedgeman, 34.

119. Hedgeman, 17–18, 28, 30; Unpublished Oral History conducted by Ellen Craft Dammond with Anna Arnold Hedgeman, Black Women's Oral History Project [hereinafter: Dammond oral history with Hedgeman], Schlesinger Library, Radcliffe Institute for Advanced Study, Harvard University [hereinafter SL], 24, 26, 40, 43, 44, 50–51.

120. Boyle; Trotter, *Black Milwaukee*, 61–63; Susan Smith, *Sick and Tired of Being Sick and Tired: Black Women's Health Activism in America, 1890–1950* (Philadelphia: University of Pennsylvania Press, 1995), 22; Countryman, 18–19. For a discussion of racist hiring policies by Metropolitan Life Insurance Company, one of the largest companies in a city of corporate giants, see *New York Age*, April 26, 1930.

121. Dabel; Sugrue; Countryman; Biondi.

122. *New York Age*, October 19, 1916; February 22, 1917; October 15, 1921; June 30, 1923; July 14, 1923; March 1, 1924; March 29, 1924; September 15, 1928; *The Crisis*, March 1923, 208–10.

123. *New York Age*, May 19, 1923.

124. *New York Age*, April 4, 1925.

125. Dawson case, see *New York Age*, February 14, 1925; October 23, 1926.

126. *New York Age*, August 2, 1917; June 10, 1922; October 7, 1922; *The Crisis*, September 1917, 227; March 1923, 213–15.

127. *New York Age*, November 18, 1922.

128. *New York Age*, May 2, 1925; October 3, 1925.

CHAPTER 2. STRIDES FORWARD IN TIMES OF CRISIS IN THE 1930S AND 1940S

1. *Afro-American*, July 25, 1931.

2. *Report of the New York State Temporary Commission in the Condition of the Urban Colored Population to the Legislature of the State of New York*, created by Chapter 858, Laws of 1937 (Albany: Lyon, 1938), 13–18. In 1930, there were 93,781 women in private/domestic work in Manhattan. In 1950, there were 42,410. The census data does not break the figure down by race in 1930 (and no comparable figure was available for 1940), but it does in 1950. In 1950 there are 106,044 domestic/private workers in the whole New York City area, and 71,373, or two-thirds, are identified as Negro. By 1950, there were more African American women under twenty-four years old (1,145) with college degrees

than African American men (555). See *1950 Seventeenth Census of the United States*, vol. 2, "Characteristics of the Population," part 32, New York, 32–231, and for domestic work figures. See also *1930 United States Department of Commerce*, Fifteenth Census, "Population," vol. 3, part 2.

3. See Robert A. Margo, "Employment and Unemployment in the 1930s," *Journal of Economic Perspectives* 7, no. 2 (1993), 43. Economists continue to debate the most effective measurements and greatest accuracy of employment statistics during the Great Depression. Here I use the figures from Stanley Lebergott's 1964 book, *Manpower in Economic Growth*, as cited in Margo. For GNP figures, see U.S. Department of Commerce: Bureau of Economic Analysis, available at http://research.stlouisfed.org/fred2/data/GDPA.txt (accessed August 31, 2011).

4. Eleanor Roosevelt Papers, "The Great Depression," in *Teaching Eleanor Roosevelt*, ed. Allida Black, June Hopkins, et al. (Hyde Park, N.Y.: Eleanor Roosevelt National Historic Site, 2003).

5. Darlene Clark Hine, "The Housewives' League of Detroit: Black Women and Economic Nationalism," in Hine, *Hine Sight*, 129–45; Wolcott, chapters 5 and 6; Lizabeth Cohen, *A Consumers' Republic: The Politics of Mass Consumption in Postwar America* (New York: Knopf, 2003), chapter 1; Sugrue, 21–29; Materson.

6. *New York Age*, March 28, 1931; October 21, 1931; December 9, 1933. *New York Red Book, 1934* (Albany: Lyon, 1934), 263; *New York Red Book, 1935* (Albany: Lyon, 1935), 276.

7. Cheryl Greenberg, *"Or Does It Explode?" Black Harlem in the Great Depression* (New York: Oxford University Press, 1991), 89–90. See also Kessler-Harris, *In Pursuit of Equity*; Linda Gordon, *Pitied but Not Entitled: Single Mothers and the History of Welfare, 1890–1935* (Cambridge, Mass.: Harvard University Press, 1998).

8. Carita Owens Roane, "Negro Relief Work in New York," *The Crisis*, January 1931, 451.

9. Roane, 469.

10. Dammond oral history with Hedgeman, 63.

11. Joyce A. Hanson, *Mary McLeod Bethune and Black Women's Political Activism* (Columbia: University of Missouri Press, 2003), 168–69.

12. Hedgeman, 67–70, 74; Dammond oral history with Hedgeman, 66. See also Shaw, 188.

13. Hedgeman, 68–69. See also Shaw, 197.

14. Dorothy Height, *Open Wide the Freedom Gates: A Memoir* (New York: Public Affairs, 2003), 55.

15. Height, *Open Wide*, 31; *Washington Post*, June 4, 2004.

16. Height, *Open Wide*, 36–37.

17. For a discussion of Communist activism and the Popular Front in the 1930s, see Mark Naison, *Communists in Harlem during the Depression* (New York: Grove, 1983). For a discussion of broader-based battles for racial equality during the 1930s, see Greenberg; Gail Lumet Buckley, *The Hornes: An American Family* (New York: Knopf, 1986), chapter 6; Michael Denning, *The Cultural Front: The Laboring of American Culture in the Twentieth Century* (New York: Verso, 1996), 310–11, 369–70; on Baker's and Height's participation in Popular Front activities, see Ransby, chapter 3; Ruth Edmonds Hill, ed., *The Black*

Women Oral History Project: From the Arthur and Elizabeth Schlesinger Library on the History of Women in America, Radcliffe College, vol. 5, "Dorothy Height Interview" (Westport, Conn.: Meckler, 1991), 59; Height, *Open Wide*, 61–63.

18. Hill, *Black Women*, 60.

19. Height, *Open Wide*, 51–52.

20. Height, *Open Wide*, 56.

21. Hill, *Black Women*, 60–62; *Amsterdam News*, April 17, 1948; *Second Report of the New York State Temporary Commission in the Condition of the Colored Urban Population to the Legislature of the State of New York, February 1939* (Legislative Document [1939] No. 69) (Albany: Lyon, 1939), 37.

22. *The Crisis*, November 1935, 330.

23. Lynd's quote cited in Ransby, 94.

24. Ransby, 95–98.

25. Genna Rae McNeil, Interview with Pauli Murray, February 13, 1976 (Interview G-0044, Southern Oral History Program Collection [#4007]), available with audio at http://docsouth.unc.edu/sohp/playback.html?base_file=G-0044&duration=05:18:41 (accessed January 14, 2011).

26. Pauli Murray, *The Autobiography of a Black Activist, Feminist, Lawyer, Priest, and Poet* [Formerly titled *Song in a Weary Throat: An American Pilgrimage*] (Knoxville: University of Tennessee Press, 1987), 102–7.

27. *New York Age*, December 2, 1933.

28. Layle Lane, "Harlem" (early 1940s), box 184–2, folder 6, Layle Lane Manuscript Collection, Moorland-Spingarn Research Center, Manuscript Department, Howard University.

29. The American Labor Party (ALP) was formed in 1936 by labor activists and New Deal leaders, including the city's Republican mayor, Fiorello LaGuardia. It gave the city's Democrats an easier way to vote for LaGuardia, who in 1936 ran on the Republican and ALP ballots. Despite its limited reach in the rest of the state, the ALP was a major political party in New York City for much of its twenty-year existence. J. David Gillespie, *Politics at the Periphery: Third Parties in Two-Party America* (Columbia: University of South Carolina Press, 1993), 257.

30. Lane's handwritten response to a questionnaire given to her from a citizens' political group [n.d.]. See also Campaign Flier 1942, box 1, folder 5; Layle Lane, "What Steps Can We Take Now toward More Democracy for the Negro?" Discussion Digest, December 6, 1942, box 1, folder 5, Layle Lane Manuscript Collection, Schomburg Center for Research in Black Culture [hereinafter Schomburg].

31. Letter to Layle Lane from Maida Springer, October 26, 1942, box 1, folder 5, Lane Collection, Schomburg.

32. Letter from Layle Lane to Mr. Solomon, October 1, 1934, box 1, folder 4, Lane Collection, Schomburg.

33. Letter from August Claessens to Dear Comrade [Lane], September 19, 1934, box 1, folder 4, Lane Collection, Schomburg.

34. Alma Crosswaith ran for the Nineteenth Assembly District seat, and Morgan ran for the Nineteenth State Senate seat. *The New York Redbook, 1935*, 451, 460, 476. See also

Campaign Literature, Layle Lane Collection, box 184–1, folder 9, Moorland-Spingarn Research Center, Manuscript Department, Howard University.

35. *New York Times*, November 5, 1936.

36. Layle Lane, "Harlem: A Challenge to Democracy," *The Guild Teacher*, 1941, 10, Layle Lane Manuscript Collection, box 184–2 Moorland-Spingarn Research Center, Manuscript Department, Howard University.

37. *New York Times*, November 7, 1934; September 16, 1936; November 5, 1936; October 31, 1937; August 17, 1938; September 1, 1942; November 1, 1942; September 1, 1943; August 18, 1945; August 29, 1946; November 2, 1947.

38. Kathleen Thompson, "Carter, Eunice Roberta Hunton," in *Black Women in America*, 2nd ed., ed. Darlene Clark Hine (Oxford African American Studies Center, http://www.oxfordaasc.com/article/opr/t003/e0057 [accessed November 25, 2008]); Faye Chadwell, "Carter, Eunice Hunton," *African American National Biography*, ed. Henry Louis Gates Jr. and Evelyn Brooks Higginbotham (Oxford African American Studies Center, http://www.oxfordaasc.com/article/opr/t0001/e0100 [accessed November 25, 2008]).

39. *New York Age*, August 4, 1934; November 3, 1934.

40. *New York Age*, November 3, 1934.

41. *New York Age*, November 10, 1934.

42. *The Complete Report of Mayor LaGuardia's Commission on the Harlem Riot of March 19, 1935* (New York: Arno, 1969); *The Crisis*, May 1935, 145; *New York Age*, March 23, 1935; March 30, 1935.

43. *Amsterdam News*, April 20, 1935; August 10, 1935; *New York Times*, August 6, 1935; September 14, 1935; Bettye Collier-Thomas, *N.C.N.W. 1935–1980* (Washington, D.C.: National Council of Negro Women, 1981), xiii, 6.

44. *New York Times*, October 24, 1936; November 1, 1936.

45. *New York Age*, November 7, 1936.

46. *New York Times*, November 5, 1936. Bolin won 4,356 votes; her Democratic opponent, incumbent Robert Justice, won 18,973 votes; her Socialist opponent, Victor Gaspar, won 265.

47. *New York Times*, July 23, 1939; J. Clay Smith, Jr., ed., *Rebels in Law: Voices in History of Black Women Lawyers* (Ann Arbor: University of Michigan Press, 1998), 282.

48. Benjamin Brawley, *Negro Builders and Heroes* (Chapel Hill: University of North Carolina Press, 1937), 262; Murray, *Autobiography*, 277; *New York Times*, December 25, 1977.

49. Campaign Literature, 1945, Ruth Whitehead Whaley Clippings File, Schomburg Clippings File; *People's Voice*, August 11, 1945; *Amsterdam News*, September 22, 1945.

50. *Amsterdam News*, August 14, 1937; September 18, 1937.

51. *Chicago Defender*, January 2, 1937; *New York Age*, August 14, 1937.

52. *New York Age*, October 6, 1934; August 14, 1937.

53. *New York Age*, August 28, 1937.

54. *New York Age*, September 11, 1937; *Chicago Defender*, September 11, 1937.

55. *New York Age*, October 16, 1937; *Chicago Defender*, October 9, 1937; October 16, 1937.

56. *New York Age*, October 30, 1937.

57. *New York Age*, October 30, 1937.

58. *New York Age*, November 13, 1937.

59. *Chicago Defender*, November 13, 1937.

60. Michael Pollan, "Farmer in Chief," *New York Times*, October 9, 2008, Sunday Magazine. While Alice Kessler-Harris's pioneering book on women in the labor force, *Out to Work*, identifies that the influx of women in the waged-labor force during WWII was far less dramatic than the wartime propaganda suggests, there was nevertheless an increase of women's labor participation of approximately 25 percent (273–77). Also on women's labor participation in defense plants see David Kennedy, *Freedom from Fear: The American People in Depression and War, 1929–1945* (New York: Oxford University Press, 1999), 776–79; Connie Fields, *Life and Times of Rosie the Riveter*, (video documentary) Clarity Films, 1980.

61. Biondi.

62. Biondi; Sugrue; Jacquelyn Down Hall, "The Long Civil Rights Movement and the Political Uses of the Past," *Journal of American History*, March 2005, 1233–63.

63. Hedgeman, 85; Dammond oral history with Hedgeman, 93; Campaign Literature, Layle Lane Manuscript Collection, Moorland-Spingarn Research Center, box 184–1, folder 9; Murray, *Autobiography*, 200–209; Ransby, 108.

64. Naison, 312–13; Biondi, 47.

65. Walter; Lewinson; *New York Times*, March 24, 1944.

66. *Annual Report of the Board of Elections in the City of New York, 1944*, 34–35. Women did not outnumber men on voter registration lists in both the major parties again until 1960. However, women consistently outnumbered men registered in the Republican Party throughout much of the 1950s and 1960s. *Annual Report of the Board of Elections of the City of New York, 1940–1968*.

67. *New York Times*, May 11, 1944; May 13, 1944.

68. *New York Times*, April 13, 1944.

69. *New York Times*, April 9, 1944; April 30, 1944. There were reportedly 310,000 African Americans in the district as well as more than 100,000 others, including Puerto Ricans, Chinese, Italians, Finns, Irish, and Jews.

70. *Amsterdam News*, July 15, 1944.

71. Naison, xviii, 11, 47, 57, 117, 194, 312; Gerald Horne, *Black Liberation/Red Scare: Ben Davis and the Communist Party* (Newark: University of Delaware Press, 1994); Biondi, 42; Charles V. Hamilton, *Adam Clayton Powell, Jr.: The Political Biography of an American Dilemma* (New York: Atheneum, 1991), 150; *New York Times*, July 29, 1944.

72. *New York Times*, May 13, 1944.

73. *New York Times*, May 23, 1944; *Amsterdam News*, June 3, 1944.

74. *Amsterdam News*, May 20, 1944.

75. *Amsterdam News*, June 17, 1944.

76. *New York Times*, October 20, 1944.

77. *People's Voice*, June 3, 1944.

78. *New York Times*, June 6, 1944; June 26, 1944; August 1, 1944; August 2, 1944; November 9, 1944.

79. *People's Voice*, August 11, 1945.

80. Horne, *Black Liberation/Red Scare*.

81. *Amsterdam News*, July 28, 1945.

82. *People's Voice*, July 28, 1945; August 4, 1945; August 11, 1945; *Amsterdam News*, July 28, 1945; *New York Age*, August 11, 1945; *Amsterdam News*, September 22, 1945; *New York Age*, November 17, 1945.

83. *New York Age*, August 11, 1945; *Amsterdam News*, September 22, 1945.

84. Biondi, 46–47; Horne, *Black Liberation/Red Scare*, chapter 9. Ruth Whitehead Whaley had 10,967 votes and ranked eleventh in a field of twenty-one candidates, followed in twelfth place by B. F. McLaurin, Republican-Liberal, with 10,381. Davis had more than 56,500 votes. *New York Age*, November 17, 1945.

85. *People's Voice*, April 19, 1947.

86. *Amsterdam News*, November 11, 1950.

87. Walter G. Farr Jr., Lance Liebman, and Jeffrey S. Wood, *Decentralizing City Government: A Practical Study of a Radical Proposal for New York City* (New York: Praeger, 1972), 16–17. See *Amsterdam News*, August 29, 1953. See also Ruth Whitehead Whaley, Schomburg Clippings File.

88. *Amsterdam News*, April 19, 1952.

89. *Amsterdam News*, July 21, 1956.

90. See Steven Fraser, *Labor Will Rule: Sidney Hillman and the Rise of American Labor* (New York: Free Press, 1991), 517–18, 520–23.

91. Biondi, 51.

92. *Amsterdam News*, December 4, 1943; December 11, 1943; *New York Times*, November 24, 1943; *People's Voice*, June 3, 1944; October 21, 1944.

93. Biondi, 6.

94. *People's Voice*, October 21, 1944. The OPA was one of Roosevelt's wartime agencies. It was established to keep inflation in check, particularly through the use of price controls. For a discussion of OPA activity in New York City, see Nat Brandt, *Harlem at War: The Black Experience in World War II* (New York: Syracuse University Press, 1996), 215; and Thomas Kessner, *Fiorello H. La Guardia and the Making of Modern New York* (New York: McGraw-Hill, 1989), 539.

95. *People's Voice*, August 19, 1944.

96. *People's Voice*, September 30, 1944.

97. *People's Voice*, October 21, 1944.

98. *People's Voice*, October 21, 1944.

99. Kessler-Harris in *Out to Work* notes that although the vast majority of women entering the waged-labor force during World War II were married, most were older women. There was almost no increase in the percentage of women of childbearing years that underscored the persistence of gender norms rather than the challenge to them (278).

100. Kasinitz, chapter 7.

101. *Amsterdam News*, July 21, 1945.

102. *Brooklyn Eagle*, October 31, 1945.

103. *Amsterdam News*, November 3, 1945.

104. *Amsterdam News*, November 17, 1945; November 24, 1945.

105. *Amsterdam News*, June 8, 1946.

106. *Brooklyn Eagle*, June 21, 1948.

107. Biondi, chapter 7.

108. *People's Voice*, August 17, 1946, 2, 4.

109. Kate Weigand, *Red Feminism: American Communism and the Making of Women's Liberation* (Baltimore, Md.: The Johns Hopkins University Press, 2001), chapter 3.

110. Biondi, 51.

111. *Daily Worker*, March 20, 1946 [Ada Jackson, Schomburg Clipping File].

112. *People's Voice*, November 2, 1946.

113. *People's Voice*, November 23, 1946.

114. *Amsterdam News*, November 16, 1946. According to Biondi, though Richardson and Jackson lost, their efforts encouraged the Democratic Party to nominate a black candidate in the next election (130–31).

115. *New York Times*, October 27, 1948.

116. *New York Times*, November 9, 1949. Borough-wide vote: Cushmore (D) = 425,872; Stark (F/L/R) = 348,216; Jackson (ALP) = 79,211. Votes in Seventeenth District: Cushmore = 12,459; Stark = 9,404; Jackson = 3,999.

117. *Brooklyn Eagle*, October 20, 1948.

118. *Amsterdam News*, August 19, 1944; September 2, 1944; "Biographical Material on Pauli Murray, Issued by Citizens Committee for the Election of Pauli Murray," box 73, folder 1274, Pauli Murray Manuscript Collection, SL; *New York Age*, January 19, 1946; *Pittsburgh Courier*, Saturday, October 29, 1949; *New York Age*, November 5, 1949; Murray, 207–8.

119. Pauli Murray, "Jim Crow and Jane Crow," in *Black Women in White America: A Documentary History*, ed. Gerda Lerner, 592–99 (New York: Pantheon, 1972).

120. Campaign Flyer (Clippings File), and Press Release, box 73, folder 1273, Pauli Murray Manuscript Collection; *New York Age*, October 29, 1949; *Amsterdam News*, October 29, 1949.

121. Campaign Letter, October 28, 1949, box 73, folder 1273, Pauli Murray Manuscript Collection, SL.

122. *Amsterdam News*, May 27, 1944.

123. Murray, *Autobiography*, 280.

124. Yvette Richards, *Maida Springer: Pan-Africanist and International Labor Leader* (Pittsburgh: University of Pittsburgh Press, 2000), 90.

125. *New York Post*, October 26, 1949, box 73, folder 1276, Pauli Murray Manuscript Collection, SL.

126. Letter from Maida Springer to "Dear Friend," December 1, 1949, box 73, folder 1273, Pauli Murray Manuscript Collection, SL.

127. Hedgeman, 86; Dammond oral history with Hedgeman, 91; *Amsterdam News*, February 5, 1944, and February 12, 1944; *Amsterdam News*, May 20, 1944; *People's Voice*, June 23, 1945. For a full discussion on the history and fate of the FEPC (though it fails to mention Hedgeman), see Merl E. Reed, *Seedtime for the Modern Civil Rights Movement: The President's Committee on Fair Employment Practice, 1941–1946* (Baton Rouge: Louisiana State University Press, 1991); and Paula Pfeffer, *A. Philip Randolph, Pioneer of the Civil Rights Movement* (Baton Rouge: Louisiana State University Press, 1990), chapter 3.

CHAPTER 3. PUSHING THROUGH THE
DOORS OF RESISTANCE IN THE 1950S

1. *Amsterdam News*, July 17, 1954.

2. Ellen Schrecker, *Many Are the Crimes: McCarthyism in America* (Princeton, N.J.: Princeton University Press, 1999); Biondi; Penny Von Eschen, *Race against Empire: Black Americans and Anticolonialism, 1937–1957* (Ithaca, N.Y.: Cornell University Press, 1997); Gerald Horne, *Black Liberation/Red Scare*; Gerald Horne, *Race Woman: The Lives of Shirley Graham Du Bois* (New York: New York University Press, 2000).

3. On police brutality, for example, see *New York Times*, March 22, 1953; on schools, see Ora Mobley-Sweeting (with Ezekiel C. Mobley, Jr.), "Nobody Gave Me Permission: Memoirs of a Harlem Activist," 1997, unpublished manuscript, Manuscript Division, Schomburg; on housing, see *People's Voice*, March 1, 1947; *Amsterdam News*, November 29, 1952; March 14, 1953; October 24, 1953; May 8, 1954; December 25, 1954; March 12, 1955; December 3, 1955; July 28, 1956; on jobs, see *People's Voice*, August 30, 1947; *Amsterdam News*, June 19, 1954; June 23, 1962; *New York Times*, April 1, 1962; August 5, 1962; on racist business practices and community safety, see *People's Voice*, August 2, 1947; *Amsterdam News*, November 1, 1947; October 2, 1954. See also Biondi.

4. Jeanne Noble, *Beautiful, Also, Are the Souls of My Black Sisters* (Englewood Cliffs, N.J.: Prentice-Hall, 1978); Giddings, *When and Where*; Beverly Guy-Sheftall, ed., *Words of Fire: An Anthology of African American Feminist Thought* (New York: New Press, 1995).

5. Pritchett, 105–7, 144.

6. *Amsterdam News*, July 7, 1951; July 28, 1951; Gerald Horne, *Black and Red: W. E. B. Du Bois and the Afro-American Response to the Cold War, 1944–1963* (New York: State University of New York Press, 1986); Carole Boyce Davies, *Left of Karl Marx: The Political Life of Black Communist Claudia Jones* (Durham, N.C.: Duke University Press, 2007); Marika Sherwood, *Claudia Jones: A Life in Exile* (London: Lawrence and Wishart, 2000).

7. Weigand, chapter 3.

8. *Amsterdam News*, February 14, 1953.

9. *New York Age*, February 21, 1953.

10. *Amsterdam News*, March 7, 1953.

11. Hill, ed., *Black Women Oral History Project*, vol. 5, 104. See also Stephen Whitfield, *The Culture of the Cold War*, 2nd Edition (Baltimore: The Johns Hopkins University Press, 1991, 1996), 21.

12. Hill, *Black Women Oral History Project*, vol. 5, 105.

13. Hill, *Black Women Oral History Project*, vol. 5, 107.

14. *Amsterdam News*, May 27, 1933.

15. *New York Age*, October 22, 1932; November 5, 1932; *Amsterdam News*, October 15, 1949; November 5, 1949; November 12, 1949.

16. Carlos E. Russell, Interview with Wesley Mc.D Holder in "Perspectives on Power: A Black Community Looks at Itself," 130, unpublished manuscript, Union Graduate School, n.d., Robert Beecher Papers, Manuscript Division, Schomburg [hereinafter

referenced as Russell interview with names of various public figures]; *Amsterdam News* March 28, 1953.

17. *Amsterdam News*, March 28, 1953; September 5, 1953; September 12, 1953; August 22, 1953; August 29, 1953; October 10, 1953.

18. Democratic primary election returns: Flagg, 4,503; Schor, 4,365; John Walsh, 2,339; *New York Times*, September 17, 1953. General election returns: Flagg, 25,913; Staves, 10,332; Schor, 6,332; *New York Times*, November 5, 1953; *Amsterdam News*, January 23, 1954.

19. *Amsterdam News*, August 28, 1954; January 1, 1955; October 29, 1955; July 21, 1956. For a discussion of the role of ethnically or racially based pressure groups as vehicles to influence public policy and party politics, see Hanes Walton, Jr., *Black Political Parties: An Historical and Political Analysis* (New York: Free Press, 1972), 29–34.

20. *Amsterdam News*, March 19, 1955; September 7, 1957; September 28, 1957.

21. Russell interview with Ruth Goring, 159.

22. Chisholm, *Unbought and Unbossed*, (Boston: Houghton Mifflin, 1970), 39–40.

23. Kantrowitz; Connolly, 129–33; Wilder, 212.

24. *United States Census*, 1960.

25. *New York Times*, June 22, 1964; June 25, 1964; November 25, 1964.

26. Roger Waldinger, *Still the Promised City? African-Americans and New Immigrants in Postindustrial New York* (Cambridge, Mass.: Harvard University Press, 1996), 12, 14, 63, 106–7; Wilder, 160, 167.

27. *New York Times*, August 24, 1966.

28. The median income for New York State was $5,407. The median income for New York City families was $6,091; for Brooklyn families, $5,816. For Brooklyn's nonwhite families, the figure was $4,149 (*United States Census*, 1960, table 86, table 65).

29. The individual median income for nonwhite men was $3,458; for nonwhite women, $2,074 (*United States Census*, 1960, table 134). Note: The table did not break down the figures between African American, Puerto Rican, and other "nonwhite" people. Black men's unemployment rate was 11.6 percent; black women's, 5.9 percent ("Bedford-Stuyvesant Youth in Action Report, 1965," chap. 2, pp. 16, 25, Robert Wagner, Jr., Papers, box 272, folder 3179, Municipal Archives of the City of New York.

30. Russell interview with Thomas R. Jones, 78.

31. Russell interview with Jones, 47.

32. *Amsterdam News*, November 14, 1964.

33. *New York Times*, November 10, 1964.

34. Russell interview with Goring, 158.

35. Author's interview with Jocelyn Cooper, February 17, 2000.

36. *Amsterdam News*, March 19, 1960.

37. *Amsterdam News*, June 4, 1960; *Amsterdam News*, September 1, 1962.

38. Bedford-Stuyvesant Youth in Action Report, 25. Robert Wagner, Jr., Papers; author's interview with Andy Cooper, February 9, 2000.

39. Russell interview with Jones, 54.

40. See Grace Jordan McFadden, "Septima P. Clark and the Struggle for Human

Rights," in *Women in the Civil Rights Movement: Trailblazers & Torchbearers, 1941–1965*, ed. Vicki L. Crawford, Jacqueline Anne Rouse, and Barbara Woods, 85–97 (Bloomington: Indiana University Press, 1993).

41. Russell interview with Goring, 161.

42. "Bedford-Stuyvesant Youth in Action Report 1965," chapter 5, p. 3, Robert Wagner, Jr., Papers, box 272, folder 3179, Municipal Archives of the City of New York [emphasis in the original].

43. *Amsterdam News*, March 26, 1960; *New York Times*, October 6, 1963; October 14, 1963.

44. Interview with Shirley Chisholm, New York, 1968, Sc Audio C-161, Moving Image and Recorded Sound Division, Schomburg.

45. Author's interview with Jocelyn Cooper, February 17, 2000.

46. Author's interview with Andy Cooper, February 17, 2000.

47. Wilder, 167–69, 233–34; Waldinger, 12, 30–31, 106–7; Biondi.

48. *New York Times*, April 1, 1962, 1; August 5, 1962; August 12, 1962; Russell, interview with Jones, 50; August Meier and Elliott Rudwick, *CORE: A Study in the Civil Rights Movement, 1943–1968* (New York: Oxford University Press, 1973), 192–93.

49. *Amsterdam News*, August 18, 1962; September 1, 1962; September 15, 1962; *New York Times*, September 7, 1962. Jones beat Stan Berman 2,686 votes to 2,465 and beat Wesley Holder for Assemblyman 3,043 votes to 2,654.

50. *New York Times*, November 8, 1962; *Amsterdam News*, November 10, 1962. Jones beat his opponents with 10,584 votes to 3,643 for Maddox, the Republican candidate, and 916 votes for Eversley, the Liberal.

51. See Weiss.

52. Russell interview with Goring, 166. See also Farr, Leibman, and Wood: according to the authors, "The City's governing scheme leaves to government officials many discretionary decisions, especially the filling of certain jobs and the selection of firms to receive certain contracts. . . . Party officials still have a say in those decisions. . . . In that way service to a party can still lead to preferment for a City job or contract" (21).

53. Russell interview with Jones, 58–60. See also *New York Times*, November 10, 1964.

54. Ransby, 108.

55. Ransby, 103.

56. Ransby, chapter 4; Joanne Grant, *Ella Baker: Freedom Bound* (New York: Wiley, 1998).

57. *People's Voice*, March 27, 1948.

58. *Amsterdam News*, September 30, 1950.

59. Ransby, 129.

60. *Amsterdam News*, February 21, 1953; September 12, 1953; *New York Times*, March 22, 1953.

61. *Amsterdam News*, November 1, 1952.

62. Grant, 98; *Amsterdam News*, September 12, 1953; October 24, 1953; October 31, 1954.

63. *Amsterdam News*, August 22, 1953; Lewinson, 88–89.

64. *New York Times*, July 28, 1953.

65. *Amsterdam News*, February 21, 1953; October 31, 1953; *New York Times*, March 22, 1953; Ransby, 157; Biondi, 205–6.

66. *Amsterdam News*, November 7, 1953; *New York Times*, November 5, 1953.

67. *Amsterdam News*, September 15, 1956.

68. *Amsterdam News*, October 13, 1956.

69. *Amsterdam News*, September 28, 1957.

70. Maurice R. Berube and Marilyn Gittell, eds., *Confrontation at Ocean Hill–Brownsville: The New York School Strikes of 1968* (New York: Praeger, 1969); Connolly; Podair; Pritchett.

71. See *People's Voice*, June 8, 1946, for an example of Bessie Buchanan's column. *New York Age*, October 13, 1951; *Amsterdam News*, August 18, 1951; July 17, 1954. See Biondi on Buchanan's friendship with Baker, 187.

72. *New York Age*, September 24, 1949; October 15, 1949.

73. In 1952 (a presidential election year), there was a record number of women registered as Democrats in the Twelfth Assembly District—23,828. In 1954 in Buchanan's district (the Twelfth Assembly District), 16,766 women and 13,853 men were registered as Democrats. *Annual Report of the Board of Elections of the City of New York, 1952*, table 7, and *Annual Report of 1954*, table 6.

74. *Amsterdam News*, October 2, 1954.

75. *Amsterdam News*, October 23, 1954.

76. See Joanne Meyerowitz, "Beyond the Feminine Mystique," in *Not June Cleaver: Women and Gender in Postwar America, 1945–1960*, ed. Joanne Meyerowitz, 233–234 (Philadelphia: Temple University Press, 1994).

77. *Amsterdam News*, November 6, 1954. See also *New York Times*, November 4, 1954. The vote tally was 23,399 for Buchanan and 6,013 for Pickett. *New York State Legislative Record and Index, vols. 1955–1962*.

78. See *New York Legislative Record and Index*, section on Individual Record Assembly Bills, 1955–1962, New York Public Library State Records.

79. "Ambitions That Could Not Be Fenced In," n.d., Hedgeman Manuscript Collection, Schomburg, 86; Dammond oral history with Hedgeman, 91; *Amsterdam News*, February 5, 1944; February 12, 1944; *Amsterdam News*, May 20, 1944; *People's Voice*, June 23, 1945. For a full discussion on the history and fate of the FEPC, see Reed (though there is no mention of Hedgeman), and also Pfeffer, chapter 3. Pfeffer discusses the tensions among the National Council's leadership and noted that Hedgeman voiced complaints "about the problems caused by the complexity of unsuspected rivalries among the supporting groups" (109). In addition, Pfeffer argues that Randolph never had "mutually rewarding working relationships" with women, and "he never treated them as equals." He often dismissed their advice, including Hedgeman's, and he appointed her as "executive secretary" because she would work for less money (301–2).

80. *Baltimore Afro-American*, February 19, 1949; *Pittsburgh Courier*, February 19, 1949; *Chicago Defender*, 1.

81. *New York Times*, February 12, 1949.

82. *Amsterdam News*, October 15, 1949.

83. Special Message to the Congress Recommending a Comprehensive Health Program by President Truman, November 19, 1945, available at http://www.trumanlibrary .org/publicpapers/index.php?pid=483&st=&st1= (accessed August 31, 2011); President Truman's Remarks at the National Health Assembly Dinner, May 1, 1948, available at http://www.trumanlibrary.org/publicpapers/viewpapers.php?pid=1612 (accessed August 31, 2011).

84. *New York Times*, July 8, 1949; *Amsterdam News*, January 9, 1954; *Pittsburgh Courier*, July 3, 1954.

85. Dammond oral history with Hedgeman, 121.

86. *New York Times*, July 28, 1953.

87. Hedgeman, 110; Dammond oral history with Hedgeman, 139–42.

88. *Afro-American*, November 14, 1953.

89. *Amsterdam News*, November 28, 1953.

90. *Amsterdam News*, January 30, 1954; Hedgeman, 116–18.

91. Letter from Edward Lewis to Mayor Robert Wagner Jr., January 4, 1954, Robert Wagner, Jr., Papers, box 76, folder 1062, Municipal Archives of the City of New York.

92. *New York Times*, March 29, 1954.

93. Dammond oral history with Hedgeman, 121. Letter from Bowles to Donald Montgomery, April 7, 1952, Chester Bowles Papers, box 89, folder 137, Sterling Memorial Library, Yale University [hereinafter SML]. Letter to Jane Hoey, Social Security Administration, Federal Security Agency (where Anna Arnold Hedgeman worked) from Steb (Mrs. Chester) Bowles, May 22, 1952, Bowles Papers, box 208, folder 124, SML. Letter from Don Montgomery to Chester Bowles, November 24, 1952, Bowles Papers, box 89, folder 137, SML. See also Hedgeman, 100, and *Amsterdam News*, January 9, 1954; Thomas Borstelmann, *The Cold War and the Color Line: American Race Relations in the Global Arena* (Cambridge, Mass.: Harvard University Press, 2001); Michael Krenn, *Black Diplomacy: African Americans and the State Department, 1945–1969* (Armonk, N.Y.: Sharpe, 1999).

94. *Alpha Kappa Mu Journal*, vol. 12, no. 2 (April 1956), box 7, Hedgeman Collection, Manuscript Division, Schomburg.

95. *Alpha Kappa Mu Journal*, vol. 12, no. 2 (April 1956), box 7, Hedgeman Collection, Manuscript Division, Schomburg.

96. *New York Age*, September 3, 1955.

97. "Four Years of Progress: A Report to the Woman's Council on The Woman's Program, 1955 through 1958," Wilhelmina Adams additions, Manuscript Division, Schomburg.

98. Letter from Myrta Ross to Anna Arnold Hedgeman, May 15, 1957, box 8, folder "Aid to Mayor Notes," Hedgeman Collection, Schomburg.

99. *New York Age*, October 25, 1958.

100. *Amsterdam News*, February 20, 1960; March 26, 1960.

101. Hedgeman, 129.

102. Hedgeman, 129–30; *New York Times*, April 4, 1960.

103. *New York Times*, April 14, 1960.

104. *New York Times*, March 7, 1960; March 8, 1960; Hedgeman, 131–32.

105. *New York Times*, April 30, 1960.

106. *Amsterdam News*, June 4, 1960.

107. *New York Times*, June 9, 1960. Gilbert won 10,333 votes and Hedgeman won 2,490.

108. *Amsterdam News*, June 11, 1960.

109. Hedgeman, 133.

110. *Amsterdam News*, July 21, 1962.

111. *New York Times*, April 4, 1960.

112. *New York Citizen-Call*, June 4, 1960.

113. *New York Times*, August 15, 1965.

114. *New York Times*, May 24, 1964; July 25, 1965.

115. *New York Times*, September 12, 1965.

116. *New York Times*, August 15, 1965.

117. *New York Times*, September 16, 1965.

118. *New York Times*, March 14, 1968, 30; June 20, 1968.

119. Constance Baker Motley, *Equal Justice . . . Under Law* (New York: Farrar, Straus and Giroux, 1998), chapters 1 and 2.

120. Motley, 58–59, 95.

121. *In the Matter of Appeal from Action of Board of Education, Union Free School District No. 9, Town of Hempstead*, 71 State Dept. Reports 161 (1950), cited in Motley, 21/265.

122. *Chicago Defender*, February 11, 1950.

123. *Novick v. Levitt & Sons*, 200 Misc. 694, 108 N.Y.S. 2nd 615, NY Supp.1951.

124. *New York Times*, February 10, 1956; March 3, 1956.

125. *New York Times*, July 23, 1958.

126. Motley, 203.

127. Motley, 204–6; Lewinson, 96.

128. Letter from Abzug to Motley, February 6, 1964, and Letter from Motley to Abzug, February 11, 1964, series 2, box 8, folder 6, Correspondence Bella Abzug. Motley Manuscript Collection, Sophia Smith Special Collection, [hereinafter SSSC].

129. Telegram to Constance Baker Motley from Geraldine P. Woods, February 10, 1964, and Letter from Motley to Woods, February 12, 1964, box 3, folder 3, Correspondence, SSSC.

130. Letter to Constance Baker Motley, February 7, 1964, from Mrs. Owens, Chair of Human Relations Committee of the Girl Friends, Inc., box 3, folder 4, SSSC.

131. Motley, 205.

132. Letters from constituents, box 4, folder; Introduction of Housing Legislation, February 12, 1964, box 10, folder 12, SSSC.

133. Various pieces of legislation introduced: box 10, folder 8; box 10, folder 11; box 10, folder 17; box 10, folder 19, SSSC.

134. Letters from constituents, box 10, folder 13, Constance Baker Motley papers [hereinafter CBM Papers], SSSC.

135. Motley, 121; unsigned letter to Motley, April 20, 1964; unsigned letter, September 12, 1975, series 2, box 8, folder 22, Correspondence: Hate Mail, CBM Papers, SSSC.

136. "Address by Manhattan Boro Pres Motley at membership meeting of United Democratic Club/Wilhelmina Adams," April 22, 1965, box 13, folder 2, Speeches, SSSC.

137. *New York Times*, January 26, 1966.

CHAPTER 4. FEMINISM, CIVIL RIGHTS, AND LIBERALISM IN THE 1960S

1. Murray, *Autobiography*, 347–48.

2. Executive Order 10980, "Establishing the President's Commission on the Status of Women," in *American Women: The Report of the President's Commission on the Status of Women and Other Publications of the Commission*, ed. Margaret Mead and Frances Balgley Kaplan, 207 (New York: Scribner's, 1965).

3. Harrison, 48.

4. State of New York, Department of Commerce, "Four Years of Progress: A Report to the Woman's Council on The Woman's Program, 1955 through 1958," in Wilhelmina Adams- Additions, Schomburg.

5. Executive Order 10980, 76.

6. Executive Order 10980, 76.

7. Background information on commission members came from *Current Biography*, 1944, 1947, 1949, 1955, 1956, 1958, 1959, 1961, 1962, 1964, 1965, 1967, and 1970.

8. Transcript of PCSW meeting, April 9, 1962, p. 188, folder 4, PCSW Papers, box 4, John F. Kennedy Library [hereinafter JFKL].

9. Rosa Gragg, president of the National Association of Colored Women's Clubs, served on the Committee on Home and Community; Lillian Holland Harvey, dean of the School of Nursing at Tuskegee, served on the Committee on Education.

10. Mead and Kaplan, 50.

11. Giddings, *When and Where*, 330. On the importance of the public sector for African American women's employment, also see Jane Berger, "When Hard Work Doesn't Pay: Gender and the Urban Crisis in Baltimore, 1945–1985," PhD diss., Ohio State University, 2007. Employment data on African American women in the public sector in New York City is extremely difficult to find. The *1960 U.S. Census*, table 3 (p. 376)—Selected Occupations and Industry Groups of Employed Persons by Color and Sex—shows that in New York City there were more "nonwhite" women in professional/technical (16,000, or 7.8 percent) and clerical (34,000, or 16.8 percent) positions numerically and proportionally than there were "nonwhite" men (12,000 or 4.6 percent and 33,000 or 12.5 percent, respectively); the table does not disaggregate the data into public- and private-sector categories.

12. *American Women*, 32–33, 78. See also "Report to the President by Mrs. Eleanor Roosevelt—July, 1962," which demonstrates how quickly some changes were made after the commission recommended them. John Macy, head of the Civil Service Commission, was a member of the PCSW (PCSW Papers, box 1, JFKL).

13. Marguerite Rawalt, co-chair of the Committee on Civil and Political Rights to the Commission, transcript of PCSW, June 16–17, 1962, meeting (p. 195), folder 5, PCSW Papers, box 4, JFKL.

14. Murray, *Autobiography*, 349.

15. Murray, *Autobiography*, 238–40.

16. Murray, *Autobiography*, 351.

17. Mead and Kaplan, 45.

18. Harrison, 136, 183; Murray, *Autobiography*, 363.

19. Kessler-Harris, *In Pursuit of Equity*, 226.

20. Report on Four Consultations, PCSW, List of Participants in Consultation on Problems of Negro Women (p. 37), folder 13, PCSW Papers, box 3, JFKL. See also *Ebony*, October 1984, 26; Biondi, 48; *New York Times*, August 28, 1964. For a detailed profile on participants of the consultation, see Harris, *Black Feminist Politics*, 72–80.

21. Statement by Dorothy Height, April 19, 1963, Transcript of the Proceedings of the Consultation of Minority Groups (pp. 12–14), folder 7, PCSW Papers, box 4, JFKL.

22. Statement by Height, Consultation Transcript, 14, PCSW Papers, JFKL.

23. Statement by Walter Davis, Consultation Transcript, 17, PCSW Papers, JFKL.

24. Statement by Cenoria Johnson, Consultation Transcript, 18, PCSW Papers, JFKL.

25. Kessler-Harris, *In Pursuit of Equity*, 227.

26. Statements by Walter Davis, Ruth Whitehead Whaley, and Dorothy Height, Consultation Transcript, 17, 24, 179. See also Report of Consultation on Problems of Negro Women, in Mead and Kaplan, 220, [and Report in box 3, folder 13, p. 29, PCSW Papers, JFKL]. Harris has also profiled the issues the Consultation dealt with including vocational guidance and community service and participation, which are not discussed herein. See *Black Feminist Politics*, 65–72. Harris has a somewhat different assessment of the discussion, seeing Alice Dunnigan as the member who first raised the issue of matriarchy and who was met by resistance from a number of others. My sense of the discussion was that there was general agreement about the fact even as it was considered regrettable.

27. Statement by Paul Rilling, Consultation Transcript, 66, PCSW Papers, JFKL.

28. Statement by Johnson, Consultation Transcript, 45, PCSW Papers, JFKL. See also Sugrue, 277–78.

29. Statement by Johnson, Consultation Transcript, 47; Report of the Consultation, 32, PCSW Papers, JFKL.

30. Statements by Ruth Whitehead Whaley and Dollie Robinson, Consultation Transcript, 38, PCSW Papers, JFKL.

31. Kessler-Harris, *In Pursuit of Equity*, 226.

32. Statements by Whaley, Robinson, and Alice Dunnigan, Consultation Transcript, 39–40, 43, PCSW Papers, JFKL.

33. Statement by Gerri Major, Consultation Transcript, 40, PCSW Papers, JFKL.

34. Report on Consultation, 32, PCSW Papers, JFKL.

35. Statement by Johnson, Consultation Transcript, 86–87, PCSW Papers, JFKL.

36. Statement by Grace Hewell, Consultation Transcript, 89, PCSW Papers, JFKL.

37. Report on Consultation, 34, PCSW Papers, JFKL.

38. Statement by Height, Consultation Transcript, 180, PCSW Papers, JFKL.

39. Statement by Height, Consultation Transcript, 179, PCSW Papers, JFKL.

40. Mead and Kaplan, 14, 35.

41. Mead and Kaplan, 4.

42. In her book *Too Heavy a Load*, White argues that the NCNW increasingly shifted

its focus from the needs of black women in society to a civil rights agenda. While there is much evidence in her study to support that argument, the role that Dorothy Height and other black women played in the PCSW in fighting for attention and action on the needs of African American women nevertheless deserves more credit than it has been given.

43. Hugh Davis Graham, *The Civil Rights Era: Origins and Development of National Policy, 1960–1972* (New York: Oxford University Press, 1990), 134–35.

44. Carl Brauer, "Women Activists, Southern Conservatives, and the Prohibition of Sex Discrimination in Title VII of the 1964 Civil Rights Act," *Journal of Southern History* 49, no. 1 (February 1983): 41–43; Freeman, *We Will Be Heard*, chapter 12; Harrison, 176–81; MacLean, 118; Kessler-Harris, *In Pursuit of Equity*, 239–45.

45. Statement by Representative Martha Griffiths (D-MI), *Congressional Record*, 88th Cong., 2nd Sess., February 8, 1964, 2578.

46. Statement by Representative Martha Griffiths (D-MI), *Congressional Record*, 88th Cong., 2nd Sess., February 8, 1964, 2580.

47. Statement by Representative Martha Griffiths (D-MI), *Congressional Record*, 88th Cong., 2nd Sess., February 8, 1964, 2580.

48. Statement by Catherine May (R-WA) *Congressional Record*, 88th Cong., 2nd Sess., February 8, 1964, 2582.

49. Cobble, *The Other Women's Movement* (Princeton, N.J.: Princeton University Press, 2004), 173–74; Statement by Edith Green, *Congressional Record*, 88th Cong., 2nd Sess., February 8, 1964, 2581.

50. Green, *Congressional Record*, 88th Cong., 2nd Sess., February 8, 1964, 2581–82.

51. For an extensive discursive analysis of the debate, see Cynthia Deitch, "Gender, Race, and Class Politics and the Inclusion of Women in Title VII of the 1964 Civil Rights Act," *Gender and Society* 7, No. 2 (June 1993): 183–203.

52. Harrison, 179; Brauer, "Women Activists, Southern Conservatives, and the Prohibition of Sex Discrimination in Title VII of the 1964 Civil Rights Act," *Journal of Southern History* 49, No.1 (February 1983): 37–56.

53. Murray, *Autobiography*, 356.

54. MacLean, 118–19; Cobble, 91–92.

55. Brauer, 54.

56. Pauli Murray, "Memorandum in Support of Retaining the Amendment to H.R. 7152, Title VII (Equal Employment Opportunity) to Prohibit Discrimination in Employment Because of Sex," April 14, 1964, 9 [hereinafter referred to as "Memo"], available at http://asp6new.alexanderstreet.com.ezaccess.libraries.psu.edu/was2/was2.object.details.aspx?dorpid=1000680941 (accessed October 25, 2011).

57. Murray, "Memo," 18.

58. Murray, "Memo," 20–21.

59. Murray, "Memo," 21.

60. Murray, *Autobiography*, 356–57.

61. Murray, *Autobiography*, 357.

62. Murray, *Autobiography*, 358.

63. See discussion of "Memorandum in Support of Retaining the Amendment to H.R. 7152 to Prohibit Discrimination in Employment Because of Sex" in Murray, *Autobiography*, 357–58.

64. Michael Katz, *The Undeserving Poor: From the War on Poverty to the War on Welfare* (New York: Pantheon, 1989), 80; Christopher Weeks, *Job Corps: Dollars and Dropouts* (Boston: Little, Brown, 1967), 59.

65. "Poverty—Message from the President of the United States" (H. Doc. No. 243), *Congressional Record*, March 16, 1964, 5287. See also *New York Times*, March 17, 1964.

66. *House Education and Labor Committee, Subcommittee on the War on Poverty Hearings*, vol. 2083, March 17, 1964, 64–65; March 18, 1964, 114–15; April 8, 1964, 367–68; April 15, 1964, 819; April 28, 1964, 1525. See also Patricia Zelman, *Women, Work, and National Policy: The Kennedy-Johnson Years* (Ann Arbor, Michigan: UMI Research Press, 1982), 80–82.

67. Weeks, 91–92.

68. Author's interview with Jeanne Noble, August 15, 2000.

69. Author's interview with Noble (Noble's emphasis).

70. Paula Giddings, *In Search of Sisterhood: Delta Sigma Theta and the Challenge of the Black Sorority Movement* (New York: Morrow, 1988), 241.

71. Author's interview with Noble.

72. Mead and Kaplan, 80–81.

73. Author's interview with Noble.

74. Author's interview with Noble.

75. Author's interview with Noble.

76. Hill, *Black Women Oral History Project*, vol. 5, Dorothy Height Interview, 180–81. Note: After the group was approached for the Job Corps contract, it changed its name from Women's Inter-Organizational Committee (WIC) which was formed in March 1964 at a meeting in Atlanta, to Women in Community Service and kept the same initials WICS. See also Height, *Open Wide*, 162–66; 202–4.

77. *Norfolk Journal & Guide*, April 30, 1960; *Industrial Statesman*, June 1960, no. 3, p. 7; *Pittsburgh Courier*, November 19, 1960, 16. Note: the Secretary of Defense established DACOWITS in 1951.

78. *New York Times*, December 17, 1964; July 11, 1965.

79. *Norfolk Journal & Guide*, February 6, 1965. On WICS, see Hill, ed., *Black Women Oral History Project*, vol. 5, 183.

80. Height, *Open Wide the Freedom Gates*, 203.

81. *New York Times*, March 1, 1966.

82. *New York Times*, April 18, 1966.

83. Zelman, 82–83.

84. *New York Times*, June 12, 1964. See also Jones; Giddings, *When and Where*, 7, 62–63, 333; Rosen, 277.

85. Nadasen; Orleck; Kornbluh; Levenstein.

86. Zelman, 84.

87. *New York Times*, July 3, 1966; *New York Times*, November 30, 1967; Harlem Youth

Opportunities Unlimited, Inc., *Youth in the Ghetto: A Study of the Consequences of Powerlessness and a Blueprint for Change* (New York: HARYOU, 1964).

88. Zelman, 76.

89. Motley, 210–12; Lewinson, 96, 98.

90. Letter from Bella Abzug to Constance Baker Motley, January 28, 1966, series 2, box 8, folder 6, Correspondence Bella Abzug, CBM Papers, SSSC.

91. Note from Pauli Murray to Constance Baker Motley, January 25, 1966, series 2, box 8, folder 18, Correspondence Pauli Murray, CBM Papers, SSSC.

92. Motley, 226.

93. Invitation from the American Political Science Association, box 8, folder 3; Misc. Correspondence, box 8, folder 2, CBM Papers, SSSC.

94. Letter from Mrs. Wallace of Shawnee Mission Kansas to Motley, February 10, 1966; and Letter from Wilhelmina Valcore of Pensacola, Florida, February 3, 1966, box 6, folder 4, CBM Papers, SSSC.

95. Constance Baker Motley, Speech before the United Church Women of Lower Middlesex County, Connecticut, April 29, 1967, box 14, folder 1, CBM Papers, SSSC.

96. Constance Baker Motley, Commencement Address, Spelman College, Atlanta, May 20, 1979, p. 3, box 14, folder 3, CBM Papers, SSSC.

97. For a discussion of women's religious organization activism around women's rights, see Susan M. Hartmann, *The Other Feminists: Activists in the Liberal Establishment* (New Haven, Conn.: Yale University Press, 1998), chapter 4.

98. Hill, *Black Women Oral History Project*, 173.

99. See Hartmann, 93.

100. Height, *Open Wide*, 61–63, 149–52.

101. Height, *Open Wide*, 195.

102. Height, *Open Wide*, 198–99.

103. White, 196–98.

104. Hedgeman, 152–53.

105. *New York World-Telegram and Sun*, August 24, 1963, Hedgeman Clipping File, Municipal Reference and Research Center, New York City Municipal Archives; Dammond oral history with Hedgeman, 181.

106. *Kalamazoo Gazette*, May 14, 1964, Hedgeman Manuscript Collection, box 5.

107. Memo from Hedgeman to Oscar Lee, January 22, 1964, Hedgeman Manuscript Collection, box 1, Schomburg.

108. Hedgeman, 194.

109. Graham, 151.

110. Hedgeman, 201–2.

111. Hedgeman, 167, 169; Dammond oral history with Hedgeman, 180.

112. *The Afro-American*, week of March 22, 1969, Hedgeman Manuscript Collection, box 8A, Schomburg. On the merging of Randolph's and King's march ideas, see Hedgeman, 169–70.

113. *New York Times*, August 15, 1965. See also *New York World-Telegram and Sun*, August 24, 1963; *Herald Tribune*, August 28, 1963; Hedgeman Clipping File, Municipal

Reference and Research Center, New York City Municipal Archives. See also Hill, ed., Height Interview, 173.

114. Hedgeman, 178–80; Dammond oral history with Hedgeman, 187–88. See Dorothy I. Height, "'We Wanted the Voice of a Woman to Be Heard': Black Women and the 1963 March on Washington," in Collier-Thomas and Franklin, 86, 87.

115. Height, *Open Wide*, 145.

116. *Herald Tribune*, August 28, 1963, Hedgeman Clipping File, Municipal Reference and Research Center, New York City Municipal Archives.

117. Pauli Murray, "The Negro Woman in the Quest for Equality," *The ACORN*, June 1964, n.p.

118. Murray, "Negro Woman."

119. Pauli Murray and Mary O. Eastwood, "Jane Crow and the Law: Sex Discrimination and Title VII," *George Washington Law Review* 34 (1965), 233.

120. Murray and Eastwood, 236–37.

121. Murray, *Autobiography*, 361.

122. Pauli Murray, Testimony, House Committee on Education and Labor, *Discrimination against Women*, 91st Cong., 2nd sess. (Washington, D.C.: U.S. Government Printing Office, 1970), cited in *The Essential Feminist Reader*, ed. Estelle Freedman (New York: Random House, 2007), 284.

123. For a full discussion on the creation of NOW, see Murray, *Autobiography*; Rupp and Taylor, 179–86; Harrison, chapter 10; Rosen, 69, 78–81. For African American women's participation in NOW, see Giddings, *When and Where*, 303–4.

124. Murray, *Autobiography*, 363. An important case Murray was on testing the use of the Fourteenth Amendment was *White v. Crook* in Montgomery, Alabama. See also Hartmann, 63–64.

125. Excerpts from Minutes, National Conference of NOW, November 1967, 3–6, Betty Friedan Papers, 1952–93, carton 44, folder 1550, Schlesinger Library, Radcliffe Institute for Advanced Study, Harvard University; Women and Social Movements in the United States, 1600–2000.

126. Anne Firor Scott, ed., *Pauli Murray and Caroline Ware: Forty Years of Letters in Black and White* (Chapel Hill: University of North Carolina Press, 2006), 138.

127. Letter from Jean Faust to Marlene Sanders, June 9, 1967, box 4, folder 8, National Organization for Women, New York City Chapter, Tamiment Library, New York University.

128. Black Women Oral History Project, Anna Arnold Hedgeman Interview, 21.

129. See letter from Hedgeman to Thelma Isaacs, Hedgeman Manuscript Collection, box 6.

130. See Winifred Breines, *The Trouble Between Us: An Uneasy History of White and Black Women in the Feminist Movement* (New York: Oxford University Press, 2006); Benita Roth, *Separate Roads to Feminism: Black, Chicana, and White Feminist Movements in America's Second Wave* (New York: Cambridge University Press, 2004); Kessler-Harris, *In Pursuit of Equity*, 267–71.

CHAPTER 5. ON THE SHIRLEY CHISHOLM TRAIL
IN THE 1960S AND 1970S

Much of this chapter appeared in Julie Gallagher, "Waging 'The Good Fight': The Political Career of Shirley Chisholm, 1953–1982," in *The Journal of African American History* 92 (3), pp. 393–416.

1. Chisholm, *Unbought*, 83–84.

2. "Statement by Representative Shirley Chisholm," container 2, Shirley Chisholm Papers, Rutgers University Special Collections.

3. Congressional House lore suggests Chisholm's Agricultural Committee assignment was made because she offended Walter Little, an African American man on Congressman Wilbur Mill's staff, when he offered her assistance. Mills was chair of the House Ways and Means Committee and responsible for committee assignments. See Senate Oral History Project, Jesse R. Nichols, Government Documents Clerk and Librarian, Senate Committee on Finance, 1937–1971, Interview with Senate Historian Donald Ritchie, April 12, 1994, 83. During the 91st Cong., Shirley Chisholm served on the Veterans' Affairs Committee. She left that post in 1971 to serve on the Education and Labor Committee. In 1975, she moved to the Rules Committee, where she remained until her retirement from Congress in 1982. See Garrison Nelson, *Committees in the United States Congress, 1947–1992*, vol. 1 (Washington, D.C., 1993).

4. *Amsterdam News*, February 8, 1969.

5. See, for example, the following documents, all available from Women and Law: Section VI Black/Third World Microfilm: Kathleen Cleaver, "Racism, Fascism, and Political Murder," *The Black Panther*, September 14, 1968, 8; Patricia Robinson, "The Position of Black Women"; Frances M. Beal, "Double Jeopardy: To Be Black and Female"; Gloria Martin, "Women in the American Revolutionary Struggle," presented at the Seattle Radical Women Annual Conference, February 1970; Pat Hecht, "Sexism and Racism in America," n.d.

6. Chisholm, *Unbought*, 14.

7. *Broeklundian*, Brooklyn College Yearbook, 1943, 1945, and 1946; *Brooklyn College Vanguard*, October 3, 1945, 7; October 31, 1945, 4; November 14, 1945, Microfilm, 1946, Brooklyn College Library Archives and Special Collection; Chisholm, *Unbought*, 26.

8. Interview with Chisholm, New York 1968, Sc Audio C-160, Schomburg.

9. Interview with Chisholm, Sc Audio C-160; Chisholm, *Unbought*, 28.

10. Essie E. Lee, *Women in Congress* (New York: Messner, 1979), 46.

11. See Chisholm's comments in *Unbought*, 71–72.

12. *Amsterdam News*, January 23, 1954, B1.

13. Interview with Chisholm, Sc Audio C-161.

14. Jill S. Pollack, *Shirley Chisholm*, (New York: Watts, 1994), 23; Isobel V. Morin, *Women of the U. S. Congress* (Minneapolis: Oliver, 1994), 69.

15. Chisholm, *Unbought*, 30.

16. Interview with Chisholm, Sc Audio C-160.

17. Chisholm, *Unbought*, 36.

18. Chisholm, *Unbought*, 28.

19. Interview with Chisholm, Sc Audio C-160.

20. Chisholm, *Unbought*, 53.

21. *People's Voice*, June 3, 1944; October 21, 1944; Ada B. Jackson speech, Yankee Stadium, New York, September 9, 1948, American Labor Party Papers, series 1, box 8, 1948, Rutgers University Library; *Amsterdam News*, July 7, 1945; November 3, 1945; *Brooklyn Eagle*, October 31, 1945; *New York Age*, November 16, 1946; October 29, 1949; Campaign Flyer, Clippings File, and Press Release, Pauli Murray Manuscript Collection, box 73, folder 1273, SL.

22. In 1964 the Seventeenth Assembly District in Brooklyn had 16,471 women registered among the three main parties: Democrats, Republicans, and Liberals. There were 11,569 men registered. *1964 Annual Report of the Board of Elections of the City of New York*, Municipal Archives, New York, table 9, 47.

23. Interview with Chisholm, Sc Audio C-161.

24. Key Women Manuscript Collection, Organization History, ed. Otha Washington, December 1, 1982, Key Women Manuscript Collection, Manuscript Division, Schomburg.

25. Key Women Meeting Minutes, February 15, 1964, and February 2, 1965, Key Women Collection, Schomburg.

26. See Higginbotham, *Righteous Discontent*, and White, *Too Heavy A Load*.

27. Author's interview with Constance Rose, Brooklyn, April 17, 2000.

28. *New York Times*, June 3, 1964. Chisholm had 4,290 votes to Brady's 1,729.

29. *New York Times*, November 5, 1964.

30. For legislation regarding a civil rights course for city police, see Assembly Bill #2553, *New York State Legislative Record Index* (NYSLRI), 1965, and Assembly Bill #745, *NYSLRI*, 1966. For legislation to eliminate discrimination in business practices, see Assembly Bill #2552 and #2563, *NYSLRI*, 1965; Assembly Bill #745, *NYSLRI*, 1966; Assembly Bill #1253, *NYSLRI*, 1967. For unemployment insurance for agriculture workers, see Assembly Bill #2561, *NYSLRI*, 1965. For unemployment insurance for hospital employees, see Assembly Bill #3080, *NYSLRI*, 1966. For minimum wage legislation, see Assembly Bill #2588, *NYSLRI*, 1968. For public housing legislation, see Assembly Bill #5538, *NYSLRI*, 1967. For the SEEK education bill, see Assembly Bill #3601, *NYSLRI*, 1965. Radical scholar Manning Marable has accused Chisholm of having "no awareness of the systematic class inequalities that are part of the bourgeois democratic state." While Chisholm worked within the liberal establishment, the legislation she proposed, her own critical assessment of it, and the issues she raised inside and outside the halls of government indicate a more thoughtful consideration of class inequalities than Marable suggests. See Manning Marable, *Black American Politics: From the Washington Marches to Jesse Jackson* (London: Verso, 1985), 176.

31. For daycare centers, see Assembly Bill #1932, *NYSLRI*, 1965; Assembly Bill #1250, *NYSLRI*, 1967. For unemployment insurance for domestic workers, see Assembly Bill #2558, *NYSLRI*, 1965. For tenure protection for female teachers, see Assembly Bill #3603, *NYSLRI*, 1965.

32. *Amsterdam News*, December 30, 1967.

33. *Amsterdam News*, November 12, 1966.

34. See Collins, 76–77.

35. Author's interview with Cooper, March 9, 2000.

36. *260 F.Supp. 207*, Andrew Cooper et al., *Plaintiffs, v. James M. Power, Thomas Mallee, Maurice J. O'Rourke, and J. J. Duberstein, Commissioners of Election constituting the Board of Elections of the City of New York et al., Defendants*, August 9, 1966.

37. See *New York Times*, August 11, 1966; May 11, 1967; *Amsterdam News*, March 25, 1967; April 1, 1967.

38. *Amsterdam News*, December 2, 1967.

39. *Amsterdam News*, December 30, 1967.

40. *Amsterdam News*, January 27, 1968.

41. *Amsterdam News*, March 30, 1968.

42. Chisholm, *Unbought*, 70.

43. Chisholm won 5,431 votes to Thompson's 4,634 and Robinson's 1,751. *New York Times*, June 20, 1968; *Amsterdam News*, June 22, 1968.

44. *Amsterdam News*, March 9, 1968; May 25, 1968; *New York Times*, March 9, 1968; May 20, 1968.

45. *Amsterdam News*, October 5, 1968; October 19, 1968; October 26, 1968; November 2, 1968.

46. *New York Times*, October 4, 1968.

47. *Amsterdam News*, September 28, 1968; Berube and Gittell; Pritchett; Podair.

48. *Amsterdam News*, November 16, 1968. See also Pauli Murray's comments on the gendered dimensions of Farmer's campaign in Murray, "The Liberation of Black Women," in *Voices of the New Feminism*, ed. Mary Lou Thompson, 89 (Boston: Beacon, 1971).

49. *Amsterdam News*, November 9, 1968.

50. *Amsterdam News*, February 24, 1968; Interview with Annie Bowen, ScAudio C-163, Moving Image and Recorded Sound Division, Schomburg.

51. Chisholm, *Unbought*, 75.

52. *New York Times*, April 13, 1969.

53. *Amsterdam News*, July 12, 1969; *New York Times*, November 6, 1968.

54. Shirley Chisholm won with 34,885 votes, or 66.5 percent, to Farmer's 13,777 votes, or 26.3 percent. *Congressional Quarterly's Guide to U.S. Elections*, 1261. Chisholm, *Unbought*, 77.

55. *New York Times*, November 6, 1968.

56. *New York Times Magazine*, April 13, 1969.

57. Adam Clayton Powell, Jr., the Congressman from Harlem, had been stripped by his congressional colleagues of his seniority on the House Education and Labor Committee and of his seat in Congress by a majority vote in 1967. He later won his seat back in a special election. In addition, the Supreme Court ruled the actions of the Ninetieth Congress unconstitutional. See *Amsterdam News*, November 16, 1968; January 11, 1969; Hamilton; Wil Haygood, *King of the Cats: The Life and Times of Adam Clayton Powell, Jr.* (New York: Houghton Mifflin, 1993).

58. Chisholm, 155–58.

59. *Amsterdam News*, April 5, 1969; August 16, 1969; October 25, 1969; November 22, 1969; April 4, 1970; July 10, 1971; July 24, 1971; November 13, 1971. See also Chisholm, *Unbought*, 63–64, 85–86, 100–112.

60. *Congressional Record,* January 14, 1969–July 28, 1969, pp. 654, 1629, 2862, 6160, 6161, 6270, 7765, 8593, 10788, 12725, 12958, 13259, 13340, 13341, 13380, 13806, 15351, 15995, 20687, 20939.

61. *Congressional Record,* March 26, 1969, 7765.

62. Hedgeman was a founding member of NOW but left the organization shortly after it got underway, frustrated at its narrow understanding of women's needs. See Dammond's oral history with Hedgeman, 205.

63. NOW Address List, box 4, folder 8; NOW-New York City Officers for 1968, box 4, folder 10, National Organization for Women, New York City Chapter Records, 1966–1984, Tamiment Library, New York University.

64. *Congressional Record,* May 21, 1969, Extension of Remarks, 91st Cong./1st sess., p. 13380.

65. *New York Times,* October 7, 1971.

66. Manning Marable, *How Capitalism Underdeveloped Black America: Problems in Race, Political Economy and Society* (Boston: South End, 1983), 84–85, 92. Marable argues in *The Crisis of Color and Democracy: Essays on Race, Class and Power* ([Monroe, Maine: Common Courage, 1992], 54–55) of the importance of the black community to fight for a woman's right to abortion as a matter of personal choice. "To do less would compound the problems of poverty, powerlessness and sexism within our community."

67. See National Abortion Rights Action League (NARAL) Records Collection, carton 1. NARAL was initially called the National Association for the Repeal of Abortion Laws and was changed in 1973. NARAL Collection, box 1, folder: Bylaws, October 25, 1973, SL.

68. Congresswoman Chisholm's Statement, Press Conference, September 29, 1969, New York, Microfilm Collection of Women and Law, VI; Black/Third World, Women's History Research Center, Berkeley, Calif.

69. Congresswoman Chisholm's Statement, Press Conference, September 29, 1969.

70. Beal; Robinson; Nina Harding, "The Interconnections between the Black Struggle and the Woman Question," position paper presented at the Seattle Radical Women Annual Conference, February 1970; National Black Feminist Organization, Statement of Purpose, 1974, Microfilm Collection of Women and Law, VI.

71. *Congressional Record,* Extensions of Remarks, 91/1, December 11, 1969, 38592.

72. Dear Legislator letter from Shirley Chisholm, Congresswoman and Honorary President, NARAL, March 1970, box 2, folder 30, NARAL Collection, SL.

73. Nadasen; Orleck; Kornbluh, *Battle for Welfare Rights*; Levenstein.

74. *Congressional Quarterly Weekly Report,* April 3, 1970, 916.

75. *New York Times,* April 7, 1971; Hon. Shirley Chisholm's Statement to the Hearing before the Select Subcommittee on Education and Labor regarding the Comprehensive Child Development Act of 1971, May 17, 1971, 71–109. Lexis/Nexis Congressional at http://web.lexis-nexis.com.ezaccess.libraries.psu.edu/congcomp/attachment/a.pdf?_m=d208a24a247899681fe01b465399f5e0&wchp=dGLbVzz-zSkSA&_md5=72c587e633da8340190c7e405d44e70b&ie=a.pdf.

76. Same link as in note 75, above, with quotes from pages 74 and 95, respectively. Chisholm cited statistics, including that black women, most often employed in low-wage

service jobs, earned $1,991 annually, compared to the average income for working women in 1969, which was $3,091.

77. *New York Times*, February 23, 1971.

78. Rudolf Englebarts, *Women in the United States Congress, 1917–1972* (Littleton, Colo.: Libraries Unlimited, 1974), 107.

79. *Washington Post*, May 14, 1972.

80. *Congressional Record*, 1973, 13846, 13847, 13856, 13857.

81. "The Black Panther Party Ten-Point Program," in *Civil Rights Since 1787: A Reader on the Black Struggle*, ed. Jonathan Birnbaum and Clarence Taylor, 615–17 (New York: New York University Press, 2000).

82. Chisholm, *Unbought*, 151.

83. Chisholm, *Unbought*, 144–45.

84. Height, *Open Wide*, 63.

85. Height, *Open Wide*, 149–51.

86. Height, *Open Wide*, 152.

87. Hedgeman, 201–2.

88. *Amsterdam News*, March 27, 1971.

89. *Amsterdam News*, March 27, 1971; April 15, 1971; May 22, 1971.

90. *Amsterdam News*, April 3, 1971.

91. *Amsterdam News*, May 22, 1971.

92. *Amsterdam News*, July 17, 1971.

93. *Amsterdam News*, July 17, 1971.

94. *New York Times*, January 30, 1972; December 2, 1973; August 2, 1981; National Black Feminist Organization, Statement of Purpose, 1974, Microfilm collection of Women and Law, VI.

95. *New York Times*, July 14, 1971.

96. *Amsterdam News*, July 17, 1971.

97. *New York Times*, July 11, 1971.

98. Giddings, *When and Where*, 308.

99. *Amsterdam News*, July 24, 1971.

100. *Amsterdam News*, August 7, 1971; September 25, 1971.

101. "Statement of Candidacy for the Office of President of the United States by the Honorable Shirley Chisholm," January 25, 1972, container 3, Shirley Chisholm Papers, Rutgers University Special Collections [RSC].

102. "Shirley Chisholm Speaks Out: Presidential Campaign Position Papers No. 1, 3, 4, 5, 6, 7, 8," container 1–2, Shirley Chisholm Papers, RSC.

103. Chisholm, *The Good Fight* (New York: Harper & Row, 1973), 50–51, 84, 104–5; *Amsterdam News*, February 26, 1972.

104. *Amsterdam News*, March 18, 1972.

105. *Washington Post*, April 28, 1972.

106. Chisholm, *Good Fight*, 107.

107. Charles Denby and Molly Jackson, *News & Letters*, October 1971. Other examples of her enthusiasts were at the Operation Breadbasket workshop on Women in Politics and the Black Expo 71 in Chicago (see *People's World*, October 23, 1971); at the San

Francisco African American Historical and Cultural Society (see *San Francisco Chronicle*, November 1, 1971, Microfilm collection of Women and Law, VI.

108. *Amsterdam News*, March 11, 1972.

109. See *Amsterdam News* regular commentators' columns from January 1969–July 1972.

110. On Dellum's endorsement, see *Amsterdam News*, November 13, 1971. For Sutton's endorsement, see *Amsterdam News*, January 8, 1972. On the hostile treatment she faced from black male congressmen, see *The Village Voice*, December 2, 1971; *San Francisco Chronicle*, February 1, 1972; *Newsweek*, February 14, 1972, 24–26.

111. *Amsterdam News*, January 29, 1972.

112. *Amsterdam News*, March 4, 1972; March 18, 1972; March 25, 1972; Walton, *Black Political Parties*, 58–59; Steven Lawson, *Running for Freedom: Civil Rights and Black Politics in America Since 1941*, 2nd ed. (New York: McGraw-Hill, 1997), 142, 219.

113. Chisholm, *Good Fight*, 25.

114. *Village Voice*, December 2, 1971, Microfilm Collection of Women and Law, VI.

115. *New York Times*, February 6, 1972. See also Katherine Tate, "African American Female Senatorial Candidates: *Twin Assets or Double Liabilities?*" in *African American Power and Politics: The Political Context Variable*, ed. Hanes Walton, Jr., 279 (New York: Columbia University Press, 1997).

116. See Microfilm Collection of Women and Law: Black/Third World, Women's History Research Center, Berkeley, Calif. Moreover, none mentions Chisholm's campaign in their respective autobiographies and histories, nor is there evidence in the presses. On King's support of McGovern, see Dorothy Townsend, "Black Support Hard for Her to Win, Republican Chisholm Says," *Times*, n.d. (1972), Women and Law, section II, Black/Third World, Women's History Research Center, Berkeley.

117. *New York Post*, May 5, 1972. Ceballos argued, "Shirley Chisholm's candidacy is part of the women's movement." See also *Denver Post*, August 4, 1971.

118. Chisholm, *The Good Fight*, 57.

119. Chisholm, *The Good Fight*, 48, 84, 90, and author's interview with James Pitts, Amherst, Mass., May 8, 2000.

120. Hanes Walton, Jr., *Invisible Politics: Black Political Behavior* (Albany: State University of New York Press, 1985), 94.

121. *Jet*, July 27, 1972, 5; Chisholm, *Good Fight*, 123.

122. *Amsterdam News*, July 1, 1972.

123. Chisholm, *Good Fight*, 106, 108.

124. See Bernice Johnson Reagon, "Coalition Politics: Turning the Century," in *Feminism & Politics*, ed. Anne Phillips, 242–53 (New York: Oxford University Press, 1998). Originally published in Barbara Smith, *Home Girls: A Black Feminist Anthology* (New York: Kitchen Table Press, 1983).

125. *CORE* 3 (Summer 1973): 18–20.

126. *Congressional Quarterly Weekly Report*, March 26, 1971, 667; March 10, 1973, 536; March 19, 1977, 496; April 25, 1981, 722.

127. *New York Times*, July 30, 1975.

128. *Amsterdam News*, January 31, 1976.

129. *Congressional Record*, 93rd Cong., session 1, February 22, 1973, 5070; *Washington Post*, February 1, 1973; *Congressional Quarterly Weekly Report*, February 10, 1973, 320; March 3, 1973, 477–78; June 16, 1973, 1508, 1511.

130. "Controversy in the Congress over Food Stamps," *Congressional Digest*, 54, no. 5 (May 1975): 131–59.

131. *Congressional Quarterly Weekly Report*, May 8, 1976, 1117.

132. *San Francisco Chronicle*, February 10, 1973, Women and Law, VI.

133. Brown, "'What Has Happened Here,'"43.

134. Rosen, 291–94; Myra Marx Ferree and Beth B. Hess, *Controversy and Coalition: The New Feminist Movement across Four Decades of Change*, Third Ed. (New York: Routledge, 2000), 99, 142–43.

135. Collins, 12.

136. "Negro Women Set Meeting on Politics," *New York Times*, September 10, 1969.

137. Letter from Melody Murphy to Shirley Chisholm, August 19, 1983, box 2, container 3, Shirley Chisholm Papers, RSC.

CONCLUSION

1. Chisholm, *Good Fight*, 1–2.

2. After the 1973 U.S. Supreme Court decision in *Roe v. Wade*, the National Association for the Repeal of Abortion Laws became the National Abortion Rights Action League, but it kept the same acronym, NARAL.

3. Weinstein; Women and Law: section VI; V: Black Women and/in Politics (image numbers 1330–1422); Full Fact Sheet by Year, Women in State Legislature, Center for American Women in Politics, National Information Bank on Women in Public Office, Eagleton Institute of Politics, Rutgers University.

4. Center for American Women in Politics, National Information Bank on Women in Public Office, Eagleton Institute of Politics, Rutgers University, available at http://www.cawp.rutgers.edu/fast_facts/levels_of_office/documents/cong.pdf (accessed December 31, 2011).

5. Women in National Parliaments, Inter-Parliamentary Union, available at http://www.ipu.org/wmn-e/classif.htm (accessed December 31, 2011). This ranking represents a drop from 61st in 2005.

6. *Boston Globe*, September 25, 2003.

7. *New York Times*, September 14, 2003.

8. *Boston Herald*, November 6, 2003; *Chicago Sun-Times*, January 1, 2004.

9. Fast Fact Sheets, Center for American Women in Politics, available at http://www.cawp.rutgers.edu/fast_facts/resources/FactSheetArchive.php#congress (accessed December 31, 2011).

Index

Abell, Bess, 138
Abyssinian Baptist Church, 52, 67
Abzug, Bella, 114, 143–44, 175, 178, 182
Acorn, The, 151
Afro-American, 84–85
Aid to Families with Dependent Children (AFDC), 174
Allen, William, 36
American Federation of Teachers, 56
American Labor Party (ALP): African American roles in 1930s and 1940s, 5, 73–74; Democratic Party alliance, 93; Jackson activism, 75, 78–80, 81–82; overview, 217n38; roots, 49
American Woman Suffrage Association (AWSA), 20, 21
Amsterdam News: on Chisholm, 158, 170, 180, 181, 185; exposure of racism in New York schools, 102; Goring interview, 95; on Jackson-Richardson race of 1946, 78; on need for black representation in New York City government, 107; Republican leanings, 69; Richardson, Maude, 76, 77, 79
Anderson, Charles, 39–40
Andrews, William T., 64, 68, 69, 71
Anthony, Susan B., 20, 21
Apollo Theater, 6
Ayer, Gertrude, 69

Baker, Bertram, 76, 168
Baker, Ella: candidacy for city council, 100–102; Chisholm presidential candidacy, 182; civil rights movement contributions, 146–47; education and background, 53–54; grassroots activism against education discrimination, 102–3; NAACP (National Organization for the Advancement of Colored People), 99–100; overviews, 3, 5, 8, 47, 88–90; political/social network of 1930s, 60; Southern Christian Leadership Conference, 148; World War II civil rights work, 67

Baltimore Afro-American, 150
Beal, Frances, 174
Beauty Owners Association, 128
Bedford-Stuyvesant, 8, 12–13, 16, 92–94
Bedford-Stuyvesant Political League (BSPL), 93, 162–63
Bedford-Stuyvesant Women's Voluntary Services, 74
Belmont, Alva, 22, 23
Berman, Sam, 95
Bethune, Mary McLeod, 43, 47, 61
Biondi, Martha, 66, 74
Black Nationalist movement, 6, 32
Black Panther Party for Self-Defense (BPP), 176, 181
Black Popular Front, 74
Black Power, 176–77
Blackstone, Irene Moorman, 1, 6, 33–34, 45
Blakeslee, Charles W., 114
Blatch, Harriet Stanton, 27, 30
Blitzstein, Marc, 52
Bolden, R. M., 28
Bolin, Jane, 61–62, 218n45
Boston Globe, 199
Bowen, Annie, 170
Braun, Carol Mosley, 199
Bronx "slave markets," 51, 54
Brooklyn, 15–16, 73–74, 84–86, 92–94. *See also specific organizations; specific women*
Brooklyn Big Sisters, 42
Brooklyn Eagle, 74
Brooklyn Interracial Assembly, 74
Brooklyn Women's Anti-Lynching Crusaders, 43–44
Brotherhood of Sleeping Car Porters, 68
Brown, Earl, 102
Brown, Elsa Barkley, 186
Brownmiller, Susan, 171
Brown v. Board of Education (1954), 87, 102
Bruce, Herbert, 20, 68
Buchanan, Bessie: background and experience, 104; Chisholm comparison, 168;

Democratic Party, 104–5; New York State Assembly candidacy, 87, 104–5; overviews, 3–4, 8, 88–90, 105; on women in politics, 87
Buchanan, Charles, 104
Buckley, Charles, 109
Burke, Yvonne Braithwaite, 188
Byrne, Doris, 55

Campbell, Grace, 29–30, 31, 41
Carmichael, Stokely, 176
Carr, Charlotte, 51
Carter, Elmer, 101
Carter, Eunice Hunton, 2, 8, 59–60, 61
Carter, Pat, 97
Carter, Robert, 115
Cary, Mary Ann Shadd, 20, 21
Celler, Emanuel, 135
Chicago Defender, 65, 115
Chisholm, Shirley, 1, 172–73; Agricultural Committee assignment in Congress, 157–58; Aid to Families with Dependent Children (AFDC), 175; autobiography, 176; Bedford-Stuyvesant political uprising of 1950s, 93; black women in politics who came before, 158–59; Buchanan comparison, 168; childhood and education, 161–62; community and volunteer work, 165; Congressional Black Caucus, 178; Congresswoman, 167–80, 184–89; on early political organization work, 163; Fair Labor Standards Act amendment, 175–76; family, 161; feminist movement roles, 173–74, 178; first day in U.S. Congress, 159; grassroots political education activism, 96–97; Hedgeman comparison, 177; Height comparison, 177; on intentions as Congresswoman, 171; legacy, 188–89, 191–92; Manpower Development and Training Act, 175; marriage, 162; as militant, 176–77; on motivation, 167; NARAL role, 174; National Organization for Women (NOW) role, 173–74; National Welfare Rights Organization (NWRPO) role, 175; New York State Assemblywoman, 165–67; overviews, 3, 4, 5, 8, 9–10, 88–90, 160–61, 186–89; political agenda, 172; on presidential campaign support, 182–83, 184; presidential candidacy, 1, 180–84, 191; publicity/public relations efforts, 171; race and sex as strategic tools,

164–65; retirement from office, 186; on sexism/racism battle for women, 186; special interest groups, 177–78; teaching career, 162; Title VII (Civil Rights Act of 1964), 179; Unity Democratic Club, 94; Vietnam War position, 172–73; on violence vs. pragmatism, 176
Christian, Helen, 23
Citizens' Advisory Council on the Status of Women, 133
Citizens' Committee for Alfred E. Smith, 26–27
Citizens' Planning Council of Harlem, 72
Civil Rights Act of 1964, 134–39
civil rights movement: Civil Rights Act of 1964, 134–39; feminism, 150–54; grassroots struggles, 42–44; Motley appointment to federal judgeship, 143–45; overview, 154–56; Presidential Commission on the Status of Women (PCSW), 121–33; War on Poverty, 139–43; women's roles in liberal establishment, 145–50
"The Civil Rights Struggle — Challenge to Religion" (Hedgeman speech), 149
Civil Service Commission, 40
Claessens, August, 57–58
Clark, Ramsey, 118
Clark, Septima, 96
Clinton, Hillary Rodham, 191, 198
Coalition of 100 Black Women, 178
Cold War, 3, 87–88, 90–94
Coleman, Julia, 34, 56
Collins, Cardiss, 188
Collins, Patricia Hill, 188
Colored Women's Civic League, 41
Colored Women's Hoover-Curtis Committee of Manhattan, 34
Colored Women's Stop Lynching League of New York, 44
Colored Women's Suffrage Club of New York City, 23
Commission on Religion and Race (National Council of Churches), 148–49
Committee for a Negro Congressman from Brooklyn (CNCB), 167–68
Committee for Democratic Voters, 97–99
Committee on Civil and Political Rights, 125–26
Committee on Federal Employment, 125–26
Communist Party (CPUSA), 5, 52, 59, 90

Congressional Black Caucus, 178
Congress of American Women (CAW), 5, 90
Congress of Racial Equality (CORE), 97, 169
Consumers' Co-operative Housing Association, 39
Cooke, Marvel, 54
Cooper, Andrew (Andy), 95, 97, 167
Cooper, Jocelyn, 95–96, 96–97
CORE (Congress of Racial Equality), 97, 169
Council of Democratic Women, 63
Council on African Affairs (CAA), 60
Crisis, The, 15, 19, 26, 32, 49
Crocker, Richard, 17
Crosswaith, Alma, 58, 59, 217n33
Crosswaith, Frank R., 52, 58, 68
Curtis, Sam, 84

Daily Worker, 90
Davis, Benjamin (Ben), 72, 90, 114
Davis, Walter, 128
Dawson, Anna, 42
Dawson, William, 67, 107
Defense Advisory Commission on Women in the Services (DACOWITS), 141
Dellums, Ronald, 181
Delta Sigma Theta sorority, 116, 122, 140
Democratic Party: acceptance of women post-19th Amendment, 214n109; African American women's loyalty, 199; alliance with American Labor Party (ALP), 93; black New Yorkers' adoption after 1936, 97–99, 104; Brooklyn electoral politics overviews by era in 1940s, 80–81; Chisholm presidential candidacy, 182–84; critical importance to black women in politics, 189; efforts to attract black women's votes, 28–29; gender and racial bias of 1930s–1940s, 73–74; importance to black women in politics, 187–89; overviews, 3, 5, 8, 16, 59–60, 62, 71; patronage system, 107, 110–11; political realignment of early 20th century, 17–20; racism/ gender bias combination, 37–38, 62–65, 71–72, 85–86, 95, 110–11; Tammany Hall, 5, 16, 17–18, 63, 71. *See also specific women*
Dewey, Harriet Alice, 22–23
Dewey, Thomas, 68
Diggs, Bertha, 69
Dirksen, Everett, 137
domestic work, 49–50, 54, 215–16n2
Douglass, Frederick, 20

Dreher, Lucille, 110
DuBois, W. E. B., 15, 18, 32, 36, 49
Dunbar Vocational Placement Service, 51
Dunnigan, Alice, 130
Dyer Anti-Lynching Bill, 43

East, Catherine, 137
Eastwood, Mary, 127, 137, 151
education access, 47–48
education discrimination, 102–3
Edwards, India, 107
electoral politics overviews by era: 1910s–1920s, 38–45; 1930s–1940s, 55–56, 65, 67, 69, 73–74, 84–86, 219n45, 220n83; 1950s, 87–90, 118–20; 1960s, 121–23. *See also specific organizations; specific women*
Ellenbogen, Allen, 27
Ellickson, Katherine, 123, 126
Emergency Citizens Committee to Save School Decentralization and Community Control, 169
Emergency Relief Bureau, 51
Empire Friendly Shelter for Girls, 41
Empire State Federation of Women's Clubs, 15, 22
employment discrimination, 39–40, 50, 97. *See also specific related organizations and laws*
Equal Pay Act of 1963, 133
Equal Rights Amendment (ERA), 126, 153, 156, 173–74
Equal Suffrage League, 22
Ewing, Oscar, 107

Fair Employment Practices Commission (FEPC), 67, 85, 107
Fair Labor Standards Act amendment, 175–76
Farmer, James, 168–71
Fauntroy, Walter, 175
Federal Employee Loyalty Program, 107
Federal Security Agency, 107
Feminine Mystique, The (Friedan), 113, 132–33
feminism. *See* Equal Rights Amendment (ERA); National Organization for Women (NOW); women's rights
First National Conference of Household Workers, 175–76
Flagg, Louis W. Jr., 92–94, 162, 163
Fleming, Sara Lee, 114

Ford, Gerald, 184–85
Forman, James, 145
Forten, Charlotte, 20
Fortune, Hilda, 128
Four Freedoms Committee of Brooklyn, 76
Freedom Summer, 146
Friedan, Betty, 113, 132–33, 153, 178
future challenges for African American
   women, 198–200

Gadsen, Maud, 127–28
Garnet, Henry Highland, 21–22
Garnet, Sara J. S., 21–22
Garvey, Marcus, 6, 20, 33
Giddings, Paula, 125–26, 140, 179
Gilbert, Jacob, 110–11
Girl Friends Inc., 116
Goldberg, Arthur, 123
Good Fight, The (Chisholm), 183, 191
Goodman, Ellen, 199
GOP. See Republican Party
Goring, Ruth, 93, 95, 96–97
Graham, Martha, 52
Grant, Joanne, 147
Great Depression, 8, 47–49
Great Society, 3. See also civil rights move-
   ment; Johnson, Lyndon B.
Green, Edith, 136, 139, 141
Greenwich Village, 15
Griffiths, Martha, 135, 179

Hamer, Fannie Lou, 179
Hanning, Helen, 38
Harding, Nina, 174
Harding, Warren, 27
Harlem: Caribbean immigration, 12–13;
   1940s political environment, 65–73;
   overviews, 6; political history, 16; popula-
   tion growth, 15; post-World War II era,
   99–118; riots and uprisings, 14, 22; south-
   ern migrant population, 6, 11, 12–13. See
   also specific organizations; specific women
Harlem Branch Cancer Committee, 100
Harlem Christian Youth Council, 52
Harlem Labor Committee, 68
Harlem Negro Settlement House, 29
Harlem Renaissance, 6, 49
Harlem United Democratic Club, 117–18
Harlem Unity Liberal party, 69
Harlem Youth Opportunities Unlimited
   (HARYOU), 128, 140, 143

Harlem YWCA, 6, 11, 15, 40–41, 53
Harriet Tubman Society, 162
Harriman, Averell, 107, 109, 123
Harris, Bertha Nelms, 165
Harten, Thomas, 20
Hedgeman, Anna Arnold: Chisholm
   comparison, 177; Chisholm presidential
   candidacy, 182; civil rights movement
   contributions, 148–49; Commission on
   Religion and Race (National Council of
   Churches), 148–49; Consultant on Racial
   Problems, 51; Emergency Relief Bureau,
   51; Fair Employment Practices Commis-
   sion (FEPC), 85; feminism viewpoint,
   112–13; on Harlem as "Negro Mecca,"
   32; Harlem YWCA, 40–41; March on
   Washington movement of 1941, 85;
   March on Washington of 1963, 150;
   McCarthyism threat, 107–8; National
   Organization for Women (NOW) role,
   152, 153–54; New York City Commissioner of Welfare, 107–10; New York
   State Assembly candidacy, 113; New York
   state report on women's employment,
   123; on organized religion and race, 149;
   overviews, 2, 4, 6, 8, 45, 47, 148, 155–56;
   political activism overview, 88–90;
   political/social network of 1930s, 60; on
   sexism, 150–51; on socialized medicine,
   107; social work, 50; trade union work,
   51; United States Congress candidacy,
   110–13; Wagner cabinet appointment
   and service, 88; World War II work for
   African Americans, 66–67, 85
Height, Dorothy: background and education, 51–52; Chisholm comparison, 177;
   Chisholm presidential candidacy, 182; civil
   rights movement contributions, 145–46;
   Harlem Christian Youth Council, 52;
   Harlem YWCA, 53; on Hedgeman, 51;
   labor reform commitment, 54; on lack of
   skilled employment opportunity for black
   women, 131–32; liberal establishment
   politics, 145; March on Washington of
   1963 role, 150; on McCarthyism, 91, 92;
   network building in 1960s, 146; on 1960s
   needs of black women, 125; overviews,
   2, 4, 8, 9, 47; political/social network of
   1930s, 60; on Popular Front, 52; Presidential Commission on the Status of Women
   (PCSW), 121–22, 124; on Problems of

Negro Women (PCSW consultation), 128; social work, 52–53; United Christian Youth Movement, 52; Women's Inter-Organizational Committee (WIC) role, 140–41; writer for *The Crisis*, 54

Henry, June, 141

Hewell, Grace, 131

Holder, Wesley "Mac," 92–93, 162, 163, 168, 170

Home Relief Bureau, 60

Hooper, Chauncey, 101

House UnAmerican Activities Committee (HUAC), 107

housing reform, 38–39, 50. *See also specific organizations; specific women*

Hughes, Langston, 32

Hunton, Addie W., 59

Hunton, Alphaeus, 59

Hunton, William, 59

Hylan, John, 35

Hymes, Viola, 145

immigration, 12–13, 30

Impellitteri, Vincent, 73, 92, 101

Industrial Workers of the World (IWW), 30

"Invitation to Action" (President's Commission on the Status of Women introductory section), 132–33

Ipothia (In Pursuit of the Highest in All), 162

Jack, Hulan, 101, 107

Jackson, Ada B.: activism for Brooklyn and civil rights, 74; education and background, 74; New York State Assembly candidacy, 75–76, 78–81; Office of Price Administration Board (OPA), 74–75; overviews, 2, 5, 47; red-baiting victimization, 90–91; U.S. Congress candidacy, 81–82; World War II era civil rights work, 67

Jim Crow north, 2–3, 22

Job Corps, 139

John, Eardlie, 68

Johnson, Cenoria, 128–29, 130–31

Johnson, Edward A., 26, 28

Johnson, Eleanor, 44

Johnson, James Weldon, 14, 15, 32, 43

Johnson, Lady Bird, 138

Johnson, Lyndon B., 118, 132, 134, 138–41, 143

Jones, Claudia, 90

Jones, J. Raymond, 20, 117

Jones, Thomas R., 93, 94, 95, 97–99, 163–64

Jones, William, 181–82

Jones, Winnie, 38

Jordan, Barbara, 188

Justice, Robert, 62

Kennedy, John F., 122, 132, 133, 134, 145

Kennedy, Robert F., 118, 143

Kessler-Harris, Alice, 129, 229n26

Keyser, Frances R., 22

Key Women of America, 165

King, Coretta Scott, 182

King, Martin Luther Jr., 150, 176

LaGuardia, Fiorello, 51, 61, 72

Lambda Kappa Mu sorority, 151

Lane, Layle: background and education, 56; March on Washington movement of 1941, 85; overviews, 1, 3, 5, 8; political beliefs and positions on issues, 58–59; political candidacies, 56; World War II work for African Americans, 66–67

Lawton, Maria C., 34

Lee, Edward L., 17–18

leftist political parties of 1930s, 56–57

Lehman, Herbert, 83, 107, 110

Lewis, Annie K., 23, 23–24, 24–25

liberal establishment politics, 145–49

Liberal Party, 73–74, 83–84, 100–103

Lilly, Mary, 27, 28, 31

lynching issue, 35, 37, 43–44, 45

Major, Gerrie, 128, 130

Manpower Development and Training Act, 129, 175

March on Washington (1963), 116, 141, 146, 148, 150, 151

March on Washington movement of 1941, 66–67, 85, 150

Marshall, Thurgood, 115

Mason, Vivian C., 92

Matthews, Annie, 23, 36

Matthews, Victoria Earle, 1, 21

May, Catherine, 135–36

McAdoo, Maybelle, 42

McCarthyism, 90–94, 103–4

McKay, Claude, 32–33

McLaurin, B. F., 68

Mealey, Margaret, 145

Meyrowitz, Joanne, 105

Million Women United to Fight Lynching, A, 43

Mississippi Democratic Freedom Party, 176

Moore, Fred, 35, 49

Moorman, Irene. *See* Blackstone, Irene Moorman

Morgan, Jane P., 58

Morton, Ferdinand W., 19

Moskowitz, Belle, 27, 37

Motley, Constance Baker: on appointment to federal judgeship, 144; background and education, 114–15; civil rights case litigation experience, 114–15; federal judgeship appointment, 143–45; feminism, 144, 155; judicial position achievement, 122; Manhattan Borough Presidency, 117–18; New York State Senator, 115–17; overviews, 3–4, 8, 9, 88–90; on progress for black women, 144; role models, 114

Mott, Lucretia, 20

Mount Olivet Baptist Church, 22

Moynihan, Daniel Patrick, 141, 169

Municipal Domestic Relations Court, 218n45

Murphy, Charles, 17, 19

Murphy, Melody, 188

Murray, Pauli: background and education, 54–55, 83–84; Chisholm presidential candidacy, 182; civil rights activism in the South, 85; Civil Rights Act of 1964 activism, 136–39; Liberal Party, 101–2; on March on Washington of 1963, 151; mentors, 54; on Motley federal judgeship appointment, 144; National Organization for Women (NOW) role, 152–53; overviews, 2, 4, 8, 9, 47, 126; post graduate labor education, 55; Presidential Commission on the Status of Women (PCSW), 121–22, 125–27; women's rights activism, 152–54; women's rights overview, 155–56; Workers Education Project, 54; World War II era civil rights work, 67

NAACP (National Organization for the Advancement of Colored People), 6, 15, 76, 99–100

National Advisory Commission on Selective Service, 142–43

National Association for the Repeal of Abortion Laws (NARAL), 4, 174

National Association of Colored Women's Clubs (NACW), 15

National Baptist Church, 42

National Black Agenda, 182

National Black Convention (1972), 182

National Black Feminist Organization (NBFC), 4, 178–79

National Council for American Soviet Friendship, 90–91

National Council of Catholic Women, 145

National Council of Churches, 122, 148

National Council of Jewish Women, 145

National Council of Negro Women (NCNW), 9, 50, 91–92, 122, 145–46

National Council of the Churches of Christ, 145

National Federation of Business and Professional Women's Clubs (BPW), 126

National Manpower Council, 123, 133

National Negro Congress, 52, 91

National Organization for Women (NOW): black women's particular concerns, 156; Chisholm presidential candidacy, 180–81; Chisholm role, 173–74; Hedgeman role, 122, 153, 154–55; Murray role, 122, 152; as political activism mobilizing force, 4, 122, 144

National Urban League (NUL), 15, 38

National Welfare Rights Organization (NWRO), 175

National Woman Suffrage Association (NWSA), 20, 21

National Women's Party (NWP), 134–35, 151

National Women's Political Caucus (NWPC), 4, 178–80, 185

Negro Civic Improvement League, 38

Negro Elks of New York, 82

The Negro Family: The Case for National Action (Monihan study), 141

Negro Labor Committee, 52

Negro Republicans of Kings County, 76

Negro Suffrage Headquarters, 23

"Negro Woman in the Quest for Equality, The" (Murray speech), 151–52

Negro Women's Business League, 22

Nelson, Alice Dunbar, 43

New Deal, 3, 8

New Deal government agency work, 49–55

Newman, Lyda, 23

New Negro movement, 32

New Patterns in Volunteer Work, 124–25

Newton, Huey, 176

New York Age: anti-discrimination battles, 42; Carter campaign coverage, 60; contributors, 32; on Dwyer candidacy, 72; editorial board, 29; Hedgeman contributions, 109; Speaks endorsement, 64; women's citizenship education, 25; women's suffrage position, 21; on women's voter education and registration work, 34–35

New York Citizen-Call, 112

New York City: demographic shifts, 5–6, 11; geographic consolidation, 17; importance, 5–6; political power, 16–17, 209n23; political realignment of early 20th century, 18; Progressive Era political geography, 16–20, 209n25; Progressive Era population statistics, 209–10n26; social and political context, 14–16

New York City Board of Estimates, 85

New York City Colored Women's Federation, 63

New York City National Association of Negro Business and Professional Women (NANBPW), 63

New York City Welfare Administration, 53

New York Post, 84

New York state report on women's employment, 123

New York State Senate, 8

New York Times, 22, 25, 112, 118, 170, 199

New York Urban League, 128

New York Woman Suffrage Party, 23

Nixon, E. D., 103

Nixon, Richard M., 171, 175

Noble, Jeanne: Defense Advisory Commission on Women in the Services (DACOWITS), 141; Harlem Youth Opportunities Unlimited (HARYOU), 140, 143; Job Corps role, 139–43; National Advisory Commission on Selective Service, 142–43; Office of Equal Opportunity (OEO), 142–43; overviews, 4, 9, 139–40; Presidential Commission on the Status of Women (PCSW), 121–22, 125–26; women's rights overview, 155

Norfolk Journal and Guide, 141

Northern civil rights movement, 4, 49, 66–67

North Harlem Community Council, 38

Obama, Barack, 191, 198

O'Dwyer, William, 71, 72

Office of Equal Opportunity (OEO), 139, 142–43

Office of Price Administration Board (OPA), 74–75

Oliver, Mrs., 41

131st Street Block Association, 41

Opportunity, 60

Owens, Mrs., 116

Palmer, A. Mitchell, 30–31

Pan-African Congress, 59

pan-Africanism, 32

Parent-Teacher Association (PTA), 58, 74, 76

Parks, Rosa, 103, 150

patronage system, 99. *See also* Democratic Party; Tammany Hall

Payton, Philip, 15

PCSW. *See* President's Commission on the Status of Women (PCSW)

People's Voice, 67–68, 75–76, 77, 78

Perkins, Frances, 27, 50

Peterson, Esther, 123, 126, 127, 168, 175

Pickens, William, 32

Pickett, Lucille, 104

Political Equality League, 22

politics: accomplishments, 192–95; activism overviews, 2–6, 10–12, 13; ideologies, 5; influence, 3–4, 8–10, 196–98; nonconformity, 5; vision, 195–96. *See also* electoral politics overviews by era; *specific political parties*; *specific women*

Popular Front, 49, 52

Portrayal of Women by the Mass Media (PCSW consultation), 124–25

poverty statistics, 223nn28–29

Powell, Adam Clayton, Jr., 52, 67–68, 68–71

President's Commission on the Status of Women (PCSW): black women's roles, 229–30n42; committee work, 125–27; consultations, 124–25; driving forces behind creation, 123; feminist movement relationship, 113; Height contribution, 121–22, 124; impact, 133, 228n12; introductory statement, 132; issues considered, 128–29; labor issues, 109; limitations, 150–51; members, 124; Murray contribution, 121–22, 125–27; Noble contribution, 121–22, 125–26; overviews, 124–25, 132–33; purposes, 123; women's rights, 155

Private Employment Opportunities (PCSW consultation), 124–25

Problems of Negro Women (PCSW consultation), 124–25, 127–33

Professional Women's Republican Club, 34

Progressive Era, 13, 16–20

Progressive Party, 18, 79, 81, 81–82

racial uplift, 28

racism/gender bias combination: Chisholm on, 174; citizenship education struggle, 25–26; Democratic Party, 160–61, 164; major political party leadership, 28–29; 1948 campaign for New York State Assembly, 82; overviews, 2, 13, 45; paternalism, 48, 225n79; post-World War II era, 88–89; public citizenship, 24–25; Tammany Hall Democrats, 26; U.S. Congress, 157–58, 159–61

Randolph, A. Philip, 28, 29, 30, 52, 66–67, 85, 150, 225n79

Randolph, Lucille, 69

Rangel, Charles, 113

Ransby, Barbara, 54, 99, 147

Rawalt, Marguerite, 126, 137, 138

Red Scare (post World War I), 30–31

"Red Summer," 31–32, 33

Republican Party: as abandoning black people, 18; African American roles in 1930s and 1940s, 73–74; *Amsterdam News* endorsements, 69; departure of African Americans in 1920s, 35; efforts to attract black womens' votes, 27–29; Jackson, Ada B., 75; 1930s overview, 59–60, 62; overviews, 3, 8; racial ties v. political ties, 35; racism/gender bias combination, 37–38; Richardson, Maude, 5, 76–80, 81–82; Speaks, Sara Pelham, 5, 68–71; women's groups, 34–35

Richardson, Maude: activism for Brooklyn and civil rights, 76; Brooklyn City Council candidacy, 76–77; New York State Assembly candidacy, 78–82; overviews, 2, 5, 47; World War II era civil rights work, 67

Rilling, Paul, 129

riots and uprisings, 51, 61

Roane, Carita, 50–51

Roberts, Charles, 40, 61

Robinson, Dollie, 126, 127, 130, 168

Robinson, James, 101

Robinson, Patricia, 174

Roe v. Wade (1973), 174

Roosevelt, Eleanor, 75, 107, 110, 124

Roosevelt, Franklin D., 49, 65

Roosevelt, Theodore, 18

Roosevelt Women's Republican League, 34

"Rosie the Riveters," 65, 76, 89, 220n98

Ruffin, Josephine St. Pierre, 20

Russell, Carlos, 98–99

Rustin, Bayard, 150

Ryan, William, 113

Sammis, Ida, 28

Saunders, Cecelia Cabaniss, 11, 35, 53, 60

Savoy Ballroom, 6

Schomburg Center for Research in Black Culture, 6

Schor, Benjamin, 92

Seale, Bobby, 176

Search for Education, Elevation, and Knowledge (SEEK), 166

sexism. *See* Equal Rights Amendment (ERA); racism/gender bias combination; women's rights

Shanker, Albert, 169

Shriver, Sargent, 139, 140, 142

Small's Paradise, 6

Smith, Alfred E. "Al," 19, 26, 35, 36–37

Smith, Coral, 39

Smith, Howard, 134–35, 149

Smith, Marguerite, 28, 29, 30, 31, 55

Socialist Party: black women's votes, 29–30; election of 1917, 212n59; exclusion from election participation, 30; history, 212n59; media coverage, 59; overviews, 5, 8; political candidates of 1920s and 1930s, 56–58; women's suffrage support, 25

Solomon, Charles, 57

Souls of Black Folk (DuBois), 34

Southern Christian Leadership Conference, 148

Speaks, Sara Pelham, 1, 5, 8, 47, 63–64, 68–71

Springer, Maida, 57, 84

Stanton, Elizabeth Cady, 20

State Commission Against Discrimination, 101

Steinem, Gloria, 178

Stephens, James, 60

Stone, Lucy, 20

Student Non-Violent Coordinating Committee (SNCC), 122, 148, 176

Sutton, Percy, 181

Taft, William Howard, 18
Talbert, Mary, 43
Tammany Hall, 16, 17–18, 63, 71. *See also* Democratic Party
temperance, 28
Terborg-Penn, Roselyn, 23
Terrell, Mary Church, 128
Thompson, William, 168
Title VII (Civil Rights Act of 1964), 134–35, 137–39, 179
Trainer, Pat, 153
Trotter, William Monroe, 18
Truman, Harry S., 107
Truman Doctrine, 107
Trumpet Sounds, The (Hedgeman), 111
Truth, Sojourner, 20, 21
Turner, Leslie, 104

Unbought and Unbossed (Chisholm), 176
United Christian Youth Movement, 52
United Colored Democracy (UCD), 18
Unity Democratic Club (UDC), 94–99, 109, 163–64, 165
Universal Negro Improvement Association (UNIA), 6, 20, 22, 33
Urban League Board of Directors, 60
U.S. Congress, 9–10. *See also* Chisholm, Shirley
Utopia Neighborhood Club, 41

Valelly, Richard, 18
Van Wyck, Robert, 17
Vietnam War, 172–73

Wade, Roe v. (1973), 174
Wagner, Robert F. Jr., 83, 98–99, 107
Wallace, Henry A., 79
Walsh, John, 79, 82
Walton, Hanes Jr., 182, 184
Warner, Louis, 75
War on Poverty, 139–43, 166, 172
war work, 65, 66–67, 76, 89, 219n59, 220n98
Washington, Bennetta B., 141
Washington, Booker T., 18
Watkins, Anne, 23

Watson, James, 115
Watts, Ed, 64
Wedel, Cynthia, 145
"Wednesdays in Mississippi," 145
Weeksville, 15
Wells, Ida B., 21, 43
Whaley, Ruth Whitehead: background and education, 35–36, 62–63; civil rights activism, 72–73; Democratic Party, 63, 71–72, 220n83; on lack of skilled employment opportunity for black women, 130; New York City Board of Estimates, 85; New York City Council candidacy, 72; New York state report on women's employment, 123; overviews, 3, 47, 49, 63; Problems of Negro Women (PCSW consultation) role, 127, 130; on professional women's difficulties, 46–47
White, Fannie, 42
Wilson, J. Finley, 82
Wilson, Woodrow, 18–19
Wishnovsky, Helen, 84
Womanpower, 123
Woman's Program of the New York State Department of Commerce, 109
Women in Community Service (WICS), 140–41
Women's Bureau, 123
Women's International League for Peace and Freedom (WILPF), 59
Women's Inter-Organizational Committee (WIC), 140–41, 145–46, 231n76
Women's Job Corps, 142
Women's Loyal Union, 21
women's rights, 13, 20–25, 154–55. *See also* electoral politics overviews by era; Equal Rights Amendment (ERA); National Organization for Women (NOW)
Woods, Geraldine, 116
Workers Education Project (WEP), 54
Works Progress Administration (WPA), 54
World War I, 13
World War II, 8, 65, 66–67, 219n59

Young, Mary Sharperson, 23, 24, 33
Young Negroes' Cooperative League (YNCL), 53

JULIE A. GALLAGHER is an assistant professor of
history at Pennsylvania State University, Brandywine.

Women in American History

Women Doctors in Gilded-Age Washington: Race, Gender, and Professionalization
   Gloria Moldow
Friends and Sisters: Letters between Lucy Stone and Antoinette Brown Blackwell,
   1846–93   *Edited by Carol Lasser and Marlene Deahl Merrill*
Reform, Labor, and Feminism: Margaret Dreier Robins and the Women's Trade
   Union League   *Elizabeth Anne Payne*
Private Matters: American Attitudes toward Childbearing and Infant Nurture in the
   Urban North, 1800–1860   *Sylvia D. Hoffert*
Civil Wars: Women and the Crisis of Southern Nationalism   *George C. Rable*
I Came a Stranger: The Story of a Hull-House Girl   *Hilda Satt Polacheck;*
   edited by Dena J. Polacheck Epstein
Labor's Flaming Youth: Telephone Operators and Worker Militancy, 1878–1923
   Stephen H. Norwood
Winter Friends: Women Growing Old in the New Republic, 1785–1835
   Terri L. Premo
Better Than Second Best: Love and Work in the Life of Helen Magill
   Glenn C. Altschuler
Dishing It Out: Waitresses and Their Unions in the Twentieth Century
   Dorothy Sue Cobble
Natural Allies: Women's Associations in American History   *Anne Firor Scott*
Beyond the Typewriter: Gender, Class, and the Origins of Modern American
   Office Work, 1900–1930   *Sharon Hartman Strom*
The Challenge of Feminist Biography: Writing the Lives of Modern American
   Women   *Edited by Sara Alpern, Joyce Antler, Elisabeth Israels Perry,*
   and Ingrid Winther Scobie
Working Women of Collar City: Gender, Class, and Community in Troy,
   New York, 1864–86   *Carole Turbin*
Radicals of the Worst Sort: Laboring Women in Lawrence, Massachusetts,
   1860–1912   *Ardis Cameron*
Visible Women: New Essays on American Activism   *Edited by Nancy A. Hewitt*
   and Suzanne Lebsock
Mother-Work: Women, Child Welfare, and the State, 1890–1930
   Molly Ladd-Taylor
Babe: The Life and Legend of Babe Didrikson Zaharias   *Susan E. Cayleff*
Writing Out My Heart: Selections from the Journal of Frances E. Willard,
   1855–96   *Edited by Carolyn De Swarte Gifford*
U.S. Women in Struggle: A *Feminist Studies* Anthology   *Edited by*
   Claire Goldberg Moses and Heidi Hartmann
In a Generous Spirit: A First-Person Biography of Myra Page
   Christina Looper Baker

Mining Cultures: Men, Women, and Leisure in Butte, 1914–41   *Mary Murphy*
Gendered Strife and Confusion: The Political Culture of Reconstruction
   Laura F. Edwards
The Female Economy: The Millinery and Dressmaking Trades, 1860–1930
   Wendy Gamber
Mistresses and Slaves: Plantation Women in South Carolina, 1830–80
   Marli F. Weiner
A Hard Fight for We: Women's Transition from Slavery to Freedom in
   South Carolina   *Leslie A. Schwalm*
The Common Ground of Womanhood: Class, Gender, and Working Girls'
   Clubs, 1884–1928   *Priscilla Murolo*
Purifying America: Women, Cultural Reform, and Pro-Censorship Activism,
   1873–1933   *Alison M. Parker*
Marching Together: Women of the Brotherhood of Sleeping Car Porters
   Melinda Chateauvert
Creating the New Woman: The Rise of Southern Women's Progressive
   Culture in Texas, 1893–1918   *Judith N. McArthur*
The Business of Charity: The Woman's Exchange Movement, 1832–1900
   Kathleen Waters Sander
The Power and Passion of M. Carey Thomas   *Helen Lefkowitz Horowitz*
For Freedom's Sake: The Life of Fannie Lou Hamer   *Chana Kai Lee*
Becoming Citizens: The Emergence and Development of the California
   Women's Movement, 1880–1911   *Gayle Gullett*
Selected Letters of Lucretia Coffin Mott   *Edited by Beverly Wilson Palmer
   with the assistance of Holly Byers Ochoa and Carol Faulkner*
Women and the Republican Party, 1854–1924   *Melanie Susan Gustafson*
Southern Discomfort: Women's Activism in Tampa, Florida, 1880s–1920s
   Nancy A. Hewitt
The Making of "Mammy Pleasant": A Black Entrepreneur in Nineteenth-
   Century San Francisco   *Lynn M. Hudson*
Sex Radicals and the Quest for Women's Equality   *Joanne E. Passet*
"We, Too, Are Americans": African American Women in Detroit and
   Richmond, 1940–54   *Megan Taylor Shockley*
The Road to Seneca Falls: Elizabeth Cady Stanton and the First Woman's
   Rights Convention   *Judith Wellman*
Reinventing Marriage: The Love and Work of Alice Freeman Palmer and
   George Herbert Palmer   *Lori Kenschaft*
Southern Single Blessedness: Unmarried Women in the Urban South,
   1800–1865   *Christine Jacobson Carter*
Widows and Orphans First: The Family Economy and Social Welfare Policy,
   1865–1939   *S. J. Kleinberg*

Habits of Compassion: Irish Catholic Nuns and the Origins of the Welfare
    System, 1830–1920 *Maureen Fitzgerald*
The Women's Joint Congressional Committee and the Politics of Maternalism,
    1920–1930 *Jan Doolittle Wilson*
"Swing the Sickle for the Harvest Is Ripe": Gender and Slavery in
    Antebellum Georgia *Daina Ramey Berry*
Christian Sisterhood, Race Relations, and the YWCA, 1906–46
    Nancy Marie Robertson
Reading, Writing, and Segregation: A Century of Black Women
    Teachers in Nashville *Sonya Ramsey*
Radical Sisters: Second-Wave Feminism and Black Liberation in
    Washington, D.C. *Anne M. Valk*
Feminist Coalitions: Historical Perspectives on Second-Wave Feminism
    in the United States *Edited by Stephanie Gilmore*
Breadwinners: Working Women and Economic Independence, 1865–1920
    Lara Vapnek
Beauty Shop Politics: African American Women's Activism in the
    Beauty Industry *Tiffany M. Gill*
Demanding Child Care: Women's Activism and the Politics of Welfare,
    1940–1971 *Natalie M. Fousekis*
Rape in Chicago: Race, Myth, and the Courts *Dawn Rae Flood*
Black Women and Politics in New York City *Julie A. Gallagher*

The University of Illinois Press
is a founding member of the
Association of American University Presses.

———————————————————————

Composed in 9.75/13.5 Janson Text
with Electra display
by Jim Proefrock
at the University of Illinois Press
Manufactured by Sheridan Books, Inc.

University of Illinois Press
1325 South Oak Street
Champaign, IL 61820-6903
www.press.uillinois.edu